"MOVING, INSIGHTFUL AND EMINENTLY PRACTICAL . . . *The Measure of a Man* shows that no one replaces the father. Dr. Shapiro encourages us to see the vital role the involved, caring father has in today's family . . . a milestone—a book for every parent."

—Carl Jones, author, *Mind over Labor*

"A MASTERFUL GUIDE TO FATHERHOOD TODAY that successfully blends Jerrold Shapiro's personal and professional wisdom. I highly recommend it to any man who wants to understand himself and improve his relationship with his own father and children."

—James A. Levine, Director,
The Fatherhood Project,
Families and Work Institute

"A VALUABLE ADDITION to the growing stack of literature designed to help men assume a more significant role in the family . . . comprehensive discussions."

—*Publishers Weekly*

"BOTH A GUIDE FOR CONTEMPORARY FATHERS and a detailed meditation on the state of fatherhood today . . . a wealth of specific information on the complexities of being a father in a time of shifting sex roles . . . witty, humane, warm, and wise, and by far the best and most inclusive book we've seen on the subject."

—*Dragonsmoke*

"A VALUABLE STUDY . . . Jerry Shapiro is both a father and a therapist, and he brings his experience and his wisdom into this book. I highly recommend it."

—Asa Baber, "Men" columnist, *Playboy* magazine

THE
MEASURE
OF A
MAN

BECOMING THE FATHER
YOU WISH YOUR
FATHER HAD BEEN

Jerrold Lee Shapiro, Ph.D.

A PERIGEE BOOK

A Perigee Book
Published by The Berkley Publishing Group
200 Madison Avenue
New York, NY 10016

Copyright © 1993 by Jerrold Lee Shapiro, Ph.D.

Book design by Rhea Braunstein

Cover design by James R. Harris

Cover illustration by James McLoughlin

Song lyrics appearing on pages 202, 225 and 226 are from "Cat's in the Cradle" by Harry Chapin, and are reprinted by permission of the Harry Chapin Foundation.

First Perigee edition: June 1995
Delacorte Press edition: June 1993

Published simultaneously in Canada.

Library of Congress Cataloging-in-Publication Data
Shapiro, Jerrold Lee.
    The measure of a man : becoming the father you wish your father
had been / Jerrold Lee Shapiro. — 1st Perigee ed.
        p.   cm.
    "A Perigee book."
    Originally published: New York, N.Y. : Delacorte Press, © 1993.
    Includes bibliographical references and index.
    ISBN 0-399-51935-1
    1. Fathers—Psychology.   2. Men—Psychology.   I. Title
HQ756.S476   1995
306.874'2—dc20   94-41668 CIP

Printed in the United States of America

10   9   8   7   6   5   4   3   2   1

In loving memory
of Myer Shapiro,
1917–1994

ACKNOWLEDGMENTS

There are so many people who were instrumental in this book in a variety of ways. They provided motivation, ideas, inestimable emotional support, and valuable critiques of earlier drafts.

First and foremost is my wife, Susan. She gave me support throughout the endeavor, time to work on it, encouragement, love, critical reading of the manuscript and, of course, my children.

My two closest friends, Drs. Michael Diamond and Larry Peltz, also provided considerable support, reassurance, and ideas at every stage of the ten-year project. They were always available for discussions of content or my feelings and their own. As professionals, we worked together. I feel very nurtured and loved by each and have for over twenty years. Both fathers themselves, Larry and Michael have been my fathers, my brothers, and my sons. Without my close friends this book would have been impossible.

I especially want to thank my brother-in-law and colleague, Robert Taylor, Dean of the Business School at the University of Louisville, and my friend Jim Pizor of IBM. Each read early drafts of the manuscript and provided me with constructive suggestions and encouragement.

My agent, Felicia Eth, who discovered this project, believed in it, and followed through on every promise she made, was of inestimable help in keeping me motivated and on target. Felicia provided literary assistance and encouragement and fulfilled the normal agent's responsibilities as well.

Two editors at Delacorte Press, Brian DiFiore and Emily Reichert, were helpful and responsive. They were able to work with me to bring the manuscript in on time. Emily was particularly helpful in improving the overall quality of the work.

Many others also deserve acknowledgment for their assistance. Some may be unaware of the impact they have had in the making of *The Measure of a Man: Becoming the Father You Wish Your Father Had Been.*

At Santa Clara University, my colleague Professor Dale Larson was supportive and particularly helpful in the project when he helped brainstorm through a critical impasse. Dean JoAnn Vasquez provided extra release time and assistance. Several graduate students also provided research support and encouragement by their interest in the project. My colleague and former student, Kate Pizor, has been a significant contributor. I also want to thank Geoff Kirkpatrick, Susan Hennings, and Judy Gier.

Certain writers in the area of parenting and fatherhood have been influential in helping shape my interest and thought in the area. Some of these I have known personally; others through their work. Among these are Robert Bly (*A Gathering of Men;* a video interview with Bill Moyers), Sam Keen (*Fire in the Belly*), Sam Osherson (*Finding Our Fathers*), Kyle Pruett (*The Nurturing Father*), Guy Corneau (*Absent Fathers, Lost Sons*), Charles Scull (*Fathers, Sons and Daughters*), Katharyn May of Vanderbilt University, Ora Strickland of Emory University, and Phil and Caroline Cowan of Berkeley, whose ground-breaking work helped establish fatherhood as a field of study. Singer-songwriter Tom Paxton also stands out as a man whose fathering made a big impression on his work and on my work and parenting.

Dr. Ron Levant, former director of Boston's "Fatherhood Project" and a key player in the American Psychological Association's Committee for the Psychological Study of Men and Masculinity, has helped open the entire field for more careful study. Psychiatrist Marty Greenberg, author of *Birth of a Father,* has been particularly influential in defining the field and in providing emotional support and guidance to me and to a whole generation of authors writing about fatherhood. Dr. Gerry Michaels, co-author of *Transition to Parenthood*, and psychologist, poet, and songwriter Dr. Brad Sachs, author of *Opening Day* and *Things Just Haven't Been the Same*, have given me ideas, friendship, and support.

Other men who have had a powerful impact on my life and my fathering over the years also deserve recognition. Friends, mentors, teachers, and role models, they have all contributed. Among these important men are John Beletsis of Palo Alto, Arne Gray of Chapel Hill, Gordon Bowie of Bangor, Dick Steffy at the University of Waterloo, Rene Tillich and Tom Glass of Honolulu, Air Force General (Ret.) Louis Wilson, the late John Kempers of Colby College, and Colonel Kelly of Boston Latin School. Above all, there is my "father" in the field of psychology, Dr. Viktor Frankl. His book *From Death Camp to Existentialism* (more recently known as *Man's Search for Meaning*) and his personal appearance at Colby College in 1960 gave me my first hero as an undergraduate and helped me define my career. For the first time in my life I felt a deep resonance for my way of thinking. Later contacts with Dr. Frankl in San Diego in 1976 and at his honorary degree reception at Santa Clara University in 1991 have reaffirmed my extreme admiration and belief in the direction his influence helped set.

I want to express my gratitude to the hundreds of men who willingly and openly talked about their personal experiences of fatherhood and manhood. In addition, my understanding of fathering has been greatly impacted by my clients in individual, couples, family, and group therapy and participants in men's groups, who courageously struggled with these matters with me.

Thanks are also extended to Dr. Rob Bischoff, SYSOP of the electronic bulletin board *Shrinktank* for allowing me access to so many men and women in my role as guest SYSOP of the Men's Conference, and to the many radio talk shows and feature writers who have featured my work on fatherhood, showed excellent journalism and genuine interest. Among these, Larry Kutner of *The*

New York Times; David Early, Mike Cassidy, and Dave O'Brien of the *San Jose Mercury News;* Mary Madison of the *Peninsula Times-Tribune;* David Gold of KDFK in Dallas; and Mariette Hartley, formerly of CBS, stand out. I also appreciate Dr. Robert Alberti of Impact Publishers for his belief in my work and for initial publication of *When Men Are Pregnant*.

A special note of recognition is extended to Steve Wozniak, Apple Computer Founder and philanthropist. As a member of my community, he has provided an unique side of fatherhood. Through gifts of computers and time to elementary schools in the district, his contributions to the Children's Discovery Museum of San Jose and his special classes and sponsored trips, he has tried to "father" youngsters by providing "opportunities to know that they can live their dreams."

I suppose I also ought to thank Samuel Langhorne Clemens, George Santayana, and George Bernard Shaw, whom I always seem to be quoting whenever I believe I have come up with a truly unique perception.

Finally, and most of all, I give profound thanks to my father, Myer Shapiro, who gave me more than he could know; to my mother, Beatrice, and sister, Linda, for their love; and to Natasha and Gabriel, my children. They had to give up their own time with Daddy so he could write a book on fathering. I will never love anyone the way I love them, nor be so transformed by another presence or being.

CONTENTS

PART II

MY FATHER, MY SELF

PART III

HARD FATHERING

PART IV

RESOURCES FOR FATHERS

PART V

DEAR CHILDREN

The labor of love that resulted in *The Measure of a Man* began with my wife's first pregnancy and the birth of our daughter in 1981. It continued and magnified with our son's birth in 1988. Fatherhood has been the single most powerful event in my life. It colors everything I do. My dreams, hopes, and aspirations have been transformed with the existence of my children. As a father I am more connected to mankind, to my own father, and to the future.

As the fascination with these changes took over much of my mental and emotional life, I felt pushed to share my feelings and ideas with other men who were in the same situation and with those who were my seniors.

This book has a very personal basis. However, my personal experience of fatherhood is probably far more fascinating to me than to anyone else. What is important is how my personal understanding matches the way men in general experience this core component of masculine identity. The power of my personal experience led me to explore fathering in scientific and personal ways. This book is an attempt to share that learning.

You will find in this book the combined input and knowledge of hundreds of men. As much as possible, I have provided examples and quotations from the men I interviewed. I am exceptionally grateful to everyone who shared so openly their hopes, dreams, and fears as fathers. They came from a wide variety of backgrounds.

The information came from several sources: scientific surveys, men's groups, psychotherapy, electronic media, lectures and workshops, literature, and personal experience.

SURVEYS. There was an initial comprehensive survey of 227 expectant and recent fathers. The men in that survey roughly matched U.S. census population groups. A second survey followed, in which another eighty men who had been fathers for at least a year were interviewed. The third survey involved 203 couples. These couples had been parents for at least a year. Ten percent had children who had grown and left home. Finally a survey of 90 experienced fathers was completed. These men each had at least one child and had been fathering for at least four years. Each of these survey studies involved a taped, structured interview and completion of questionnaires.

CLINICAL SOURCES. Data for the book also came from clinical sources. As a leader of men's groups since the mid 1960s, I have been privy to the rawest expression of the delights and pains of maleness and fatherhood. It was in such groups that I began to understand the fact that fatherhood was a core of masculinity, and the influence of a man's children in his life.

In addition to the men's groups I have been in the private practice of individual, couples, family, and group psychotherapy for over twenty years. In that time I have been able to get to know in very intimate ways scores of single and married men, fathers who were present for their families and those who were absent, single fathers and stepfathers, older fathers and new fathers. In this process I have become aware of the influence of these men in their families and the centrality of their families to their personal lives. Over three hundred of my clients' lives are represented in the work in this book.

ELECTRONIC MEDIA. Information on fathering has also come through my computer conversations with hundreds of men and women on electronic bulletin boards. These BBS's offer people a forum to air their concerns and grievances in a semi-anonymous way. Among the BBS's that I have regularly used to communicate with others and to be able to observe conversations among men and women are Prodigy, America Online, and Shrinktank. I have been the host of the men's conference on the last for over two years.

Telecommunication has played another role in helping me better understand fathers. Since the initial publication of my book *When Men Are Pregnant,* in 1987, I have appeared on over one hundred radio and television programs. Many of these were call-in shows. These forums allowed me an opportunity to talk to scores of people across the country whom I otherwise would not have met.

LECTURES AND WORKSHOPS. In the past several years I have been giving talks and conducting workshops on male psychology, fatherhood, and family issues. At these talks I have been able to hear the concerns and questions of a great number of fathers and mothers and potential parents. I am sure that they have given me as much as I have given them. Ideas, questions, pragmatic solutions to everyday problems, and their life stories have all sharpened my understanding of fathering as it exists in North America today.

THE LITERATURE ON FATHERHOOD. Finally there is a small but growing literature on fathering. I have attempted to give a reasonable summary of my colleagues' work here and to build on it. Their perceptions, research, and conclusions have added immeasurably to my personal understanding of myself, of men, and of fathers.

I feel honored to be privy to the most central aspects of men's lives and feelings about fatherhood. I have endeavored to treat their conversations with the respect and admiration with which I hold them. Because of that, unless men specifically requested that I quote them directly or agreed to be quoted when I asked, no personal identification of any individual is provided. Personal information is disguised to protect confidentiality. Names were changed, and any specific correspondence with an individual is purely coincidental.

THE
MEASURE
OF A
MAN

BECOMING THE FATHER
YOU WISH YOUR
FATHER HAD BEEN

I

FATHERING
TODAY

1

WHAT IS A FATHER?

"If you build it, he [Daddy] will come."
—KINSELLA

December 1987

Dear Dad:

I hope you have the opportunity to read this. I am waiting at the hospital for the surgeon with news of your bypass operation. My mind and emotions are so jumbled with fear, great sadness, and anger. Memories flood my consciousness seemingly of their own accord. We have been connected for the entire forty-four years of my life; more than sixty percent of your lifetime.

I don't think I ever cried as hard or felt such helplessness or despair as I did a few hours ago when they wheeled you away from me, into the operating room where your life now hangs in the balance.

It was so gratifying to see you enjoy the party Linda and I threw to celebrate your seventieth birthday, just a week ago. I'm glad you liked the keyboard. It has never been easy buying you a gift, you never seemed to need or want much for yourself. I guess that's one of the frustrating things about our relationship. So much of what you taught me by your actions was to delay gratification. I'm afraid I got too good at that. It's been a struggle for me to let myself want in the here-and-now. I wonder if you've had to grapple with that also, or whether it's just part of your being that remains unquestioned.

As scared and unhappy as this crisis has made me, I'm pleased that I could be present: not three thousand or six thousand miles away, as it has been for so many years. I'm glad that I could drive you to the hospital—some kind of repayment for the thousands of times you drove me to one place or another. Have I appreciated that enough? I doubt I did as a kid or at least doubt that I told you. The truth is I would have preferred a trip to the Coliseum or Candlestick. Hopefully we'll go to Fenway Park or the Garden again someday. As I sit here and wait, I can recall the first baseball game you took me to in old Braves Field with exquisite detail: the pavilion, Sam Jethroe stealing home, Bob Elliott, Sibby Sisti, Tommy Holmes, Sid Gordon, Earl Torgeson, Walker Cooper, and that incredible home run Ralph Kiner hit off Bickford. I don't think that ball ever came back to the ground. You began to teach me how to score the game that night.

There's a frustrating part to that memory too. In recent years you have been so reticent about doing anything much with me, begging off at the last minute from baseball games and other places where we could have shared. I know you do that to avoid conflict with Mom, but it has always bothered me that you were more tuned in to her desires than to your own. I also worry that I share that tendency to hear my wife's spoken and unspoken wishes as commands.

I'm angry at you for not taking better care of yourself. The smoking is particularly irritating, especially after all the heart and circulation problems. I worry a lot about my own self-destructive tendencies. I, too, delay pleasures far too long, I feel responsible for others' happiness far more than I should, I am too eager to please. I have taken as my mission in life that I must bring excitement and

*happiness to yours. Somehow I understood at a very deep level that
I was your protector as much as you were mine.*

*Dad, I really need you to live. Your first grandson will be
born in less than two months. Knowing how much you love your
granddaughters, I know this will be important for you as well. Is
this another example of my taking care of you—taking care of me
as well?*

*I am not ready to let you go. There is so much I want to say
to you. So much I want to ask you. I can't write it here because I
have no words to express it, no way of probing and unearthing my
innermost thoughts. It is like when my daughter begins to ask me
a question, mostly to connect, and gets lost in her content. Tongue-
tied, emotionally overwrought, I sit here feeling my love for you,
my yearning for more of you, my unknown and unasked questions.*

*What can you teach me about this job of fathering that you
have done? What can you help me do better as a father and as a
son? Where is the piece of absolute wisdom that will silence the
questions and satisfy my longing for true understanding and
peace? I know there is precious little time left.*

This letter remains unfinished. Although I have shared most of the
content with my father, I have not sent the letter. He survived his
bypass operation and several other life-threatening scares. Like
this letter, our relationship remains unfinished. I cannot think of
anything particular that I have left unsaid, yet know down deep
that there is much more. Most of all I do not know if my father has
said everything to me that he wants to say. Sometimes I hang on
to those rare moments when we converse at length, hoping for
whatever message a father gives his son.

This book is about my dad and yours. It is about our impact
on our children. Mostly it is about you and me, the fathers we are,
the fathers we want to become. As you become increasingly open
to, and involved with, your children, you may rediscover your own
childhood sense of father hunger.[1] This may be very important.
Those of us who remain unaware of the personal hurts and rejections of our boyhoods will tend unconsciously to pass them on to

our children. Introspection and awareness of our personal motivations and history are prerequisites to good fathering.

There are many ways to be a father, some better than others. I hope that this book will serve as a companion, providing support for what you are already doing well, information about how other men approach and struggle with fathering, a pathway to looking within yourself for the deeper elements of fathering, and a theoretical perspective on good fathering. At times it may seem that you are being made privy to the most intimate discussion of a men's therapy group. The many men to whom these chapters give voice were remarkably open about their thoughts, feelings, fears, disappointments, and joys. Fathering was so important to them that they freely opened their hearts in interviews, letters, and conversations. Some of the quotations actually did come from men in individual and group therapy.

As fathers we have firsthand knowledge and experience to pass on to our successors. For this reason much of the book relates to the relationship between fathers and sons. However, our job with our daughters is just as important. A father is the first male our little girls experience. We become in large part the prototype for her future relationships with men and women. During the course of the book women's voices, remembrances, and feelings about their fathers are included. Many of the most significant researchers and writers about fatherhood are women.

Although this book is designed to be a close friend, at times it will be a distant, more erudite companion. Complex psychological issues do not readily translate into day-to-day language or concepts. This is especially true in Chapter 8, "The Father Within," which looks at the way we internalize fatherhood as children. At other times, such as in Chapter 7, "Our Fathers: The Importance of a Man's Own Father on His Parenting," there are specific suggestions and questions that only a close friend could ask. There are also times, such as in "A Declaration of Interdependence" where I summarize the input of hundreds of fathers, as well as the available literature, in order to take a strong position about how one can best approach good fathering.

I hope you will allow me to be your companion for a while on this most important journey we take as men, each following our individual paths, connected by a biological, social, and psychological brotherhood. We begin here.

WHAT IS A FATHER?

Margaret Mead has called him "a biological necessity, but a social accident."

Andrew Lloyd Webber portrays a father as "the first man you remember, the last man you forget."[2]

Louise Bates Ames of the Gesell Institute wrote, "He is the protector, the provider, the supporter. He is the one the rest of the family looks up to and depends on. He is an essential point in the father/mother/child triangle. Others can share the burden, but his is the responsibility."[3]

Is a father the abusive or neglectful ogre, that ever-popular caricature of talk shows and pop-psych literature? Is he the "perfect" image who did everything right, or the model for Dagwood Bumstead? As a child did you have to "wait till your father gets home"? Is he Alan Alda or Archie Bunker?

When it comes to describing a father, experts are not the only ones with opinions. Ask a thousand fathers and you get a thousand different answers. Ask a thousand children and you get multiples of a thousand answers. During the past ten years I have asked this question to almost that many fathers, sons, and daughters, who were more than eager to respond.

Daniel, five, had one of the best answers: "My daddy reads the newspaper . . . buys me presents and frozen yogurt. He goes to work. He gets tired. Sometimes he plays with me and he kisses me and reads and tucks me in at bedtime."

Asked if Mommy did the same things, he replied, "Mommy is different when she 'do's' them. She doesn't let me get toppings on the frozen yogurt."

Four-year-old Allison said, "I have the best daddy in the

whole world. He rides me on his shoulders. He tells me he loves me every day. . . . He lives with Mommy and makes her happy too."

Surveys of college students produce a host of definitions of "fathers." A 1990 questionnaire completed by undergraduates in a psychology course at Santa Clara University in California generated some interesting definitions of fatherhood:

"My dad is warm, loving, strong, religious, has high standards, consistent . . . a good provider."

"I barely know my father. I lived with him for seventeen years, but don't think we ever talked."

"Most girls talk to their mother. Well, my dad is the listener in our family. He's surrounded by females (me, Mom, and four sisters), and he's the nurturer."

"He's the worrier. Until I came here, he was always awake when I came home late from a date or whatever."

"My dad's my model and my hero. He works real hard, is successful, and he's always been there for us kids."

"My father deserted my mom and me when I was born. I never got to meet him, and my stepfather molested me before he left. I think all men are jerks."

"He's a workaholic and an alcoholic."

"My father is my best friend and advisor. I hope to grow up to be just like him."

Finally, in a classic example of the larger-than-life quality fathers symbolically represent, a mature businesswoman in her forties explained her hesitation in confronting her father's continuing overinvolvement in their family business by stating, "My father is God, the founder, the beginning. Nobody questions '*Sir Charles*.' "

"Sir Charles" may find it difficult living up to that performance standard, but good fathering is no easy task for any of us. Researcher and author Sara Gilbert, commenting on some of the travails of fathering, writes, "It's not just your kids who drive their father crazy—all kids do it. Our society makes tremendous demands on a man, especially a father. As a result, more men commit suicide than women, they die younger, get sick oftener. And no wonder—we expect a man to earn a good living (and improve his "status" by continually advancing his career), finance the raising of his children, make like a father, emancipate his wife, mow the lawn, and carry out the garbage."[4]

It comes as no surprise that while there is no shortage of applicants for the occupation of father, there are also no clear-cut ways to do the job well.

Each man has his own unique form of fathering. What is "fathering" for you as a man? What meaning does it have for you? How would you like it to be different? What are the unconscious pressures that enhance and interfere with your fathering? How are you, as a parent, different from other men and women? What kind of father would you choose to be?

Changing Roles of Fatherhood

As recently as one generation ago the typical father was portrayed as being uninvolved in pregnancy, childbirth, or child care. His role during the birth was to nervously pace the waiting-room floor and chain-smoke unfiltered cigarettes until the news was brought to him. He was neither a diaper changer nor a child feeder; his role was rather to provide the opportunity for his wife to rear the children with as few distractions as possible. Ross Parke, an early and eloquent spokesman on the fatherhood experience, wrote of these men, "Specialized to their role as family breadwinner, these mythical fathers provided a strong but distant model for their children and moral and material support for their wives. Otherwise, these fathers truly were something of a social accident, and hardly active participants in the rearing of their children."[5]

There is considerable reality to this distant-father stereotype. Many adults today readily describe their fathers this way. Most men of the previous few generations shared at least some of these traits. My own father, who was quite involved in my childhood in the 1940s, commented a few years back that I had changed more diapers in one afternoon than he had in his children's lifetime.

Whatever the actuality of yesterday's stereotype, it no longer holds in Western society of the 1990s. Consider some of these modern "facts of life":

- Over 80 percent of today's fathers in intact families will be present at the birth of their children.
- They will most definitely share the chores of diaper changing and feeding their infants and children.
- If they stay married, it is unlikely that they will be the sole breadwinner in the home. Their wife will probably be working while the children are still in diapers.
- With increasing frequency, fathers of young children will be single parents, stepfathers, or living away from their natural children. Some will become the primary child-care person, even in intact families.[6]
- Finally, previous support from extended-family members and close-knit neighborhoods will be much diminished from prior generations. The somewhat isolated nuclear suburban family is much more the norm than ever before in human history.

THE CORE OF FATHERHOOD

With the nature of fathering so much in flux, you may wonder if there are certain core traits common to effective fathers. How do good fathers differ from poor ones? What can a father do specifically to improve his relationship and effectiveness with his children? How does father involvement contribute to children's growth? My interviews with over eight hundred fathers and adult children indicated the following twelve core factors of fathering:

1. Protecting and providing: The prime directive
2. Loving and being engrossed with children

3. Facing performance fears
4. Being encouraging and supportive
5. Being courageous
6. Being trustworthy
7. Honoring male compassion and warmth
8. Developing flexibility
9. Administering discipline
10. Demonstrating and teaching teamwork
11. Understanding and honoring personal limits
12. Facing yourself and your own fathering

Protecting and Providing: The Prime Directive

Of all the traits common to modern fathers, none is so deeply ingrained or influential as the traditional male protector role. No longer the hunters of prehistoric days nor the farmers of earlier generations, modern fathers most frequently fulfill this role by being the financial provider.

In a survey of expectant fathers I asked the question "Do you ever expect to be supported by someone else during your adult life?" Of the 227 respondents, all 227 answered no. What is particularly interesting about this result is that at the time of the survey, thirty-one of the men were being supported by someone else.

These men were not simply lying. The thought of not being the provider is so psychologically unacceptable that it was unconsciously denied. It was not something that could be considered. Their need to provide financially (protect) their families was so intense that failing to do it well constituted a shameful inadequacy.

Remember, these were expectant fathers. Once men get to know and hold their children, their protectorship becomes even more intense.

It is easy to understand why the male roles of protecting and providing have become so salient to our society. Historically biology, division of labor, and differential abilities constrained men to be hunters and women to be child bearers and nurturers. As society developed, these mandatory roles became less necessarily divergent. However, eons of biological necessity and cultural heritage continue to consign women more to the home and men more to the outside role of protector.

Despite dramatic social changes, including women's increasing presence in the marketplace, men continue to feel the major burden of financial providership in the family. Fathers do generally spend much more time away from the home than mothers. On average they are more likely than their spouses to work full-time or overtime or to moonlight on a second job outside the home. To their children they are the one who deals with the trials and tribulations of the "work jungle."

Chris, a thirteen-year-old "latchkey" son with two working parents, expressed it this way: "My mom works too. She tries to help out with the 'extras,' but Dad is the one who puts in the hard time. He has to travel and he's the one who pays for the basics. When I was ten, he got laid off. That's when she went to work the first time. We had hard times then, but once he got the new job, it's okay again."

For Chris and his younger sister Mom's job is secondary to Dad's. In fact Dad does earn the lion's share of the family income. His hours are longer, and insecurities in his workplace present much more jeopardy during shifting economic times than in their mother's workplace.

Several cultural factors amplify this awareness: For one thing men grow up expecting to work their whole lives and to support a family. The extent and depth of this emotional commitment are addressed in depth later in this book. For most men there is no choice about full-time work. It is a given. The majority of women today also have to work to support the family, but they grow up with an expectation that they will have a choice involving the relative amounts of time they will spend in child care, homemaking, and career.[7] The intensity of a father's sense that he *must* "bring home the bacon" is surely conveyed to the children.

This sense is reconfirmed throughout our culture. It is common for most organizations in our culture to consider a woman's work as secondary to her partner's. She is the one who is expected to leave work to pick up a sick child from school. She is the one whose schedule is expected to be changed for car pools and projects. There is a clear cultural norm that women, not men, can place the family before the job.

This point is regularly made poignant for me because I work several days a week in my home. One morning as I was writing this chapter, I received a phone call from my son's preschool teacher. Having established that I was the father of the child, she promptly asked to speak with my wife. When I told her that Susan was not at home and asked what the problem was, she slowly and very circuitously informed me that my son was not feeling well. When I asked if she thought I should pick him up, she replied by asking for Susan's work number. When I arrived at the school to get him, she made a huge fuss about "disturbing me at work," as if my son's welfare and school health regulations were secondary to my job. It was a clear message that fathers' work is less interruptable than mothers'.

Finally, fathers tend to earn more than mothers. There are a number of realities that contribute to this discrepancy: (1) men are in higher-paying positions than women (the "glass ceiling"); (2) women, more than men, tend to marry up the socioeconomic ladder, often finding partners who are older, more experienced, more educated, more advanced in their field, and so on; (3) more men work full-time in their career; (4) there is continuing discrimination in the workplace that rewards men in some (particularly blue-collar) industries more than women for equivalent work.

The sum of these realities makes single mothers, as a group, the most financially oppressed. However, fathers do not escape the financial oppression. To quote Ben, a chemist, "There's just no question about who gets to work part-time when the new baby comes. Jeanine makes $25,000 full-time, and I make $45,000. If we try to live on her salary and part of mine, we don't make the bill payments and we lose the house. We don't even discuss it seriously. She gets the extra time with the children, and I get to be away at work."

Whatever the social changes, most of us are reluctant to relinquish traditional roles. As providers and protectors, men acquire status, meaning, and direction. They also pay a significant price.

The Price of Breadwinning. Some men actually have work that they love, including good remuneration that also allows for as much time as they desire with their family. For these men the price of breadwinning is minimal. They are definitely in the minority.

Most of us cannot claim such good fortune. We feel the burden of financial responsibility for our families. Most of us are forced to take on more work than we desire or to work entirely for money, with emotional gratification and meaningful challenges being luxuries.

When a man has his first child, this responsibility becomes extremely pronounced. Mark, a former music teacher at a New England high school, is one example. "When David was born, I knew that I'd have to leave music and get work that would pay. I entered the business world. I didn't much like it, but I just had to do it. With a teacher's salary and my wife at home (which we both wanted for the first two years) . . . I just didn't want him to grow up in some apartment. I wanted him to have the best . . . so it meant that music and teaching had to go and twelve-hour days of playing the game were necessary."

Most men have to go to work every morning whether they want to or not. Many come home from work most days unprepared for instant involvement with the family. The "workday" clearly includes actual work hours, frustrating commuting time, and transition time as well.

The transition time can be particularly difficult for a family. Dad's body is home. Isn't it reasonable to expect that he will also be present and available? For wives who have already been with the children for hours, their husbands' arrival portends potential adult contact, relief, and partnering. For children who haven't seen their daddy all day, his arrival could mean playtime (or at least a new adult to wear out). Most fathers want to be there fully. However, it is not always easy. One woman, reflecting on the reception she gives her husband after being home alone with their five-month-old daughter, joked, "He throws a piece of raw meat in the door as a test. If I attack it, he puts on his armor before coming in. . . . I don't want to rush him, but by the time he gets home, all I want is for him to take Katy and let me take a long, hot bath. I just don't have the reserve to wait for him to change his clothes. He understands, but he doesn't like it."

How one makes the transition from work to home varies with the individual. Each person needs to do it in his or her own way and time. Normally anybody who has been at work during the day needs to take some symbolic step to shed the emotional work environment. It is not always convenient for the family when a father, or mother, needs to change into home clothes, watch television, read the newspaper, open the mail, eat, exercise, or all of the above.

The fact is that most work environments are not "human friendly." They are geared more toward production than personal fulfillment. In addition, for many workers the commute home is often harrowing and frustrating. Crowded public transportation, or being on the Nimitz Highway, Lakeshore Drive, Beltway, San Diego Freeway, East River Drive, Southeast Expressway, or the like, has left many a worker far more stressed than the hours on the job.

Anybody who is in such situations for several hours a day needs to unwind before being able to react lovingly to others whose expectations are that he will slip comfortably and immediately into his role as Daddy.

The work environments of our fathers and grandfathers were generally far worse than are those of today. It is little wonder that their transitions were more acceptably assuaged by alcoholic beverages and a stay-at-home wife, whose job it was to make the home hospitable after a hard day's work.

Social changes have reduced the acceptability or likelihood of these modes of support. Furthermore, fathers of today can look forward to more years of work. Few men today have a twenty-five-year work life, retirement party, pension, and gold watch from a single employer. A baby boomer can legitimately look forward to a forty-five-year work life, with shifting careers and job sites, and will have to rely on a self-funded pension. For many men this financial concern adds a significant emotional tension. It is not the only emotional stressor.

The Emotional Toll. A man's actual work time may not be entirely contained within the hours he is at the office or workplace. Many jobs demand a great deal of allegiance and thinking between actual hours where one is "punched in." Most white-collar workers carry substantial emotional demands home with them.

Willie was talking about his job as a financial planner: "I don't mind the on-job hours so much. It's a fifty-hour week, but it just doesn't end there. When I go home, I'm always taking a pile of papers to read. Then sometimes when I'm driving or watching the tube or doing pine time (sitting on the bench) at the basketball game, I'll start worrying about some client's investments or about how I'm going to tell them they made a bad move or something, and I just can't let it out of my mind."

This is added to the emotional energy required to keep in mind the kids' schedules, lessons, Home and School days, birthdays, when to get the dry cleaning, and when or what groceries need to be bought.

All of these concerns seem like normal vagaries of modern life and not unusually demanding. However, keeping each of these in mind requires some mental and emotional energy. Work that comes home with you remains work. Modern life may well be less physically precarious than caveman days, but it nevertheless takes a significant emotional toll. For a father like Sal, it can become almost overwhelming:

It must have been two weeks ago Wednesday, I think, when I just wanted to chuck the whole thing and split. Gina had to be out of town with her mother, so I had to get the kids after school. So my boss decides at the last minute to schedule a meeting at four-thirty in the afternoon—so we don't have to meet during work hours. I tell him I've got to get the kids and he looks like I blew off the whole project. Then my daughter, on her own, goes over to a friend's house, and I don't know where she is until the other mother calls. So I get dinner, and at nine o'clock, I start dealing with the mail and there's a credit card error, but I can't call until the next day, and then Gina calls at eleven P.M. and tells me her mother needs her for two more days. All night I'm awake worrying about my job, the credit company, how to teach my daughter not to make her own plans, and my son's report card. Then Wednesday morning I wake up and start to get the kids breakfast and there's no milk in the house, the youngest one is screaming, the other one won't get dressed in time, and the boss's secretary calls me at home to tell me that they rescheduled the meeting because of me to first thing in the morning, and "could I come in early" . . . that's when I wanted to just run away.

Individually none of Sal's pressures is too demanding. Most of them seem pretty average to most parents. The problem is that the sum is a prescription for what we now euphemistically call "burnout"; one generation ago it was referred to as "a nervous breakdown."

Sal is trying to meet multiple demands from work and home life. Like most of us he can keep juggling for some period of time. However, as the demands continue, his ability to satisfy them decreases. He will begin to feel less competent. His feelings of self-esteem will diminish.

In addition to the problems of unending work days and the total number of demands to keep in mind, most men experience a host of emotional pressures.

There are, of course, the financial worries. Will I be able to provide enough for my family? Will we have a decent home, a car, vacations, extras for the children? We also worry about the impact of our "obsession" with finances on our relationship with our wives. Is she dissatisfied, bored, angry, or resentful? Are we growing distant from each other? Am I available for my children? Am I so involved with breadwinning that my children have to enjoy the benefits of my wage earning without me? How do they feel about me?

We are committed to protecting and providing. We must also balance the costs of that commitment for us and our families.

Loving and Being Engrossed with Children

When men are pictured in literature, portrayed on television or the movies, and described in advertising, they are commonly depicted as aggressors or buffoons; not as warm, loving, competent parents.

Yet when men do talk about their feelings for their children, the first word they say is *love*. Judging from my interviews with fathers, my work as a therapist with them, my personal conversations with other men, the messages I read on electronic bulletin boards, and my personal feelings about my own children, I can only conclude that a father's love for his children is deeper and different from any prior emotional experience.

Martin Greenberg, in *The Birth of a Father*, describes the intense, multifaceted connection between fathers and children at the moment of birth:

> He feels stunned, stoned, dazed, off the ground, ten feet tall, taken away, taken out of himself.
>
> *Engrossment* refers to a father's sense of absorption, preoccupation and interest in his baby. He feels gripped and held by this feeling. He has an intense desire to look at the baby, to touch and hold him. It is as if he is hooked, drawn to his newborn child by some involuntary force over which he has no control. He doesn't will it to happen, it just does.[8]

Dr. Greenberg describes a sense of exhilaration and harmony with the child that may emerge suddenly or develop slowly over time. Whatever the nature of any man's personal love for his children, the bond is often the strongest that he has ever felt, except perhaps as a child to his own parents.

Being a parent is hard work. A combination of factors helps us endure it: biological drives, cultural dictates, discipline, loyalty, guilt, and most of all love for the child. A man who desires to be the best possible father needs to access the love feelings within *and learn how to express those feelings to his children.*

Bret describes his love and frustration with that component:

Nothing matters at all except Lisa and Teddy. They're my whole life, my reason for being. Sometimes at night I just watch them sleep and get filled up with tears—joy, love . . . I don't know. Maybe relief that they're alive and asleep. I think a lot of my part in bringing such perfect little beings into the world . . . knocks me out how great they are. . . . Mostly my feelings come out by taking care of their needs for food, shelter, fun. I don't really have much myself anymore. The pressure to do the best for them just keeps me going. It isn't like I resent it, you know . . . I . . . just know that it's what I'm here to do . . . I love when they laugh or are happy and especially when they yell, "Daddy's home," and come hurtling through the door. . . . You know what bothers me? . . . I regret that my dad never said he loved me, but I have such a hard time telling my kids how I feel about them—love them . . . sometimes I feel like all I do is yell at them to do what they're supposed to do. Why can't I just tell my boy that I love him without both of us getting so embarrassed?

Bret spoke these words at a weekend men's group. Each of the other thirteen men in the room had wet eyes as he spoke and each related similar feelings about their own children. Frank and Steve summed up a great deal of the frustration in the ensuing conversation:

FRANK: The biggest issue is that I tell my kids that I love them, but it never seems like enough. I'm probably waiting for some kind of reply, and it never comes.

STEVE: Yeah, you want them to say the same thing to you. It's the same for me. I tell my daughter I love her and if she doesn't tell me she loves me, too, I feel empty.

FRANK: When they do say it, though, I think maybe it's only because I did. I devalue it because it wasn't spontaneous. I can't win for losin'.

STEVE: I know that one well. But the good part is that when I say it first to them, they get to feel it spontaneously and get to hear it. I hope they grow up knowing that they had a loving father.

BRET: I gotta believe that they will. But it makes me think maybe my dad loved me, too, but he couldn't say it either.

FRANK: I believe my dad did love me. He never said it directly, but he used to brag to the guys at the barbershop in town about us all the time.

When men talk honestly and openly about their children, they describe deep love and caring. Many do not share those words with their children or feel unsure that they've been heard when they do.

As one man wrote on an electronic bulletin board, "I know my father loved me. Only he rebuffed all my attempts to love him back. Now I have two children of my own. I guess an incident in a K mart can sum up the progress so far. My daughter and I were in line buying paint for the living room when she spontaneously gave me a big hug and in an audible voice said, "Daddy, I love you." Now everybody in the K mart just about stood still to see what I was going to say next. Fact was I did not have to say anything. She piped up and said, "I beat you this time, Daddy, I told you I love you before you could tell me."

I know that I had never experienced the kind of love that I've felt for my children. It has a different depth and feel than the very real love I knew for my parents and sister. It is also qualitatively different from the love I feel for my wife.

The normal modern father's love for his children is very deep.

Facing Performance Fears

Modern fathers often have an excessive concern with achievement. Warren Farrell, author of *Why Men Are the Way They Are,* persuasively demonstrates how men in our culture are characterized and treated as "success objects." Unlike women, who are essentially assigned benefits in our culture based on appearance (and treated as "sex objects"), men are trained to believe that they must achieve success. Affluence, prosperity, and power—the rewards of success—allow men to acquire the best (i.e., "most attractive") partners. Because every aspect of a man's being is evaluated on performance criteria, there is considerable concern among men that they won't perform sufficiently well.

These values predispose us to compete with each other, especially for riches, jobs, and females. We grow up with the expectation of competing at work, at home, and at play. Being a father is no different. Men are frequently trapped by the need to be good performers as husbands, fathers, and lovers.

We believe that we will be loved and accepted only if we are winners. To lose is to invite rejection. Because the fear of rejection is so powerful, we often compete even at home. Instead of attaining the love we desire through respect, which presumably accompanies success, we actually alienate the people with whom we most desire closeness.

In the film *The Great Santini* the father cannot drop the competition even when he plays basketball with his son. He plays so hard that he is willing to hurt his own son if that is a cost of winning. He will even deny a loss to maintain his ego.

Santini and Hollywood caricatures of the Marine Corpsman are not always farfetched. Consider Rolland's memory of his play with his father: "I guess I was about sixteen when I realized that I could take my father at tennis. I did it only once. He said I was lucky, and stopped playing with me or coming to my high school matches that year. The next year I let him win so he would play more. Then when I beat him in front of my college freshman coach, he never played with me again."

In response to a question about how he plays with his own sons he responded, "I can take Martin, and Billy is still only fourteen (although he may be the best of all of us—he beat Martin last summer). Tim is on the team at college, and we don't have matches much anymore. You know, as you mention it, I guess I'm as bad as my dad. I can't let Tim beat me, so I resort to an old hamstring injury as an excuse. I don't think I could beat him even with a thirty-love handicap."

Rolland's fears of being discarded by his sons if he lost to them at tennis led him inadvertently to create the consequence he most feared. By withdrawing from his sons when they became better at tennis, he lost the contact with them he so desperately sought. Rolland clearly felt that if he lost at tennis, he was less worthy as a man and a father.

As a salesman for a large national firm, he was rewarded for being better than others at his level of sales. Success meant bettering his own and his peers' sales for the prior fiscal quarter. His personal self-esteem was directly tied to his sales numbers; his destiny symbolically aligned with that of Willy Loman, the hero of Arthur Miller's classic *Death of a Salesman:* He was unable to find any value in life without victories.

Rolland carried this ethic to an extreme, but he is not so different from many fathers. He believed that his value as a person was related directly to his performance in every realm. His desperate fear was that when he could no longer compete and win, he would be discarded by his company, by his wife, and by his children, a fear that was realized just prior to his forty-sixth birthday during the 1990 economic recession. Two months after he lost his job, his wife filed for a divorce and asked him to move out of their home. She shared his expectation that his value was inextricable from his successes.

Many men carry that fear. "If I fail, I'll be rejected." As fathers they honestly believe that their children's love is contingent on their accomplishments or what they provide for them. Often, like Rolland's father, they convey the same values to subsequent generations. It doesn't just happen to sons. Tammy, a thirty-three-year-old woman, reported one week after receiving a substantial promotion and raise,

> I became the engineer that my dad wanted and I've been very successful. I know how to play the system. I know how to get ahead and I'm a damn good engineer and manager. But you know what? Ever since the announcement of the promotion came out, I've been sad and angry . . . mostly taking it out on Greg [her husband, who nods in acknowledgment], but the one I'm angry at is my dad. I don't want to be an engineer. I don't want to be the son he never had. I've been thinking about quitting and going back to school in psychology—my first love. But, you know, I'm afraid to call my dad and tell him about the promotion or about the wish to quit. He'll just tell me I'm afraid I can't handle the extra responsibility. He may be right too. Maybe I just don't think I can compete as a level-three manager. The worse thing is I also think I'm letting women down if I don't do it, because this will make me the fourth-highest-ranking woman in the company.

It is very important for all fathers to recognize our susceptibility to these performance fears. It is also crucial for us to leave our work ethos at the job site. The work world may well be very competitive; home life by contrast is best when it's supportive.

When a father brings a performance orientation into the home, he will be more of a "Mr. Fix-it" than a father and husband. For many family situations problem solving often works in reverse. Unlike bosses at work, when our wives or children bring us a problem, they are not looking for a solution. What they want is for Dad to be involved with them, sharing their concerns.

Rico, for example, claims that his wife "drives me crazy with her conflicting demands. She says we have a problem, so I solve it for her. Then she gets mad at me and argues with the answer I came up with . . . telling me I don't listen to her. The next thing, she does what I suggest and it works out and she gets mad at me again, or decides that she was the one who thought of it."

His wife, Angie, nodded while he was describing this, then laughingly admitted, "What he says is true. I do get angry at him. He doesn't understand that what I want is for him to work with me, not be such a 'know-it-all.' It infuriates me when he knows the answer right away. It makes me feel dumb for not thinking of it myself."

Angie and Rico have a solid sixteen-year marriage. At the conscious level they agree on a partnership. At an unconscious level, however, they continue to play out old roles. At times of stress she approaches him as if he were an authority figure, and he acts like one. He gets to be the informed parent and she the cute daughter. Their discomfort with these events is both about the seeming unfairness of her anger at him for giving her what she requests and a corresponding dissatisfaction with being in those roles.

Rico needs to learn two things: He needs to learn how to respond to her unasked message for assistance by *sharing* the problem, and he needs to put aside his automatic problem-solving (performance) response for a more appropriate empathic one.

Being Encouraging and Supportive

Men are not alone in learning that success is rewarded and failure punished. Children at very young ages are quite cognizant of the social reactions to failure. They learn early that errors are to be avoided and that making mistakes can lead to ridicule and either punishment or rejection.

Preschoolers avoid tasks in which they expect to fail, they lie about outcomes, and they feel embarrassment at less-than-optimal performance. Before the age of four my son was embarrassed to let his preschool mates see him crying or being disciplined by his mother in front of them. Many children in kindergarten and earlier will disdain somersaults, rings, hopscotch, or card games if there's any chance of failure.

It is also true that the way we learn most skills is through some form of trial and error. How can a father convey to his children the need to strive for excellence, to do the best job they can, while helping them learn some tolerance for making mistakes and learning from them? It is a father's special job to be able to encourage his children to risk failure by making any experience, successful or not, an opportunity for learning.

How does a father teach a child to compete successfully and simultaneously to make efforts to learn new things by trial and error? How can a father defuse the embarrassment our culture puts on error? The answer involves three traits: modeling, empathy, and patience.

Among the semi-enjoyable tasks that often fall to fathers is teaching their children how to ride a bicycle. It is a rare child who simply jumps on a bicycle the first time and rides off with perfect balance. For most, several falls are the norm.

How does a father help the child endure the scrapes, bruises, and falls long enough to master the riding skills? How does a dad endure his own empathic hurt with his son or daughter who is scared, crying, or feeling hopeless?

Demands to "suck it up" and keep trying don't seem to work unless there is some context of caring and sensitivity that goes along with it. The effective bicycle teacher conveys to the child that progress is more important than immediate success.

I recall with great warmth the first time I helped a child learn her bicycle skills. She was the seven-year-old daughter of a close friend, who was a single mother. Tanya was a very academically successful little girl who was far less sure of her athletic skills. Her outstanding report card was of little help in mastering the skills that her friends and (far worse) her younger brother were already beginning to acquire. Her mother tried running alongside, but her own need for Tanya's success and her anxiety and frustration made extra falls inevitable.

One afternoon Tanya and I designed a plan. In secret we would "sneak out," away from Mom and the other kids, and practice. She took to the secret lessons readily and within two hours was riding with regular, if shaky, balance. My own wind was far less sure than her ability to keep the two-wheeler upright. The next weekend she and I (amid much giggling and near bursting with knowledge of a secret that wouldn't keep for long) went out for a bike ride past her surprised mother and down to the local park. It was a remarkable accomplishment for both of us.

Later she confessed to her mom that it was easy to learn because I was so certain that she could and because when she fell, I checked to see if she was okay but didn't make a big scene out of it. It was the first time in my life that I approximated the wonderful "daddy" feelings (joy at her excitement and pride of accomplishment, happiness at the closeness, etc.) that sustain me since the birth of my own children.

At age eight Jessica was a bright, accomplished, and friendly child, but she had a strong tendency to pursue only those interests that she did well. She would give up on many new tasks at the hint of a single mistake or potential difficulty. Efforts by both parents to push her to persevere produced pouting and stubbornness and ultimately withdrawal of privileges or "time-out." What they didn't produce was motivation and renewed effort.

After several months of observing the diminishing range of Jessica's activities, her father began a remodeling project in the home. Encouraging her to keep him company, he allowed her to observe his errors, frustration, and perseverance. He modeled for her how he learned by making mistakes. Soon thereafter she began taking small risks of failure on her own with her father's encouragement. He patiently allowed her to approach her challenges slowly. Several months later a report from teachers indicated that Jessica had made a major shift at school, becoming far more experimental. In Robert Bly's terms, her father shared his temperament as well as his discipline with her.

Eric McCollum, describing a conversation with a friend as the two of them watched Jack's young son catch and release fireflies, remarked that the conversation haunted him for weeks afterward. What did his friend say that so focused on the hard lessons fathers teach sons? " 'I want my son to know that there is a choice in life, to hurt and to kill, and that exercising this choice is not glamorous,' " he told me. " 'If you want to give a boy an antidote to Rambo and Dirty Harry and all the rest, you can't deny that violence exists.

You have to teach its reality. I want Peter to know what it's like to shoot a rabbit. I want him to see it screech and kick and die. And I want to be with him to comfort him when he learns the truth of violence.'"

Mo recalls his own father: "He was a Russian Jew, who worked hard as a kosher butcher and read constantly when he was home. He'd read the Yiddish newspapers, of course, two every day. . . . When I was in grammar school, he learned English with me. Even at the time I knew how much harder it was for him. He never got some of the sentence structure right. . . . But what he gave me was his struggle. . . . He was never embarrassed to get something wrong . . . he just asked to be corrected. If it weren't for him and his strong ego, I'd never have become a writer or a psychotherapist. I never would have understood that an error was a way to learn something new, instead of a personal failure."

Being Courageous

Being a father means teaching your children about courage. Because children learn to emulate our behavior rather than our words, courage demonstrated is most likely courage learned. What courage must men pass on to their children?

In the words of Mark Twain, "Courage is resistance to fear, mastery of fear—not absence of fear." To many men, exhibiting courage is acting as if there is no fear. Broad back, strong, silent, the expendable soldier.

Dr. Joan Shapiro writes,

My husband kills the bugs in our house. I don't think I am unusually squeamish, and we did not have a discussion about whose job it should be to get rid of nasty-looking creatures. All that happens was that I would say, "Ooh, what a big, awful spider!" and before I could even look around for a shoe or newspaper, my husband would be there, tissue in hand removing the offending bug without a noise or complaint. What I found out . . . is that he hates bugs, and would rather not have to look at, let alone touch insects. . . . He sees it as his job. He perfected his talent while raising his children. He didn't want them to be frightened. And he especially didn't want his sons to see his fear . . . he wanted them to be more "manly" than he was.[9]

My childhood friend, Harvey, took this ethic to a far greater extreme. Afraid of bullies in the neighborhood and of violence of any kind, he joined the Marine Corps soon after his marriage. In 1971, at the age of twenty-eight, he died in a Vietnam jungle, leaving behind his wife and two young children.

Such "counterphobic" demonstrations may only teach our children denial, or underscore their feelings that they are not like us. Children have many fears. The lesson they need to learn is how to face the fear of the unknown, being mindful of safety considerations, choosing battles carefully. There is a difference between being foolhardy and being brave. The foolhardy face predictable danger that could be avoided; the brave accept danger with all necessary precautions, because it is unavoidable or because it is important to make a statement at that time.

Fathers do need to teach children to stand up for beliefs in the world at large, but they must also demonstrate courage at home. One of the places that fathers most need to show courage is with their wives. Mothers understandably believe themselves to be the better parent and as such the correct one. There will be times when you truly believe that your wife is proceeding in a manner with which you disagree. It is at those times that you must point out what you believe and take on any wrath that may follow, stand up to it, don't escalate or leave, and work it through by staying and discussing your concerns. It will take some courage to listen to her opinion, to share your own perspective, to stand up for your beliefs, and (the extreme courage) to acknowledge openly when you are wrong.

This is in direct contrast to the "typical macho" male stereotype in which "courage" in the face of a perceived spousal attack is an aggressive escalation of the conflict through demeaning language and accusations, leaving the scene, or physical abuse.

It is not uncommon for wives to "correct" their husband's form of parenting. This "correcting" may be delivered in public. It takes courage for a husband who is scolded in this way to inform his partner of his feelings about her treatment of him and to reaffirm that his ideas and methods as a parent may well be as valuable as hers.

Consider the following interaction between this husband and wife. The discussion occurred when Nancy returned from work to find that Ted had disciplined their three-year-old son for playing with matches by depriving him of dessert and sending him to his room early after a swat on his behind. When she walked in the door, the little boy was crying on his bed.

She asked their son what had happened, and he replied, "Daddy hit me." Without another word she marched in on Ted, who was then involved in helping their older son with his homework.

NANCY: I will not have you abusing my children. You will restrain yourself and never again strike any of the children.

TED: What are you talking about?

NANCY: Don't you dare play stupid with me. I know what happened. I just talked with Kevin.

TED: Did Kevin tell you why he was punished?

NANCY: I don't care why. I am his mother and I won't have him hit by you.

TED: There are two things going on here that I don't like right now. First of all I will not talk to you until we can both talk and be listened to. Second, you do not make the parenting rules around here. I have just as much say as you do.

NANCY: I'm the mother.

TED: Yes, you're the mother, but you are not the queen. I'm the father here. Now, when you're ready to talk to me about this privately, we can decide about what we'll both do in the future.

NANCY: It'll be a cold day in hell before I'll let you abuse my children.

TED: I did not *abuse* anyone. I'm trying to teach him a lesson about playing with matches, and right now you're ruining that lesson. If anyone should be angry about this, it's me . . . besides the temperature is falling, and hell could freeze over by morning.

She didn't laugh at his attempt at anger-diffusing humor, but two hours later Nancy came back into the room and asked to talk. She began by saying that she had had a really rough day, felt guilty about being away from the children, and couldn't stand to come home to her crying baby. Ted was understanding but firm. After indicating that he felt for her position, he reiterated that he needed to be treated as the parent he was. He said, "When you came home and started disciplining me, I felt like the baby-sitter who was about to be fired. You need to understand that I love the boys as much as you. I wouldn't do anything to hurt Kevin or Tony. And I believe that a single swat on the behind may well stop him from hurting himself in the future."

Ted's reaction seems almost too good. It's the kind of response most of us would wish we had said at the time but didn't think of until an hour or two later. After all, it did wind up in a book on fathering. It was not easy for Ted either. He admitted that he was scared when he said those things, "scared of making her angrier, scared of more rejection, worried about regaining face with my children." He claimed that he was very proud of that particular interaction because he felt "courageous, doing it right for a change."

Being Trustworthy

Among the important lessons children need to learn is how to trust themselves and others. Self-trust is evident in a person's self-esteem and confidence. A suitable trust of others and the outside world allows for appropriate risk taking and experimentation.

The more unavailable, unreasonable, inconsistent, or unreliable a father, the less likely his children will grow up in a stable environment. Without stability a child is hard-pressed to trust self or others.

Research on fathers who are not available to their children is quite instructive. Among the most common findings in the literature on the effects on children of absent fathers is the subsequent inability of those children to develop trusting relationships as adults. The frequent conclusion drawn from these data on absent fathers is that present, involved fathers play a significant role in helping their children develop trust as adults. How might we do that?

Imitation is one way that children learn. Fathers who are themselves trustworthy will encourage the same in their children. A sense of quiet confidence elicits admiration and emulation. Because we normally spend less time with our children than mothers do, our actions may be more influential. A father with high self-esteem will be less threatened by his children's extreme and disconcerting behavior. This will allow for more patience and understanding. He can also demonstrate an orientation to problems that exemplifies good sense, perseverance, and the ability to learn from errors. He will not be put off by failures.

Children who emulate his behaviors and do not fear his reactions to their failure will be more readily able to develop a sense of personal self-confidence.

Another way that fathers teach trust is by being reliable. We must keep promises to our children or at least explain why we do not. We must keep appointments with them, be available when we are supposed to be, and stand up for them when they need us. We also need to maintain firm, fair limits.

One of the domestic arenas in which fathers offer such stability is discipline. Normally the man's role in family discipline is to hold to the rules, being less flexible or responsive to fluctuating mood states. If a father is firm and fair, not rigid, in the application of reasonable regulations and consequences, he supports a more predictable environment. A CBS survey of fourteen hundred high school seniors, reported by Charles Osgood in May 1992, indicated clearly that the thing most children wanted more from their parents was time and limits. These teenagers wanted their fathers to say no in a consistent way.

Children who can anticipate what their dad will and will not do are far more free to develop their own unique ways of being (individuate) and to grow independent (separate): the two primary tasks of childhood.

Many experts in the field of child development argue that because Mom is the primary attachment figure for children, it is more threatening to separate from her. Without an alternative attachment figure such as Dad, a child attempting to separate from Mother is faced with a feeling that he will be completely alone if he is not with Mother. When Dad is available, the child can experiment with distance and reduced dependence on Mom and still feel supported. In addition, a mother is far more likely to encourage her child to be close to the father than to release her child to find his or her own way in the world. The father thus offers the child an intermediate step; the child can still be somewhat connected while increasing independence and exploration of the outside world. The father provides a safety net while encouraging his children to experience personal growth. They can have the confidence to risk new adventures because they can count on Dad to bail them out if necessary.

A second form of trustworthiness by a father is in his translating the outside world to his children. Stanley Cath, a pioneer author in the field of fatherhood, writes that despite the increasing role of women working out of the home, Dad still stands as the primary representative of the outside world to children.

Because that is considered Dad's area of expertise, he is the parent who is best suited to teach his children about the joys and dangers in the world outside the home. If a father misrepresents the outside world as a way of self-aggrandizement or fear, his children develop a distorted perspective of what to expect.

Les described his personal unreadiness for college at a small liberal arts school: "In my family, I was always taught it was 'dog eat dog.' Dad was always coming home with stories about tricky situations and dangers. He never trusted anyone, and he was himself an accomplished liar and con man of sorts. When I arrived at college, I questioned everyone's motives and competed ruthlessly.

It took me a long time to figure out that they were just being friendly. I was the one who tried to win at all costs. Mostly everyone else was ready to cooperate. I must have seemed like a real jerk when I got there. I was just unprepared for trustworthy, helpful, caring people."

Les was ready for a world of danger as described by his father. Having taken his father's perception to heart, he went to his college prepared to be mistrustful, looking for competitiveness.

Grant's father provided him with an equally debilitating expectation. "My father told us since we were little that we were special. You know, better than other people. He was always coming home with stories about how he was more noble, more ethical, more successful than others. . . . When I got to high school, I discovered that he was pretty ordinary. I had a long fall from grace. I went from feeling superior to feeling worthless and inferior. I no longer knew who I was or who I was supposed to be. If my father was a nobody, who was I? . . . I don't think it bothered me that we weren't special as much as how [discrepant] that was from how I thought it was."

What fathers convey about their personal experience of the outside world will affect their children's expectations. If a child cannot trust his father for a realistic viewpoint, he may find himself ill-prepared.

Honoring Male Compassion and Warmth

Chucky and I sat on the curb talking. We were talking about how the Cubs were sure to win the pennant this year, about the other kids at school, and occasionally in little bits and pieces about how my mother was drinking again. He never said anything directly, but the offer to have dinner at his house was genuine, and the way he looked down at the ground made me know he felt for me in special ways. When I broke my leg, he somehow got to the hospital and just sat there in my room, arguing with me over which TV program was better, and I forgot the pain and argued back.

I miss the curb and Chucky. We don't talk much any-more. He called me last Christmas and said he had a son and the boy's middle name was Steve. I knew he was named after me. We didn't talk of my divorce, but I knew it hurt him. Next time I go back East, I'll see him. Maybe we'll go to Wrigley and assure ourselves that this year the Cubbies will surely win. I cried after that call.

Men may experience emotions similarly to women, but they share emotion in very different ways. Often what is said is far less important than what is not said. The shorthand that we use as men is very different from women's conversation. The best communication is not necessarily face-to-face, feelings-oriented discourse. Sometimes that form of communication is essential. Other times indirect communication is far more effective.

When I want to talk to my ten-year-old daughter about some-thing that is important to her, it is best when we are alone in the car. Sitting side by side, she can tell me what she wants at her speed, in comfortable increments. She can change the subject back and forth. She can tell me in the form of a metaphorical story about imaginary characters or other children we both know. She is also most receptive to information from me when I am not "in her face."

There are also times when she most responds to quiet, distrac-tion-free heart-to-heart, eye-to-eye conversations. I don't know how much I adapt to her way of communicating or she to my own. I do know that I often prefer to discuss intimate things side by side rather than face-to-face, my wife's preferred style. Obviously this occasionally calls for some negotiation and compromise for "home court."

Men have long been criticized for either having no feelings, having the wrong ones, or being unable to describe them. It is true that males in our society are trained to deny, ignore, cover up, and rise above feelings. However, we do have them all the time. It is important that we express our feelings to our children in male ways. It is customary for men to be most open, for example, while they are working on a joint project together (i.e., shoulder to shoulder).

Openly expressing feelings is particularly hard for men because we are well trained to contain these feelings to protect our loved ones. Fathers have to serve as the buffer against the harsh realities of the world. When things get tough, the buck is supposed to stop with us. We have been taught that "real men" do not share their worries with their children. Yet to be a good father, we need to reveal ourselves and our internal struggles to our children. We do not have to give them our problems, but we do have to share our inner lives and our caring as we experience them. Our children need to understand male modes of being open and caring.

Developing Flexibility

As a man I have been taught to understand and obey rules and guidelines. I expected that parenting would also be governed by certain appropriate "correct" principles. Unfortunately it has not turned out to be so easy (predictable or dull). One of the benchmarks of parenting is that you are regularly unprepared for something the children will do.

Carl Whitaker, a noted family therapist, said, "Parents have only one choice. They get to choose how they want to be wrong."

Given a job for which there are few appropriate models, outdated personal experience, and a goal of becoming obsolete, it is no surprise that parenting feels like a series of constant readjustments. It is quite a problem to hold on to basic values while responding to shifting needs and situationally determined predicaments.

Robert, speaking for many fathers at a workshop, told the group, "I finally got it figured out. If I say it to my wife, it's 'naive.' If I say it to my son, it's the equivalent of a red flag to *el toro*, and if I even consider telling my sixteen-year-old daughter anything, it causes an involuntary reflex; her eyeballs roll up as if trying to leave their sockets."

It isn't that whatever Robert says is discarded. He lives in an environment in which the operative rule is *whatever Dad suggests must be met with a negative reaction*. He will not be credited with finding the solution to a problem. For some men this represents a serious challenge. Will replied to Robert with the following: "Well, I know how that is, but I'll tell you, I don't stand for it. I don't care if it takes all night or if I have to talk till I'm blue in the face, they are going to listen to what I say or face the consequences. My seventeen-year-old son knows that if he crosses that line once more, he's grounded for a month."

Will did acknowledge that he has been relatively unsuccessful to date with that approach. Dealing effectively with the changing needs of family life requires flexibility, awareness, and creativity. If Robert is to communicate effectively, he needs to know when his family members are open to listening. He also needs to keep the sense of humor he displayed at the workshop.

It seems a verity of modern life that any solution to problems will be time-limited. What worked in a relationship last year may well not be effective tomorrow. For men who are trained for most of their lives to be problem solvers, this can be particularly frustrating. We expect to solve a problem once and for all and then move on to the next. Fathering doesn't work that way. Most "fixes" tend to be temporary.

Furthermore it is not always easy to determine exactly what our children desire. It's important for fathers to develop the ability to read between the lines. As a father, rigid or fixed responses seem to be effective only a small percentage of the time. Sometimes when my daughter asks me a question, she wants my best factual answer. Other times she wants me to be with her while she figures it out for herself. As much as I try to discern which of these two it is at the moment, it remains a trial-and-error endeavor, with my first response being the desired one approximately 50 percent of the time.

Being flexible means adjusting to situations as they occur, not implementing solutions that will not apply.

How would you respond to a call in the middle of the night

like the one Phil received in 1990? His daughter, a college sopho- more, was calling from a jail in the Midwest. She had been arrested for "soliciting." A minister with "strong fundamentalist leanings," Phil felt shocked, disappointed, guilty, angry, and very worried. He had thought that she was in a protected college environment. Phil's reaction was to jump on the first plane to see her and take care of things. He was able to square things with the police and the col- lege. It took a lot longer to iron out differences with his daughter. "Every fiber of my being told me to yank her out of school and bring her home. I had to fight all my impulses to try to reteach her all the lessons she missed. It's a good thing that when I saw her, my heart went out to her. All I really did was listen, cry with her, help her get some spiritual guidance at college. Then I left, scared to death. It was gratifying that my wife and my congregation ap- plauded what I did. I guess God needed me to learn a lesson about forgiveness and love. It all worked out, but to this day I don't know where I got the strength to overcome my own sense of personal hurt and to pay attention to my little girl." Until that night Phil believed that he would have had a different response to such a predicament.

Cal had a quite different dilemma. When his wife left him "abruptly" in 1986, he had to immediately change from being "the distant disciplinarian" to being the sole parent of his two school- age boys. He changed his job, which had required a lot of travel, and his lifestyle, "which was hands off. She was the real parent at home, and I was on the road. I only saw the boys on weekends and two nights a week usually, and they were all fed and bathed most of the time. What a change to being responsible for all their needs. We're living on a lot less money now, but the three of us are a good team."

Being flexible does not mean losing one's basic values. As a therapist I have experienced, a number of times, parents who were shocked that their children were using drugs like cocaine. Yet these same parents smoked marijuana with their teenagers. Normally teens rebel by doing parents one (or two) better.

Administering Discipline

"Wait till your father gets home!" These words can bring terror into the hearts of children. The grand executioner will be told of my misdeeds, and punishment will be painful, perhaps capital.

Fathers did not get to be the disciplinarian in the home because they are bigger and could mete out grander and more painful punishments. At least two factors coalesced: the mother's symbiotic relationship and the father's role as the outside person in the family.

By virtue of their biological connection and in their role as primary care giver to infants, most mothers bond with their children in a particularly intense and personal way. The connection encompasses physical, emotional, and psychological ingredients. Psychologically and symbolically the child remains a part of the mother. Where they once shared a single body, they continue to share an intense interrelationship. Emotions are experienced jointly. They are in regular and lengthy physical contact. If she is breast-feeding, she remains a source of sustenance for her child. The psychological attachment defies easy separation for mother or child. Where the child ends and the mother begins is not always clear. In such a symbiotic relationship a mother will have access to the child's feelings and emotional state on a consistent basis. Her discipline will reflect that knowledge.

As the person in the family who had the most contact with society and the outside world, it fell on Father to bring home those social values and train his children to fit into their culture. He was also less present on a moment-by-moment basis and therefore more mysterious. Finally, the father lacked the unbreakable invisible emotional umbilical cord that allows the mother to discipline more on a moment-by-moment, event-by-event basis.

Many couples do notice the difference in their natural approach to disciplining their children. For men, adherence to rules is often primary. In the example of Ted and Nancy, cited earlier, Ted's response to three-year-old Kevin's playing with matches was to follow a certain course of action: a smack on the behind, no dessert, and time-out in his room. No matter what the circumstances, that was the punishment for that misconduct. Nancy was much more focused on what Kevin was feeling and would have adjusted her discipline based on that understanding. What is important here is that Ted's approach was neither generically worse nor better than Nancy's. It is different and more typically masculine. It is easy to see how each form of discipline would benefit Kevin. If you are unalterably opposed to corporal punishment, you would predetermine punishments that do not include spanking.

It is curious that the same word, *discipline,* means "punishment," a "field of study," and "a noble motivation for work." For a father, conveying a sense of a proper work regimen is often quite important. As Clint recalled, "When I was growing up, there was no sense of doing things right or sticking to a job till it was done. We just took whatever shortcut we could. I suffered in school because of that and was not a very good worker until I had to run my own business. That's where I had to learn discipline and perseverance. Mostly I learned from this old guy who lived in my neighborhood. He made kids' toys out of wood. The thing is, he was a real perfectionist. Never made any money, I'm sure, but he was always proud of his toys. . . . So the thing is I want my kids to have that kind of pride in their work. I want them to have some of Emmett's style. . . . The only way I know how to help them do it is to let them watch me struggle to do jobs right and fully . . . to stay at it until it's really done."

Demonstrating and Teaching Teamwork

It is a fact of modern work life that teamwork is crucial in surviving and getting ahead. Children need to learn how to be part of organizations larger than themselves. They need to learn how to subordinate their own ego for some greater good. Typically the job of teaching this teamwork belongs to men.

Normally females in our society are discouraged from learning teamwork skills. This occurs very early and persists through many formative stages of development. Watch the children on an elementary school playground at recess time. Gender differences are immediately evident. First of all, boys and girls are separate. In addition boys are together, playing in groups, whereas the girls are often alone or with a single partner. These values, conveyed before puberty, begin to explain one of the prejudicial elements in the "glass ceiling" that limits women's advancement in many segments of the business world. Many adult professional women have never developed the teamwork skills so necessary in the corporate world. They have mastered the skills to be a supporter of the leader or to be in charge themselves. One of the reasons that women's support groups and consciousness-raising groups were so helpful in advancing the women's movement is that they provided a place and methodology for women to learn those skills, denied them elsewhere.

Growing up, Dad had the opportunity to hang out with the gang. He was offered the opportunity, or was consigned against his will, to participate in team sports. Whether he was the star athlete or was chosen last because he was inept by comparison with his better-coordinated mates, his experience with team sports gave him the opportunity to experience the role of cooperation as part of competition.[10]

He learned that victory can be tasted by playing a small role in a larger endeavor. With enough games most of us actually get to experience the role of hero, honored by our peers, if only for a moment. Such memories and training allow us to subordinate personal desires to play a role in our combat unit, corporation, team, or family as adults.

They also tend to stay with us as moments of splendor in an otherwise drab existence. For many men heroic victories as a high school football player stand out as an epitome of success, long after others have ceased to remember or care.

Greg was a gifted athlete as a high-schooler. Bigger, stronger, and better-coordinated than most, he lettered in four sports. His academic prowess did not match his physical abilities, and he "retired" to a lifelong job as a laborer right out of high school. Married with three children, he worked hard to make ends meet, played sports on the weekends, and devoted some time to coaching as an adult. When asked what was most important to teach his children, he replied, "How important it is to seek the glory. My boy Chris, he has real talent—he can throw, hit, run. He's got the makings of a real star. I work with him to involve his teammates more. Sometimes he thinks he can do it all himself. I tell him if he doesn't reward the guys who work hard to let him be the hero, they'll stop. I guess he's a little like me. I remember the 'Wilson' game. We were three touchdown underdogs. I remember what it was like being city champions after we beat them. God, I can still taste that victory."

Greg continued with the story of that game twenty years ago for several minutes. He was obviously reliving the joy of his moment in the sun.

Some men who have been very successful in other fields recall team memories as being the sweetest. In an interview several years ago award-winning musician and songwriter Paul Simon described, as his greatest thrill, getting the winning hit in a baseball game when he was in junior high school.

It is from the perspective of a life of being part of group efforts that fathers can teach their children how to succeed. Consider the differences in the ways fathers and mothers typically play with their young children. A mother naturally *joins* the child at play, gauging the child's needs and level of play. It is the child who chooses what to play, how to play it, and when to play. From this children learn how to be in charge and how to be creative. They feel accepted for who they are. By contrast a father is most likely to engage in play with a child by *allowing the child to join him.* For a father, play can involve the child handing him the motor oil or a screwdriver. If the father is whittling a stick, his child can whittle along with him. If he is going to a sports event or watching television or making lunch, the children get to play with Dad by doing what he's doing. This teaches a child how to be part of a team. It allows the child to practice group effort leading to a common goal. Whereas a mother is likely either to encourage a child to do chores or to give up and do them herself, a dad may well invite the child to do the chores with him.

It is obvious that both forms of play are quite important and valuable to a developing child. It also underscores an additional dilemma for single parents. Nonetheless the father is most often the central point for teamwork training in the home.

Teamwork by Example. In the traditional home, children observe mothers doing tasks alone or with the children, and with Father when he is available. By contrast, and by virtue of his out-of-the-home commitment, Father is constantly doing things with others in the world. Whether he works on an assembly line or in an office, his work is only part of a greater production. He is a team player most of his waking time. When he is home, he must coordinate his efforts with the children with the rest of his team: his spouse.

Understanding and Honoring Personal Limits

From a psychological perspective childhood is a training program for independent adult life. Growing up means taking one's own place in the adult world. To be a successful adult, a child must develop a clear sense of personal psychological boundaries. Without a clear set of boundaries a child may feel too closely connected to or too distant from others. When a person is unclear as to where he or she psychologically ends and others begin, that person will have great difficulty with intimacy as an adult.

How does a father foster his children's development of psychological boundaries? The answer lies in how he nurtures a child's development of independence and connectedness.

All children are born with a need for security and a need for freedom. These must be kept in balance. Too much freedom becomes a sense of abandonment; too much security becomes suffocating. A father must promote a child's sense of independence, all the while advocating safety. Similarly he must promote appropriate safety measures, but not too many to inhibit experimentation and creativity. It is not easy to do. Many families eschew freedom for security or vice versa.

Parents who are too closely linked emotionally with a child

may inhibit the child's ability to become separate. These "enmeshed" family systems foster excess dependence.

Guilio is a forty-year-old man who grew up "in this unbelievably close Italian family. To this day when my mama gets sad or cries, I involuntarily begin to cry also. My wife, who grew up in this Norwegian Midwest family, thinks we're all nuts. She may be right. . . . Last year I made four trips to New York that I didn't really want to make because my mama said she needed me. . . . I took six trips all in all. . . . We just could have used the time and money here. It's just with Mama I can't say no."

By contrast, parents who are completely disconnected inhibit the child's ability to merge with others as an adult. Children who grow up in such "detached" families may well never develop an ability to share. They tend to be excessively cautious about their personal boundaries.

Philip admits, "I know I have a problem with commitment. Clarissa is at her wits' end. We've been engaged for four years and I just can't seem to get myself to actually say 'I do.' To me it's like a trap, a death sentence. We've been living together for six years now, so it's not like there's any surprises. If I don't decide soon, I may lose her. . . . When I asked my father about what to do, he just said, 'Be careful of entangling alliances.' "

Because of the intense emotional bond a mother may be ill suited to establishing emotional boundaries between herself and the children to whom she is so connected. This is a place for the father to validate the child's separateness. He does this by being personally separate from, but connected to, his child and his wife. A child can set individual boundaries by imitating Dad's respectful presence. A father who can love the child without a need for the child to fulfill his own needs fosters a child's ability to learn adult intimacy. Incidentally this is one reason why it is such a violation when men cross a sexual boundary with children. The child must be able to experiment with closeness and distance with an adult, confident that the adult will maintain the proper personal boundary to allow the child to be vulnerable and learn.

Bonnie, a thirty-six-year-old engineer expecting her first child, described her dad:

> Dad was the safety net. Mom would always be in my room, going through my things. . . . I think she used to read my diary. . . . She always took everything so personally. Like when this guy dumped me, she cried so much, I lost track of whether he dumped me or her. Daddy would just come over and say, "Let's go for a walk (or a drive)," then we'd not say that much. He'd tell me about how once he was broken-hearted in a failed romance, but he wouldn't say too much and he wouldn't ask so many questions about me. It's like I always felt like he believed that I was competent to take care of myself. That was something because I sure didn't feel so confident. But, you know, after being with him on our "walks," I sort of lived up to his higher expectations of myself. . . . He's seventy-seven this year, and he still loves me but knows where to stop. Like last year when Jim and I were having all that trouble. Mom wanted to know all the details, and she got mad at him for me, but Dad just told me that he'd be there and that he knew I'd do the right thing. It was hard for him, because he really likes Jim, and if we had broken up, he'd lose a good friend. . . . We didn't . . . it's a lot better now. Jim is just too much like Mom. . . . He gets scared when I pull away for a while to work on problems.

A peculiarly American version of unclear boundaries involves a sense of unlimited potential. In a culture that encourages all adults to be all things to all people, which emphasizes victories and wins, it is common for men and women to compare themselves constantly to "stars" in each realm.

Vic is a successful computer software engineer. As one of the original employees in a Silicon Valley start-up company, he became suddenly wealthy when the company went public. A self-described "computer nerd," he has a decent life with his live-in girlfriend, enjoyable work, and high compensation. He has been in individual psychotherapy for four years. His basic concern is that he feels inadequate and unhappy in most of his life.

Vic has the unfortunate habit of comparing himself with the experts in any field and coming out the loser in his comparisons. When he plays center field for the company softball team, he feels inadequate to the way he believes Willie Mays would have played.

In the software business he compares his income unfavorably with that of Microsoft founder Bill Gates, a man whose annual income rivals that of many countries' gross national product. In addition he finds himself less adequate than many innovators in his field.

Nor is it different when he makes a dinner, runs a mile or two, or makes love. He simply always sets up mental comparisons in which he is the loser. Vic describes growing up in a home in which both his parents encouraged him to strive for excellence and in which his father was never satisfied with his work. As an example, he described the biggest event in his high school career: "I won the science award as a junior and then the city and state competitions as well. Me and this other kid who won for English actually went down to the capital and got these medals from the governor. But even though he was proud, you know what my father said? He said as a senior I could probably win the English award and the science award. It bummed me out, but you know I actually tried to write poetry that whole year. So what happened was I didn't give enough attention to science and didn't place in either."

A father needs to help his child recognize personal limits and choose his battles carefully. Vic's father's suggestion that his son could demonstrate the same excellence in English ignored his son's abilities and aptitudes. It is not up to a father to determine that his child succeed in a particular arena, it is to encourage a son or daughter to follow his or her own dream after experimenting.

Lars described his daughter: "Leilani loves gymnastics. She just thrives on the physicality of the thing and stretching her body to its limits. I know she'll never turn the gymnastics into anything. She'll have the same chunky body her mother and I both have. She'll also probably have her mother's proclivity to music. I think she could be a great pianist, and I do encourage her, but only when she's ready. For now she can enjoy what she's doing and find her way. I wouldn't support her joining the gymnastics team if it meant a string of losses. I would like her to practice music more. So what I do is listen to her when she practices piano and let her know that I enjoy it a lot."

Facing Yourself and Your Own Fathering

"I'd like to spend a lot more time with the kids."

"I know that the kids would rather have me than a nicer home, but I can't shake the feeling that I've failed if I don't get it for them."

"Sometimes I just wish I was single again."

"I feel guilty, but lately I just can't stand being around the kids, the noise, my wife."

Sound familiar? These quotations came from hundreds of men who were interviewed for this book. Have you also said similar things or thought them? We all must come up short in our fathering. What do you really believe would make you the father you wish your father had been? How do you inadvertently fail to do the right thing, all the while trying to do things right?

Such questions have no easy answers. They require a serious look in the mirror as well as an exploration of the internal pushes and pulls that influence our feelings and actions.

Every father needs to look closely at what he believes and compare it to his actions. Where they are discrepant, a change is in order. Usually the behavior is what must change. If you believe that your children need more contact with you, you need to find time and energy for that contact. If you cannot accomplish anything when you are around the children, perhaps you shouldn't try to get anything done but be with them.

Many men have decried how quickly their children grew or how they never got to know them. By contrast I can't think of anyone who said mournfully on his deathbed, "Damn, I wish I had spent more time at the office!"

THE FATHER I HOPE TO BE

Parenting is one of the two toughest jobs that we normally encounter; maintaining a long-term intimate relationship is the other. What makes these jobs particularly tough is the lack of an adequate training program. Fathers commonly lament the errors that typically accompany on-the-job training. Fathers who love their children all want to be better at the business of fatherhood.

If you are such a man, you would be well served by the experience of your predecessors and peers to complement your personal knowledge gained from hard knocks, good luck, and observation. Many men have generously contributed to the knowledge of fatherhood by sharing their thoughts, feelings, and experience for this book. As you progress through the book, you may become increasingly aware of the proud heritage and noble pursuit of fatherhood as well as the difficulties and mishaps.

Our journey continues with a description of the modern context of fatherhood.

THE CONTEXT OF FATHERING

All the world's a stage,
And all the men and women merely players;
They have their exits and their entrances;
And one man in his time plays many parts
—SHAKESPEARE

In *As You Like It* William Shakespeare described seven "ages" of man: infant, schoolboy, lover, soldier, justice, pantaloon, and finally second-childishness; "sans teeth, sans eyes, sans taste, sans everything."

He doesn't mention fathering.

He is not alone. Sigmund Freud, Erik Erikson, Gail Sheehy, and Daniel Levinson, the most prominent writers of male psychological development, also neglect to include any stage of fatherhood. Common parlance is also instructive. One is far more likely to hear a woman described as "wife and mother" than a man as "husband and father."

Why is fatherhood of such little interest that it doesn't merit a place in psychological theory? Why does fatherhood seem an afterthought to our characterizations of men in modern society? It is common to introduce a man solely by reference to his work.

At a recent party I had the familiar experience of being introduced by the host as "Dr. Shapiro, the psychologist and professor."

My wife, who also has a professional career, was introduced as a "therapist and mother." Why wasn't I presented as "Natasha and Gabriel's father"? Was the host, himself an involved father of four, simply presuming that my role as father was of such secondary importance that the people I was meeting would be uninterested? Did he think I would be less impressive to other guests? Was it just convention—fatherhood is not a usual way of thinking about men?

In fact at a social gathering I would much prefer to talk about my children and my experiences as a father than to be thrust into my professional role. As a dad I can share my personal feelings and perceptions and learn from other parents. As "the psychologist" I expect to be approached for a professional opinion or advice on personal problems; I usually hear anxiety expressed that I would instantly "psychoanalyze" or diagnose someone on the spot; and I am often asked to engage in discussions of other "shrinks."

My profession is not unique. My brother-in-law, "the engineer," will inevitably find himself in a conversation about computers, whether he wants to or not. Once a man is defined as a "plumber," a "surgeon," a "businessman," or a "mechanic," he will be pressed into conversation about his work rather than his home life.

It is not unusual for people to find comfort and enjoyment in discourse about their work. Yet the typical exclusion of the man's role as a father may minimize the possibility for men to broach openly a topic of great meaning.

For many modern men fatherhood is the cornerstone of their male identity and intimacy. Surveys of men's values consistently point to their desire to be more connected to their children. In a 1991 workshop entitled "Why Men Are the Way They Are," Warren Farrell asked a group of almost one hundred men, "If society permitted it, and if it were financially feasible, how many of you would choose to remain home with your infant child for the first six to nine months of his or her life?" The show of hands shocked the women, and most of the men, in the audience. All but seven men raised their hands.

The workshop participants, a group interested in gender issues, obviously were not representative of the entire population,
but I doubt that the results of his informal survey would have been
completely different in other groups. Two of my own more scientific, lengthy surveys included interviews with over four hundred
recent and expectant fathers. The results clearly indicate that men
today experience deep yearnings for greater connection to both
their families of origin and families of procreation. Such longings
typically revolve around a man's feelings about being a father.

For modern men in Western cultures, becoming a father is a
biological, social, and emotional process. It is, however, one for
which there is little consistent training, norms, or guidelines. Most
men learn very early that the predominant role of fathering is to
be the *financial provider* for the family. They also learn, in a variety
of ways, that fathering is somehow secondary to mothering.

When I became a father for the first time in 1981, I had already been a psychologist, professor, and family therapist for over
a decade. My career was successful and stable. I was in a good
relationship. I very much wanted the child growing in my wife's
womb, and I thought myself "ready" for the change in status and
lifestyle. It therefore came as a surprise to discover how emotionally unprepared I was. I didn't fully expect the array of anxieties or
outpouring of love that accompanied the pregnancy and birth of
our daughter.

Why the surprise? Why wasn't I emotionally better prepared?
Having researched the process of becoming a father for the past
ten years and written about it in my book *When Men Are Pregnant*,
I am fully aware that my concerns were shared by the majority of
expectant and recent fathers.

WHY ARE MEN SO ILL-PREPARED EMOTIONALLY FOR FATHERHOOD?

Two explanations seem apparent: (1) a peculiar lack of professional
and popular interest in men's psychology; and (2) a dearth of traditional supports for learning about fathering.

Lack of Interest in Fatherhood

The lack of interest in and information about fathering is evident in any bookstore. There are whole sections of popular psychology books on women and mothering. Yet few bookstores devote even a single shelf to men's issues and fathering. A recent trip to a large bookstore was indicative. Under the "Gender Studies" rubric, there were almost 120 books on women and only 3 on men and women. There were none that addressed men alone. In the "Child-birth" and "Parenting" sections almost 200 books addressed motherhood, pregnancy, and birth. There were only 2 books on expectant and early fathering.

This lack is mirrored by the professional psychological literature. For its century-long history, since the early clinical studies of Freud, Breuer, Charcot, and others, the major focus has been on women and mothers. Although dominated by the influence and research of Caucasian males, psychological theory has primarily been based on clinical work with female patients. For one thing female patients were more available. They had more time to be in psychotherapy, and it was culturally more acceptable for women to seek such help. The dramatic influx of female therapists into the field in the past twenty-five years has only heightened this imbalance. For the most part this new group of women therapists and writers have helped to normalize female psychology. Instead of viewing women from a medically oriented, male perspective, a more appropriate broader view has been established.

However, male psychology has yet to catch up. Not only is there no lengthy history of studying males but there is a newer tendency to reverse the earlier prejudice, holding male behavior up to a female standard.

If fathering is so central to men's lives, we would expect that men would thirst for knowledge about the topic. For many years the publishing industry has widely believed that men don't buy many psychology-type books. Although literary interest in men's issues is on the upswing in the 1990s, the average man wanting to know more about fathering is confronted with a drought. How are we to know which fathering feelings or behaviors are normal? Where do we learn about the experience of our peers and our predecessors?

The Anti-male Bias. Although it is problematic, the scarcity of knowledge is far less damaging than the biased message favored by the popular media. The information on men and fatherhood that is commonly presented is almost entirely negative. In many "pop-psych" portrayals, the words *man* and *perpetrator* are virtually interchangeable. Somehow, as a society, we seem locked in a competitive duality. In order to honor traditional feminine traits centered on relationships, connectedness, and mothering, we compare them with masculine traits revolved around doing, producing, or acting. Having created such an arbitrary comparison, we typically demean one by reference to the other.

Popular-psychology literature and media reflect a twenty-year trend in our culture.[1] In general, men and fathers are commonly blamed for most of the ills of children, women, and society in general. Precious little in the popular media is supportive of fathers. In fact there is a greater tendency to portray fathers as dangerous to children than to define them as an integral part of their growing up. Men have been required to support the family financially and to protect them from outside harm but have not been particularly recognized for their emotional, intellectual, relational, or teaching roles. To some extent the typical male caricature for our time is Homer Simpson, a sometimes good-hearted cartoon character who is foolish, loutish, scheming, ineffective, and the butt of jokes.

The popular press and electronic media bombard us with the message that women are victims and men are scum. We are told that we talk too little or incorrectly, we have no feelings or the wrong ones, we think too much or too little, we act inconsiderately or solicitously. In short, when it comes to relationships and family, men are inadequate and quite possibly dangerous.

There is no need to reproduce the long list of male-bashing books, talk shows, and TV sitcoms. They were matched already by similar attacks on women for decades or centuries. The quintessential quotation for me came from the book jacket of a 1990 guide for women in relationships. In her book *Why Women Shouldn't Marry* Cynthia Smith posits, "There are only two basic reasons for women to marry: sperm and support." Men and fathers are reduced to providing money and genetic material. Phil Donahue, and a legion of other nationally famous talk-show hosts, have had phenomenally successful television careers predicated on an anti-male ideology.

Frederic Hayward has studied the representation of males by the media. In 1988 he wrote, "By far, male bashing is the most popular topic in current talk shows and interviews. . . . The trend is particularly rampant in advertising. In a survey of 1,000 random advertisements, one hundred percent of the jerks singled out in male/female relationships were male. There were no exceptions."[2]

It is tempting to continue the trend of gender competitiveness, unfair comparison, and blame by laying responsibility for this male-bashing trend at the feet of feminism. Haven't excesses from the women's movement and political rather than scientific data provided material for a legion of talk shows, magazine articles, and advertisers? However, such a characterization would be unfair, inaccurate, and hypocritical.

As early as 1961, before the dawn of the modern women's movement, statesman and social critic Adlai Stevenson said in an address before the National Father's Day Committee:

There was a time when Father amounted to something in the United States. He was held with some esteem in the community; he had some authority in his own household; his views were sometimes taken seriously by his children; and even his wife paid heed to him from time to time.

In recent years, however, especially since World War II, Father has come upon sorry times. He is the butt of the comic strips; he is the boob of the radio and TV serials; and the favorite stooge of all our professional comedians.

In short, life with Father seems to have degenerated into a continuous sequence of disrespect or tolerance at best. It appears that the poor fellow is unable to hang a picture or hit a nail without some mishap; no radio or clock will ever work again after he fixes it; he can't boil water or even barbecue a steak, at least not without burning it. Every time the so-called head of the household attempts to assert himself or express his opinions, the whole family is convulsed with indulgent if not scornful laughter.

This book does not attempt to delve into the reasons for a social reversal of victim and oppressor roles nor to balance such prejudice. What is crucial here is that when we have only negative models, we have no useful information on positive fathering. The overwhelming message is that whatever a man does as a father or in relationship to a woman will be examined critically and will ultimately be considered faulty.

When we are regularly reminded that we are unlikely to be good parents, that we are secondary to mothers, potential abusers of children, and do most things wrong from a "politically correct" perspective, it is not surprising that we become more silent about our perceptions and feelings or withdraw to the garage, den, workshop, office, or personal computer.

This reinitiates a reciprocal cycle. Fathers withdraw from the pressure, are then viewed as uninvolved or uncaring, which in turn propels the mother to do even more of the child care, which gives the father a greater sense of his own undesirability and a corresponding increased withdrawal.

It is of little value to attempt to untangle this "chicken-egg" cycle in order to assess blame for the initiator. What is important is that fathers recognize their role in this pattern, determine how they want to make it different, and do so with the cooperation of mothers. The media will reflect a change in this trend, but only after it occurs in families across the land.

Lack of Traditional Support

The dilemma for a father who seeks a close, important relationship with his children is caused not only by media representations. He must also cope with dramatic cultural changes and a lack of effective models. The problem is compounded for fathers because our culture doesn't furnish the necessary learning through other natural sources, such as modeling or an oral tradition. Normally we would learn significant roles in our lives from others who have preceded us. We would look first to our own fathers.

Unfortunately most fathers today cannot rely very heavily on what they learned about fathering from their own fathers. My dad's world was quite different from mine. The expectations, pressures, and cultures in which he plied his own craft of fathering were quite dissimilar.

Are there other sources of guidance? Mothers may provide some clues to parenting. Other men may also. Perhaps cultural institutions will provide viable paths? Unfortunately each of these sources is limited or flawed for one reason or another. Let's look at some of the reasons why there is such a lack of traditional support for learning about fathering.

1. SECOND-STRING PARENT. Although women's social roles have also shown a dramatic shift in the past generation, women have maintained one significant aspect of motherhood: the biological basis of becoming a mother. Although male sperm is necessary to create a child, the male's experience of parenting, which begins during pregnancy, is a sociocultural rather than a biological experience. It is far more subject to social trends.

Guy Corneau, looking at the different biological experience for men and women, points out that "Mothers are; Fathers are made!"

Because a man's early experience of fathering is necessarily "secondhand"—his partner, who is carrying the child inside her body, is clearly the gatekeeper—he learns a great deal about fathering from, and with the permission of, a mother. It is unreasonable to expect any woman to be an expert on how to father; that is a male responsibility. Unfortunately for many men the most likely teacher—his own father—cannot offer much in the way of modeling or advice.

2. RIGID MALE STEREOTYPES. Perhaps other men will provide such an answer? Unfortunately until recently men have somehow adopted, and been assigned, the "silent" role in the family. Men are supposed to act, women to talk.

One of the dominant American male role models could be described as the Teddy Roosevelt Syndrome: "Speak softly and carry a big stick." Gary Cooper, John Wayne, Clint Eastwood, and countless other screen heroes emulate and create this value. The good man is wise, powerful, just, defender of the appropriate moral standard, *and is quiet about it.* Complimented on his prowess, the "hero" is supposed to refer to duty and "aw shucks" himself out of the uncomfortable situation. He is not supposed to discuss it at length. As a generation of men we have been carefully taught to be out of touch with, and unable to discuss, personal feelings. If we are to learn from our fathers, it will not likely be from their verbalizations.

Nonverbal communication has not been much better. What Robert Bly calls the "male mode of feeling," which was in prior generations transmitted from father to son by virtue of their side-by-side work, has been a casualty of post–Industrial Revolution work demands. Fathers are not available for their sons. Most of the time fathers are away from the home at work and sons are in someone else's care and tutelage at school.

3. ECONOMIC CHANGES. Fathers of dependent children today grew up in the economic climate of the 1950s to 1970s. These years were characterized by general economic prosperity, particularly for middle-class America. Of course there are millions who grew up in terrible and inexcusable poverty, but middle-class America has not known personally the trials of massive poverty that our own parents likely experienced in the Great Depression. For most of the country the decades in which they were coming of age promised upward mobility.

Many men who were born into the America of the 1920s and 1930s espoused a predominant value: that their children would have a better life than themselves. Martin, a grandfather several times, born in 1918, described this: "It's all changed today . . . when my children were born, there was one, just one rule—that they wouldn't have to live like I did . . . and I had it a lot better than my father, who was a dirt-poor farmer. I got away from the farm . . . got a job in the city and made sure my kids went to college. . . . I always wanted them to not have to work with their hands like I did. My son is a college professor, and my one daughter is going back to finish up her schooling now that the kids are in school . . . glad I could help her there too. The other one is back on a farm, but she's educated and happy about it. In our time we never had no choices . . . work was to be done and food wasn't always plentiful."

The great immigration during the early years of this century meant that many of our fathers were the first generation born in North America. Their job was to make the transition from the Old World values brought here by their parents to the demands of American life. Their job was hard, but values were more clear-cut. Immigration continues, but a greater proportion of men becoming fathers today are the second or third generation here. They have always been acclimated to this world, and for most of them economic times were better. Indeed current forecasts suggest that we have a different dilemma to contend with. It is unlikely that our children will be able to live as well as we have.

4. PHYSICAL MOBILITY AND THE RISE OF THE NUCLEAR FAMILY. In our parents' generation it was far more common to live in an extended family in an ethnic neighborhood than it is today. The modern model is the nuclear family. Parents and their children, separated from their relatives by many miles, share neighborhoods with people who share similar work and standards of living rather than values or racial or ethnic backgrounds. Ghettos still exist, of course, but they are not the "desired" localities that characterized prior generations. With these changes have come a great loss of family support. Grandparents and other built-in baby-sitter relatives are nowhere nearly as available. Similarly, fathering models and male role models within the family are also less available.

As the ethnic neighborhoods break down, intercultural marriages increase. More than ever people are coming into contact with others who have very different backgrounds, traditions, and religions. With increasing contact at work and at play comes greater understanding and attraction. Choices of marital partners broaden with greater familiarity. Within some groups a majority of members now marry someone from another traditional culture (i.e., American Jews, Hawaiians, Native Americans).

The advantages of such unions include the strength of diversity, openness to change, and less prejudice. The major disadvantage is that the world in which we are likely to live is discrepant enough from the world of our fathers that lessons from the tradition in which we grew up no longer apply.

5. CHANGES IN THE WORKPLACE AND HOME. One of the changes in the workplace is the change in the nature of the work that men do. Manufacturing and production have taken a backseat to information and service. Most basic production for Americans is performed offshore, in countries with less expensive labor. Working men are producing less with their hands and sweat. Service professions are the most prevalent and preferred.

Another major change in the family is the increasing likelihood that both parents will work outside the home. In my childhood years the expected norm was that Mom would stay at home and make the home a warm and safe place for Dad and the kids. Dad would work at one job (maybe moonlight occasionally when we needed or desired something special). Family life was supposed to reflect the words of the song "Lucky, Lucky Me": "I work eight hours, I sleep eight hours, and have eight hours for fun." Fun was playing with the kids, being with the "boys," and of course special time with the wife. Work was a duty, "the job"—it was hardly considered a privilege. Many men took pride in the fact that their wives did not have to work outside the home.

That norm (or promise) is long past for many upwardly mobile families of the eighties and nineties. It is now common to have as many wage earners as there are adults in the home. Women have entered the marketplace out of desire and necessity. Most families require the income from their work. In many parts of the country public education is in such disarray that the income from one parent's job is used entirely to fund private schooling or "extras," such as lessons and tutors, to provide their children with an adequate and safe school.

Women are likely to work outside the home even in families where a single income is sufficient for their economic needs. The dramatic social upheaval that began with the civil rights movement of the 1960s and progressed into the women's movement has made it possible for women to have greater choice over their lifestyles. Many women choose careers for personal fulfillment and dedication to their interests. They are exercising their deserved and long-overdue freedom to have more personal say over their lives.

6. THE CHANGING FAMILY CONSTELLATION. Since the mid 1960s the family of two parents and 2.85 children has ceased to define the average family constellation. Divorce strikes 50 percent of marriages today. It is estimated that 50 percent of all children will live with only one biological parent during their school years. Most often these children live with their mothers. This has a big impact on fathering. Single-parent families and blended families are now as common as intact families. Indeed the *Ozzie and Harriet–Donna Reed* household, with a husband who worked out of the home, a stay-at-home mother and homemaker, and their biological offspring characteristic of 1950s television sitcoms, represent less than 20 percent of American families in the 1990s.

The fact of wives working outside the home has also affected the family constellation. Most homes do not have the luxury of a full-time homemaker or family caretaker. Able to survive financially on their own, more women can opt to be single parents. The end of their dependence on a husband for financial support has allowed for more choices. However, with the increasing freedom has come additional breakdown of traditional supports.

Furthermore there has been a reduction in family size in the Western world. Fewer children has not necessarily resulted in fewer demands. For one thing fewer children means less physical or emotional help around the home from siblings. The smaller families also seem to place more pressure on each child and parent for excellence.

7. THE INFLUENCE OF TELECOMMUNICATIONS AND THE MEDIA: THE NEW RELIGION. Another cultural change that affects the support traditionally granted to fathering involves what is commonly called the Information Age. With satellite-based telecommunication, fiber optics, computers, and cable networks most Americans have instant access to much of what is happening anywhere on the globe. So much information comes at children so fast that fathers are unable to keep up with or mediate what their children are exposed to.

With the abundance of information available, we become more dependent on editors, censors, interpreters, and presenters. News and entertainment have become inextricably linked. As Marshall McLuhan warned, packaging has become as important as the message (the medium is the message). We make political decisions based on "sound bites." Even recent wars and environmental policies have reflected the political concern "How will it play in Peoria?" Reflecting on this trend, Dr. Robert Taylor, dean of the University of Louisville School of Business, commented that as a culture "we have become receivers of information rather than seekers."

Our elected officials and heroes are increasingly more likely to come from the fields of entertainment or sports than from commitments to statesmanship. Parents have learned to use television as an electronic baby-sitter, less concerned with the input given their children than with the need for peace in our noisy and very busy world.

One of the powerful messages promoted by electronic media is that the father is unnecessary or foolish. Traditional fathering skills, such as the ability to demonstrate patience, to commit to hard work, to seek truth, and to endure difficulties have been replaced with slick, well-packaged images and an expectation that there are quick solutions to most of life's problems.

THE CONTRARY CULTURAL TREND: MEN AND CHILDBIRTH

In direct contrast to the exile of men from family life is the powerful revolution that has occurred in birth practices. Today fathers are expected to be an integral part of pregnancy and the birth of their children.

Modern society has a way of sanitizing life and anesthetizing us into psychological and emotional denial of the most crucial of life's moments: birth and death. The movement toward husband-involved childbirth is an amazing counter to that trend. As the direct result of the women's movement; a few brave, pioneering obstetricians; childbirth educators; and to the credit of millions of parents, 85 percent of all American men in intact families expect to be present at the birth of their children. This figure is up from 15 percent in the mid 1960s.

Most men who have become fathers in the past twenty years are the first men in their families' recent history actually to be present at the birth of their children. This change in cultural expectations has produced amazing opportunities for fathers to be deeply involved in family life from its earliest moments.

By being present at the birth of his children, a father has the opportunity to experience the struggle and pain through which we humans are born and to bond with his partner and baby from the moment of birth. Of course, because this experience is different from that of recent prior generations, our models for such experiences are also sorely lacking.

We begin fatherhood with sexual intercourse. During the pregnancy we have access to our baby only to the extent allowed by the mother. We are present at the birth of our children, wanting to help, yet feeling helpless. Soon we are home with our family and we feel the pressure of being sole support and protector of the people we most love. Where in the world can we learn how to do these well? What models of fathering can we emulate?

EXTANT MODELS OF FATHERING

Despite the social changes and inadequate models, fathers do not grow up in a vacuum. Cultural models of masculinity or fathering are not altogether absent or deficient. Every man does learn about fathering from a host of sources over his life span. From our earliest recollections there are fathers or other male figures in our lives (coaches, teachers, bosses, relatives, heroes, etc.). What do we as men learn about fathering and how do we learn it?

POSITIVE MODELS OF FATHER. Positive roles for fathering include financial provider, representative of the outside world, disciplinarian, family protector, dreamer, problem solver, genius, motivator, tough-minded parent, moral standard-bearer, and hero.

NEGATIVE MODELS OF FATHER. There are also a host of negative roles attributed to fathering. Among these are oppressor of the family; aggressor; slave (yes-man to mother); perpetrator of physical or sexual abuse; alcoholic; unemployed; poorly motivated "leech"; deserter; good-natured simpleton; obstacle to mother and children; nonverbal, unemotional, uninvolved member of family; and overgrown little boy.

Each of these unidimensional "models" is insufficient to describe any person's behavior in a role as complex as fathering. In truth most men have some of the positive and some of the negative ones. Many of us are aware of the negatives and honestly desire to alter them. When we are aware of the positives, we often attempt to increase their frequency.

Of course, oftentimes fathers are unaware of how others view them or how they think about themselves as fathers. As Clarence, a father of three sons and a daughter, says, "I don't know much about what the kids think about me. They love me, I guess. I know that the little girl does, she's always tellin' me and huggin' me. I try to do my best, but, you know, I never knew my own father . . . died before I was old enough to know anything. I just play it by ear. Don't have much complaints about how the boys are turnin' out. You never really know these days. Just got to do the best you can . . . raise 'em to believe in God and betterin' themselves and to love their family and be good to others."

Will was less sanguine about the process. Describing himself as "a worrier," he was "constantly evaluating and reevaluating everything I do and don't do with the kids. I'm the more conservative one in the family. I was an only child and I'm really risk-averse. My wife is more laissez-faire. I think it's so important to teach them the rules of safety first. I monitor their schoolwork and grades closely. When I was a kid, that was the first thing to go when I was upset. I also teach them as much as I can about respect for others and the environment. Mary Ann thinks I'm too controlling with them. Maybe she's right, but I just don't feel right until I know that they're considering all the dangers."

Neither of these men got their models of fathering from their own fathers. Clarence never really knew his father; Will's dad, a blue-collar worker in a manufacturing plant, held the powerful ethic that his son should have a better life.

TO BE A FATHER

The father that I am involves what I learned from my father and other men; what I know about myself and my needs, beliefs, and values; the values held by the mother of my children; the influence of my social circle and cultural background; and of course trial-and-error learning.

Despite my lack of models, handbooks, courses, or other resources, I have a need to do this fathering job very well. I want to keep improving in this most central aspect of my male identity. My training isn't what it should be. A person with such a poorly defined training program would never be allowed to "tinker" with the car engine or repair a washing machine. Yet it is the only training I have, and the time for fathering well is now.

In Steven Spielberg's film *Hook* a grown-up Peter Pan has lost touch with his inner child and is losing his precious connection with his children. Confronted with their kidnapping by the evil Captain Hook, he learns that he will do anything to save and re-claim them. Peter is not alone. It is easy for fathers to succumb to the innumerable pitfalls that lead us away from the essence of our relationship with our children and from the core of what's most important within ourselves.

Before looking more deeply into my goals as a father and the traits of good fathering, let's examine how fathers and mothers differ.

3

WHY CAN'T A FATHER BE MORE LIKE A MOTHER?

Women have choices. Men have responsibilities.
—STEVE MARTIN, in *Parenthood*

Snapshot 1: Roger was "roughhousing" with his two children at a local park. The younger of the two (two years old, by appearance) began to cry. As the father was assuring himself that his son was unharmed, the child's mother appeared from nowhere, swept up her baby in her arms, comforted him, and cast a fearsome glance toward her husband. Clearly he had done something wrong. He turned to his older child and said, "Come on, let's go get an ice cream" as his wife's eyes rolled upward.

At home later the same day the older child misbehaved. Her father quickly ordered her to the agreed-upon "time-out." As she went to her room, however, Mother gave her a hug, told Father he had acted impulsively, and overrode his punishment. The father shrugged, walked into the living room, picked up the remote control for the television, and turned on ESPN.

Snapshot 2: Tad emerged from his workshop weary from long hours fixing broken home appliances, toys, and furniture. As he proudly informed his wife of his mixed success, she, having spent six continuous hours with three needy children, retorted, "I wish you would spend more time with the family." To the chagrin of both, he swore at her, grabbed a beer from the refrigerator, and walked back to the garage, muttering.

Snapshot 3: When their teenage daughter arrived home tearful, past curfew, and reported that she had been mistreated by her boyfriend, her mom tried to comfort her, her dad asked several specific questions.

It is gratifying to me that my wife is the mother in our little family. She's quite good at it, seems to come by it naturally. I, on the other hand, am not much of a mother. I don't think I could ever be very good at it. As a mother the best I could hope to do is *act like* Susan. Despite this, I think I'm a good parent to my two children. I hope to improve continually, but even now I'm pleased with a lot of the parenting I do. I approach my children very differently than my wife does. After all, *she doesn't know much about how to father.* That's where I am the natural.

Fathers are different because we are male. Our biology is different. Our traditions are different. We encounter different sociocultural expectations and we communicate differently. Understanding fathering requires a knowledge of the uniquely masculine experience of the world.

FOUR BASIC GENDER DIFFERENCES

The Influence of Biology

We must make at least one assumption: *Boys and girls are born different.* This is not to say that we are unequal, have different basic human rights, or that either gender is the lesser. It is to acknowledge a very basic biological reality. Maleness and femaleness are complementary, not identical.

Parents who have both boy and girl children have no difficulty distinguishing many gender differences that seem to be genetically acquired. In my own family a great effort was made to avoid violent television and stories when the children were little. Unisex toys were always available. Yet, from their earliest play, our daughter used traditional boy's toys such as trucks to make beds for her dollies, whereas our son primarily appreciated dolls as obstacles to run his truck into. He made "weapons" from sticks, other pointed objects, and even mashed potatoes and flowers, without any particular exposure to guns, spears, or knives.

We are all biological beings, and one of the predominant biological realities is our gender. It is true that within each gender there is wide variation, perhaps greater differences than that between genders. However, there are general stereotypes that aid our understanding of gender differences.

For example, men are physically larger and stronger, are better suited to short, intense bursts of energy, and have better spatial abilities. Women can grow babies in their uterus and can feed the newborns with their breasts. Anatomically the male and female brain are different. Sections of the corpus callosum, which connects the two hemispheres, are significantly larger in women. This greater connectivity between right and left hemispheres allows women to more readily integrate thinking and emotion. It may also encourage more verbalization. By contrast men will be more predisposed to separate affect and thinking and to think more specifically or task-relatedly.

It can be argued that millennia of disparate tasks for men and women have resulted in evolutionary changes in brain and body function. Whatever their genesis, there are real differences today. It matters not whether men's biology was more suited for hunting or that they became suited to hunting. Probably both were true. The reality of men's history, and the Y chromosome that we carry, have left us with an orientation toward hunting. In his *Knights Without Armor*, Aaron Kipnis enumerates many such male skills:

quiet, nonverbal, side-by-side communication; dependence on teamwork; courage; speed; strength; hand-eye coordination; visual-spatial abilities; gross motor skills, and so forth.

According to Kipnis, women as gatherers were able to be verbal: "Unlike hunted prey, plants do not run away if they hear, see, or smell their pursuer . . . superior verbal skills were needed to organize and catalogue the many different foods, medicinal herbs, and plant materials they collected. Thus women also required a much more complex symbolic language . . . for their work and childrearing."[1]

Biosocial Differences

Maturation is also different. Girls become women differently than boys become men.

In his best-selling book, *Fire in the Belly*, Sam Keen states, "The cycle of human life naturally suggests that there are at least four major rites of passage for every person: birth, coming of age, marriage, death. The rites celebrating our beginning and end, are necessarily conducted without our consent by those who are on the stage before and after our time. But between the parenthesis of birth and death, the most important rites are those when we separate from the opposite sex to learn the mysteries of our own gender, and when we return to join in marriage and create new life."[2]

According to Guy Corneau, girls become women physically by the onset of menstruation. For females the cultural initiation is primarily biological: Her womanness is affirmed by her menses and confirmed by giving life. By contrast, lacking such a biological confirmation of their coming of age, boys must be initiated into masculine life more socioculturally. Male initiation has traditionally been the cornerstone of a boy's coming of age.[3]

In primitive cultures the male initiation often involved a violent separation from the tribe and mother, instigated by the elder males, followed by an ordeal that required courage, discipline, and endurance of pain. This ordeal communicated many things to the boy-man: (1) that he must be courageous in the face of fear; (2)

that his life belonged to the larger society; (3) that he will be expected to sacrifice for the greater good. In short the initiation was a training for war. He would be a soldier and would have to be disposable.

In his time away from the world of the tribe and women, he would also be taught his productive role, craft, or work and the lessons of his culture for ceremony, ritual, and social skills by the older men in his society. Only after he had learned these lessons could he take his place as an adult.

Modern society is notable for the relative absence of such initiation rites. Military basic training or making the football squad provides some components of male initiation, but these are hardly universal. Many modern initiations may have only the form of traditional methods. Devoid of its essence, adolescents go through some limited ceremony without developing a deep sense of connection or mission in society. Larry described his own "coming of age": "I went to Hebrew school for four years to read and speak Hebrew, but was taught no comprehension. My bar mitzvah was at a temple that my parents were not members of and did not attend services (there or anywhere). I was initiated into nothingness. Weird!"

Despite his inadequate "initiation," Larry and the rest of us must come to grips with and incorporate the basic male values of courage, duty, sacrifice, and productivity.

What happens to a boy who is not initiated into adult life? Corneau and Robert Bly believe that uninitiated boys might not fully develop into men. This point mirrors the many "complaints" about males who act like adolescents or children in adult relationships. Corneau believes that boys' maturation must go beyond the basic biological ability to reproduce. It involves a training process and an acceptance by the world of adult men. For many adolescent boys male models are absent or unavailable. Lacking proper male initiators for adult sex roles, they naturally seek to be initiated by the available adults or more mature peers, who happen to be female. This has led to at least two difficulties. First of all, these women, albeit well intentioned, naturally rely on biological forms of initiation, especially sexuality. In a sense she can only teach him how to experience things in a feminine way, a way in which he will always be subordinate and out of place. Thus a male initiated by a woman learns the process of being dominated by, and unequal with, women. He also learns to place a high premium on sexuality for both connection and competence.

Historical Differences in Parenting

History and culture reinforce the biological gender differences. Major alterations in the nature of parenting have evolved over the past three and a half centuries in America.

Anthony Rotundo of Phillips Academy identified two major periods of American fatherhood: Patriarchal Fatherhood, which ran from the settling of the colonies until 1800; and Modern Fatherhood, which precedes our current period.

Patriarchal Fatherhood, 1620 to 1800. In agrarian culture production of basic supplies (food, shelter) dominated life. Families were primarily economic units; the larger the family, the greater the production. As the adult who was unencumbered by numerous pregnancies or necessary care for young children, the male assumed leadership. When children reached the age of helping, the father served as the foreman and children as the workers on the family farm. Social traditions gave him ownership and dominion over all property, including family members. Because he could veto or delay marriages of his children, he could control the time when they would leave home. The father's power was unquestioned.

The man also held most of the responsibilities that accompanied such power. It was his duty to *provide* for their physical necessities and to *protect* his children. He had to ensure that they learned appropriate lessons and skills to take their role as adults. He was responsible for the moral and spiritual growth of his children. He was the family *disciplinarian*.

From birth until approximately age three, children belonged

to the mother. After that time, the boys were taught by father, and the girls remained with mother. The father-son relationship primarily resembled a master-apprentice relationship. Not affectionate or emotional, it was characterized by approval and disapproval. If a father were to express emotion directly, it would be to his daughters rather than to his sons.

By the time of the American Civil War cities were emerging, farm life was not the only calling for a son, and the combination of a growing population and limited land necessitated smaller farms in populated areas. With these changes paternal authority began to lessen. At the same time a new concept of womanhood emerged. It was then believed that women were inherently more moral, spiritual, and tender than men and thus better suited to teach children.

Modern Fatherhood, 1800 to 19??. By the early 1800s many farmers were growing cash crops. Villages became marketplaces. As towns grew into cities, an urban middle class emerged. This middle class developed newer forms of family life. In this new society, work became separated from the home. Businessmen of the 1800s left home every day to pursue their work in offices, shops, and factories. Since this time the middle-class father became much less of a presence in the home.

In this emerging society, the company replaced the family as an economic unit. The male who worked away from home became the expert on the world at large, while the mother's sphere of influence in the home expanded. As economic necessity for large families diminished and mothers extended their influence, the family became more of a place for nurturance and socialization.

As the Industrial Revolution took hold by the mid nineteenth century, the mother became the linchpin of family life, and the father increasingly became more of a specialized outsider. He remained "head of the household" by virtue of his economic necessity and somehow retained the role of disciplinarian (e.g., "Wait till your father gets home"), but his role as educator was reduced to teaching (primarily his sons) about the world of work, ethics, politics, money, and competition.

As he was away from the home for longer and longer work-days, a father's deep connection with his children was severely reduced. He became increasingly an outsider. This trend has continued through the middle of the twentieth century. As one child put it, "Me and Jennifer and Mommy live in the house. Daddy lives in the garage."

During this period the father's role became more specialized. Protecting and providing remained, but they evolved to be essentially synonymous with "breadwinner," and "model." Fathers taught their children, especially their sons, problem-solving skills through sports and home projects. Because most of these were outside the center of the home—mother's realm—the boys also learned how to "live in the garage."

With greater physical and psychological absence, paternal authority subsided. However, emancipated from the constraints of the role of "master," the father was freer to enjoy warmth, play, and closeness with his children when he was available.

The mother's role in the home continued to expand as the father's input diminished. The home and childrearing became her domain. She ran her mini-kingdom according to her personal knowledge, tastes, and intuition. Thus a new conflict began to emerge. While mothers focused on chores and "home work," dads were out enjoying their free hours with their children. The tension created by this contradiction rapidly expanded in recent decades.

Current Fatherhood 197? to 20??. Dramatic social changes are again influencing the nature of fathering and gender roles. A child's experience of his father is increasingly discontinuous. With work and home so separate, children are less privy to the manner in which their father approaches life. However, fathers are not the only parent who is subject to the vagaries of the workplace.

In the current generation women have left home to enter the marketplace in record numbers.[4] Whether through economic necessity, freedom from rigid and demeaning sex-role expectations, a need for creative adult stimulation, or a drive for equality, the majority of Western women are no longer primarily mothers and homemakers.

As women leave the home empire, a shift in power within the marriage is inevitable. Women demand equality on the job and expect it at home. When mothers are not home all day caring for family needs, fathers are pressed into additional household duties. As the empires and power shift, there is confusion and difficulty in interpersonal relationships. There is also fertile ground for marital power struggles. What new duties should each partner assume? Who gets to decide?

Recently women have begun to bring the country's awareness to "the glass ceiling"—an unspoken, but very real limit of advancement for women in the corporate world. Of course, most men experience this corporate glass ceiling as well, not being members of the "right club," nor willing to engage in certain demeaning, time-consuming, or political games required to be chosen to advance.

In this changing environment many men are becoming aware of another "glass ceiling": one at home. Boundaries and roles are less clear. Their job description has been changed without much warning, awareness, or consent.

Many feminist writers have correctly noted that the woman of the house still feels the responsibility for homemaking and child care, even after a long day's work outside the home. Husbands "help" around the house and with the children. While women are pressured and burdened by the responsibility, they claim it as their own turf. As long as men are the "helpers," women are the "bosses." As a man I am not expected to set policy or to make decisions. I carry out orders. In such an inequitable situation it is natural for me to avoid extra work and to revisit the old army rule, "Never volunteer." A psychological cycle is set in place. I play the role of the "lazy husband" to my wife's role of "nagging wife." Neither of these roles is attractive, satisfying, or desirable.

This is especially problematic for men who feel oppressed and suffer indignities at work, holding on to the hope of a safe harbor at home. When the home demands and feelings of powerlessness replicate the work environment, a man may feel trapped and angry. He may well react to this by withdrawal or expressed rage.

Women may not exactly welcome the emotional responsibility

for homemaking and child care, but it does in some ways emotionally empower them. It may be the only place where a woman feels in a powerful position. Although it is unpleasant, many working wives are reticent to relinquish it. Unfortunately, while it is present, fathers will feel like second-class parents.

It is important to distinguish here between responsibility and power. Most fathers would readily connect better with their children *on their own terms.* It is the sense that they have responsibilities without power that creates the problem situation.

With the changing times, fathers are faced with new quandaries and possibilities. We have an opportunity to be much closer to our children than men have for generations. We will be present at, and participatory in, their births. We will be more involved in early child care. The separation between the workplace and home life will increasingly become blurred. A father will have to negotiate with his partner for their relative responsibility for child care, homemaking chores, and income. Most fathers of today will have to overcome the powerful notion that they are less credible as parents by virtue of gender alone. Most of all, today's fathers must personally determine what roles they wish to play and be willing to negotiate with their partners.

Such negotiations are predicated on him knowing what he wants. Fatherhood history does not provide many of these answers to the father of today. The social context complicates this matter substantially.

Social Context of Fathering

Males are treated differently as parents than are women. We have different cultural expectations, demands, and realities. These differences emerge in a host of circumstances including the relative perceptions of work and family.

Following the historical changes in the way men and women work are a set of somewhat changing attitudes and motivations toward work. In ancient times work and life were synonymous. Everyone worked all the time. "Free time" is a modern concept applicable only to cultures of plenty, specifically to certain elite classes of citizens in those societies.

Despite major changes in the equalization of work and pay over the past three decades, there remain significant differences between men and women vis-à-vis work and attitudes toward work. In most of the world today work and life remain synonyms. In much of America and the West a large proportion of the population still must work to survive. However, among middle-class and upper-class denizens of developed countries there are some choices about career.

Women have correctly pointed out that many career opportunities are closed or limited by gender prejudice. There is no question that their assertion is true. However, there is another truth as well: *Almost all men are constrained powerfully by the work ethic.* In his book *Why Men Are the Way They Are,* Warren Farrell succinctly states that many American women today have choices about the relative value of career in their lives; specifically they have three options: (1) full-time career; (2) full-time child care and homemaker; or (3) a part-time mixture of both. Men's choices are somewhat more limited: (1) career; (2) career; (3) career.[5]

Farrell's view may seem extreme, but it is not altogether inaccurate. At least from a male perspective our partners seem to have far more freedom of choice in this arena. When men talk openly about the frustrations of fatherhood, they usually describe an increasing work load in the home with no corresponding reduction on the job site.

In most middle- and upper-middle-class, intact, two-parent families, the arrival of the first child produces a host of role changes. Most couples go from two incomes for two people to one income for three, at least temporarily. For clear biological reasons it is naturally expected that mothers will be the prime care giver during the early months of the infant's life. Sociocultural forces support this. Men who wish to be primary care givers are not supported by our culture, their workplace, or their own personal history.

Men do not have the freedom of choice that many middle-

and upper-class women claim as their basic right. There is no question that single women, particularly single mothers, are deeply oppressed and limited by demands of job and career. However, married men experience quite similar pressures. To the extent that his wife has choices about the relative weight she will put on career and home, his is reduced. It is simply not okay for men to decide to work part-time and have their wives work full-time to support the family. Neither men nor women will allow for that.

The Impact of Social Values on Masculine Identity. The relative differences in job and home life for men and women are not the sole social constraint on fathers. Certain socially driven masculine values are also quite influential. Three values dominate a male's experience of his world: man as problem solver; man as protector and provider; and man as contributor to future generations.

Remember, males are viewed in this culture as success objects. Our status is linked to an ability to solve problems. Whenever there is an obstacle, a man naturally dons his "Mr. Fix-it" outfit.

Thus when my partner or my child comes to me with a desire, I automatically perceive it both as a challenge and as an obligation. If my wife says something as innocuous as "My car is making a funny sound," I am duty bound to listen to the sound, investigate it, and get it fixed for her. It immediately has a higher priority than anything I may be doing for myself. If my son's battery-driven robot or flashlight croaks under his unique brand of toy torture, Dad is the one who stays up all night with the glue and soldering iron.

What is most interesting is that these obligations feel like desires. We want to do it. The accomplishment of fixing the toy is great, and we expect recognition and love in return. The problem is that we feel that it's the only way we are worthy of our family's love. Failure at problem solving translates in the male mind as unworthiness and rejection. For most men our acceptance is based entirely on our competence.

Another dominant male value involves the traditional role as family protector. There is no question that in American society men are supposed to protect their families from physical and fiscal harm. Most fathers take this commitment very seriously. As Peter described his recent eight months of unemployment, "It's not me or even Carole so much. I had no idea how much I'd feel like a failure. I hated that job and really had mixed feelings when I got laid off, but after a month of résumés, six A.M. newspaper classifieds, and interviews, I started to feel this awful dread. We won't starve, because Carole's got a job, and the building is rent-controlled, but it's in me. The feeling that I'm hurting my children . . . letting them down. It's way beyond realistic . . . almost a primitive feeling of failure . . . like a caveman who comes home without the kill for the winter."

Peter is well socialized. He knows at a very deep personal level what is expected of him as a man. It is his job to be the good soldier. Even when his wife is the one earning the family income, he feels the responsibility to provide. That psychological tension doesn't exit easily.

Being the good soldier also means that men will put their lives at risk to fight wars, to protect our society. Combat aside, each male grows up with the expectation that he should sacrifice himself for others. Whether it's Damon and Pythias, the young Dutch boy with his finger in the dike, the Lone Ranger, or (Iwo Jima hero) Ira Hayes, our lives are suffused with the glory of safeguarding the larger group. From a social perspective this works. From a personal psychological level it may drive men to feelings of failure, by holding out an unreachable standard, or to feelings of inferiority, because their own lives are less valuable than those of their female counterparts.

In the words of one person on an electronic bulletin board, "We can always get more sperm. Save the egg. It's what's valuable."

Another powerful social expectation for males is to leave the world a better place than when we entered. What contribution will a man make? Work is one place where he can be creative and responsive to social needs.

Fifty-five-year-old Abraham responded, "When I look back

on my life as a rabbi, I can see the comfort I have helped others to find, and I'm proud of the translations I did of the old Polish documents, but what stands out is the new chapel. It took me ten years to raise the money and to convince the board, and I designed it. That's something this community will have for generations."

Whit, an eighty-year-old former auto maker, recalls that he was part of a team that developed a new valve. He also feels proud and thankful for his early work with trade unions.

One of my clients, a computer software engineer, has a vision of bringing computer use to each child in the schools. He works tirelessly at his quest, writing software and raising funds from local businesses.

Other men make their contributions in the family. Many men of my father's generation took great pride in making it possible for their children to have the higher education and career possibilities that were denied them personally. They sacrificed for the next generation.

Zeke spent eight hours a day in painstaking rehabilitation with his crippled daughter in the hope of seeing her graduate from high school. She subsequently dedicated her master's degree to him.

By the time a man is fifty, he normally becomes very interested in how he will give something important back to the world. Men who feel unsure of what their contribution has been may feel a deep sense of failure. Many therapists who work with "mid-life" men focus a great deal on the contribution a father will make in the remainder of his life.

Rick was, in his own words, "a hard-nosed businessman," who had managed to start up and lose three companies and two families. He was angry and depressed when he finally came into therapy. "I was about to begin a new venture and then started to wonder, why bother? I'll only lose another one. . . . My kids don't know me, or don't care. I never see them at all. . . . That's partly my fault. . . . Last month I was browsing in a bookstore and I saw this statement: 'The unexamined life is not worth living.' For some stupid reason I can't get those words out of my mind. What is my life about? What does it all mean? What have I ever done for anyone else? That's why I'm here. I want a new direction. I want my life to mean something."

For men like Rick this social expectation is maturational. It evolves later in life. For most men, and particularly for fathers, the requirement that we make a difference is deeply felt and strongly motivational. It is often a burden as well as a means to personal gratification.

Social Expectations for Men in Relationships. More than anyplace else in his life the burdens social expectations place on a man's life fall most powerfully on his intimate relationships. There is no question that traditional couple and parenting relationships have dramatically changed in the past two decades. Men cannot rely on their predecessors to help them define normal relationships. In place of history they have to rely on trial and error. Too often the evaluation is done by women, who are ill equipped to understand relating from male perspectives.

The past doesn't provide many clues for contemporary marriage and family life. Most couples are struggling with redefinitions of their relationships with each other and their parenting responsibilities. By forcing communication, negotiation, and compromise, the struggle itself may foster a great deal of intimacy in the family. Unfortunately in the process there is a lot of anxiety, confusion, and disruption.

Whenever there is prolonged social flux, any strong, repeated position may be particularly seductive. The predominant message espousing "politically correct" changes in American culture has a distinctly anti-male message. This position, promulgated by self-help books, therapists, feminist writers, and the popular media, and supported with questionable statistics,[6] is that male ways of relating and parenting are equivalent to wrong ways.

Conventional wisdom is particularly critical of male forms of intimacy. We are led to believe that men avoid intimacy, whereas women seek it. We are told that we are worse at intimacy than women because we don't talk about our feelings the way women do, that we frequently abuse women in relationships, that we are primarily interested in sex, and that we are unromantic.

A plethora of popular books,[7] magazine articles, and television programs explore women's frustration with men who run away from relationships, fail to talk properly, change (or don't) after marriage, take only a passing interest in their children and housework, and resort to violence without provocation. What is the truth of these assertions?

Do some men act in these ways? There's no question that some men do. Is it true of all men? Absolutely not.

Let's examine the reality. In fact, when it comes to the direct communication of emotion, few people of either gender are particularly articulate. Often the word *feelings* is used to camouflage the delivery of a judgment (e.g., "I feel that you're a jerk").

Many women are more accustomed to using the words of feelings. They often express opinions or judgments using feeling words. For example, a wife might say to her husband, "I feel that you don't help enough around the house." She is probably feeling some anger or frustration, perhaps justifiably. Unfortunately by using feelings words while delivering a judgment, she takes a more righteous stance, and he has no way of responding. In general, men are no better. Most of us are well trained to ignore our feelings, and if that fails, to keep them to ourselves. It does seem important that intimate partners share their emotions as well as their thoughts, behaviors, and bodies. As men, when someone asks us *what* we are feeling, we may be truly lost for an answer and have to begin a laborious search to determine precisely what we are feeling about a specific issue.

Are men less likely to discuss their feelings than women? A lot depends on which feelings. Normally speaking, men and women talk about different feelings. Men have relatively little difficulty expressing anger. Women are better at expressing sadness than men. Neither gender is particularly good at directly expressing fear or love—emotions that reflect greater vulnerability.

Are men more reticent to be intimate than women? A lot depends on who is defining what constitutes intimacy. Intimacy requires vulnerability. If one member of the couple determines which behaviors reflect intimacy, the spouse is being asked to be vulnerable without a corresponding openness by his or her partner. It's akin to being naked in a roomful of well-dressed people. Many men in my surveys described exactly this concern. They experienced their wives as the self-appointed director and judge of their intimacy. If she determined that intimacy involved the expression of sadness, for example, he was being asked to do something for which he has limited skills. By contrast, in expressing her own sadness, she was responding in a way that was more familiar, accomplished, and comfortable. This is one-way intimacy. Wouldn't it be more interesting if he were to struggle with his acknowledgment of sadness or fear, while she struggled to acknowledge her own fear and anger?

These men also reported that their wives insisted that intimate conversations had to be face-to-face, reflecting an assumption that face-to-face discussions are more intimate than side by side interactions. For many men the greatest closeness comes from doing something together, talking as we do it shoulder to shoulder. Face-to-face conversations are perceived as either provocative or disciplinary.

Do men use sex in place of intimacy? Not from a male perspective. Because men have experienced a great deal of rejection in intimate relationships (from his original family and from having to be the initiator in relationships), we fear abandonment most prominently. For many of us sexuality is a pathway to intimacy. When we feel so accepted that our partner will literally invite us into her body, we begin to remove the armor to our deeper feelings. This is in sharp contrast to a woman who feels sexual as a culmination of other forms of closeness.

Are men less romantic than women? Again the question of who defines romance is important. If romance involves buying greeting cards or noticing nuances in makeup or clothes, the answer is generally yes. In some large ways, however, men are far more romantic than women. For example, a number of studies of married couples indicated that women tended to be far more pragmatic and less romantic than their husbands when it came to their reasons for choosing a mate.[8] There are understandable cultural reasons why a woman would be more concerned about a man's earning power or social station, but the fact remains that depending on what criteria are used, either the man or the woman could be viewed as more romantic.

Finally, in recent years we have become aware of widespread abuse in relationships. This abuse includes a wide range of heinous acts, such as physical and sexual violations or a pattern of psychological humiliation. Survivors of such abuse must receive appropriate psychological care and legal redress. Victims need protection and understanding. Unfortunately many men who would never perpetrate such crimes feel painted by the same brush as true abusers. No small number of men have been accused of being "abusive" for a steadfast unwillingness to appreciate or agree to his partner's point of view or for confronting her behaviors. One man in my survey had been reported for abusing his wife when he discovered and destroyed her stash of illegal drugs. Another was called abusive for cutting up the family credit cards after his wife went on a compulsive shopping spree.

At the 1991 American Psychological Association Convention in San Francisco, one speaker proposed that all women who were convicted of killing their husbands should be set free if the killers "felt they had been abused." One commentator opined, "Why not just make it open season on males?"

When such excesses occur, many men become very gun-shy in relationships. Fearful that they could be labeled "abusive" for almost any confrontive interactions, they retreat from the potential condemnation, and in the process from relationships and intimate interactions with women altogether.

I am not suggesting that men are better than women at intimacy. I don't think we are. However, I believe that improving intimacy is a personal challenge. It is unfair and ineffective to use gender to dismiss personal responsibility. Men can accept that we do not do intimacy well at times. When things go wrong, we have to fight the tendency to blame others. Sometimes when we're scared, we tend to withdraw. Other times our anxiety automatically switches to anger, as if on a hair trigger. Often we worry more about solutions than about being. Frequently we become too job- and money-centered for our own or our family's good.

Each of these shortcomings in intimacy could be traced in part to our male physiology, ancestry, or socialization. Yet it is not fruitful to blame gender. Every female partner has an equivalent list of traits that interfere with her development of intimacy. This list is ours to overcome. With insight and motivation we may improve. Indeed unless we view these as our own list, our own responsibility, we may never change.

The Myth of Male Superiority. In addition to the negative cultural stereotypes men experience in our daily life are a few complicating factors. Particularly problematic is the incongruous message that we are the privileged group in our culture yet we feel both oppressed and unhappy. Both men and women commonly believe that being male comes with more advantages. For most men there is quite a discrepancy between the belief that we are better off than women and the actuality of our lives. Notwithstanding the outrageous gender imbalance in political offices or in corporate leadership in America, it is a spurious argument that "men have all the power." The fact is that a very small minority of wealthy, white males are inordinately represented in positions of power.

For the average male the acquisition of such a position is both out of reach and a major irritant. That power is unattainable for a person who makes the median income (under $30,000 per annum). He works at a job that holds little intrinsic interest or creative possibility. Advancement is limited. He cannot afford to buy a home[9] or a new car. His children will not have a wide range of educational possibilities. His health care will not provide him with the technological advances available to others, and his life will be eight years shorter than that of his female counterpart.

The unattainability of power is not a surprise to most. So why is it an irritant? Two reasons stand out: personal expectation and social expectation. First and foremost, men are trained to believe that they should advance despite the "stacked deck." Ian Harris, in a 1990 article in *Media and Values*, comments, "They blame themselves for their failure to live up to standards set forth in the culture, while envying other men for achieving success, when they cannot achieve their goals."

In addition the media bombard us with examples of success and promote the notion that an average life is substandard. Our values often reflect this belief.

Feeling inadequate by comparison with society's "winners," inundated by the general negative social evaluation of males, and simultaneously believing that we are the better-off gender creates conflict for many, despair for some. It is very likely to affect our self-esteem, impact on our feelings as fathers, and inhibit our willingness to try to be with our children in a natural, masculine way.

Double Binds. In addition to this conflictual message, there are two others that are even more paradoxical: being sensitive at the same time one is protective, and being simultaneously considered inadequate and strong. Unless a man understands the impossibility of satisfying opposite demands at the same time, he will be trapped by his desire to be a problem solver and by his feelings of inadequacy when he fails.

To be acceptable in the world of women, I am encouraged to be understanding, accepting, sensitive to her needs, and willing to talk about feelings, especially hers. I am also clear that I am to protect her and my children from economic or physical harm. Most of us accept these roles as if there were not an intrinsic paradox. This is because we are taught to compartmentalize and express them sequentially during different conditions.

It is possible to be both protective and sensitive at different times. The problem comes when the expectation is that they be simultaneous. In my practice I commonly see couples in which the woman demands that her partner be open and vulnerable to her, that is, be sensitive to her needs while she is expressing anger toward him.

No matter how hard any man tries to live up to this standard, he will fail. Being a protector and being an equal partner call for opposite reactions, responses that are incompatible. One cannot face the strange noises downstairs in the middle of the night as a "sensitive New Age man." That job calls for the "Neanderthal." It is no small feat to discover that the noises were of little consequence, shut off the high adrenaline, return to bed, and sensitively inform one's sleepy partner that she is okay.

Perhaps the grossest example of this on a cultural level was the reaction we give our male warriors. The men we sent to Vietnam to "protect" our interests and way of life did their best to do that. The memorial wall in Washington is testimony to the tragic sacrifices they made.

The victims of that political and social nightmare were not only the dead, wounded, and missing in action and their families. Nobody returned from Vietnam the way they went. Not only was each man's life altered by the dreadful experiences of war, but there were few rewards or acknowledgments of his sacrifices. Indeed many of the returning soldiers received a substantially negative reaction when they returned. There is no question that those of us who stayed in America during the sixties and seventies were unprepared to accept the "Warrior" as he was on his return.

He didn't fit in anymore. He was too violent, and he frightened us. He wasn't sensitive in the age of love-ins and peace demonstrations, so he was psychologically exiled. The Southeast Asia veteran may have been valued as a protector, but he was unacceptable as an equal. By contrast his counterpart at home who was gaining acceptance as a sensitive, equal partner often found himself rejected as "a wimp."[10] No man was truly fully acceptable; no man could be all things at once.

The second double bind involves the contrast in role expectation. How does a man return from long days of servitude to his family's economic needs and his own psychological needs to provide and succeed and still have legitimacy in the home environment when he is considered the second-string parent? Where is he to develop the sufficient ego strength to be a good model and parent for the children?

Most men experience a kind of double servitude: one to his boss at work and a second to his wife at home. At work we feel as subordinate as do our female partners. Furthermore, men are also faced with coming home to another second-class status. He is given to believe that he is not the "expert parent"; he fails to talk correctly to his spouse; he is told he is inadequate. Yet he is also supposed to be the "man of the house," the "king of the castle."

How does a father teach his children when he feels as critiqued and evaluated at home as he is on the job? This is no easy dilemma. Some men, well trained in perseverance and problem solving, keep trying to serve all these contradictory masters, always waiting for word of their success, hopeful the love they crave will follow.

Many men, despairing of ever getting it right and feeling fully accepted, opt out of the quandary completely. Some leave their homes physically. Far more respond by leaving psychologically. Their bodies may be at home, but their consciousness is elsewhere. They become denizens of the garage, all-night computer hackers, or masters of the remote control. They do not relate to their families in ways that they would prefer because it is too fraught with failure. Others, frustrated by the impossible demands, express their anger in verbal assaults and physical violence.

While we may understand the causes of these paradoxes, there is no real justification for the common male solutions. Certainly mothers can be as frustrated as fathers at the conflictual demands. Is there any way out?

The answer to this question involves developing the skills to be a better father. These involve knowledge about fathering, psychological work to better comprehend our personal needs and our motives, relational work with our partners, and developing pride in male modes of relating and parenting. We need to eschew any notions of being "Mr. Mom." Fathers need to understand a quite basic truth: *Male ways of parenting and relating are different. They are not more right or wrong!*

The remainder of this book explores pathways men may take to acquire the necessary skills and understanding. However, before turning to the solutions, we will explore one additional gender difference that not only underscores all the others but complicates all attempts to resolve relationship issues.

GENDER-BASED COMMUNICATION DIFFERENCES

Biological, historical, and social differences between men and women provide fertile ground for misunderstanding and frustration. With understanding, negotiation, and compromise these discrepancies can be ameliorated. This involves communication and goodwill. Unfortunately men and women often speak different languages in their intimate conversations. This greatly impacts on our ability to get together.

Four of these major differences are described in the following section. Each is based on stereotyped perceptions of men and women. It is possible that some do not apply precisely to you or your spouse. It may even be reversed in your relationship. Whatever form the communication takes, awareness of the differences may be valuable to you in reducing miscommunication and enhancing your connection with your partner.

1. In discussing emotional topics men normally prefer to talk shoulder to shoulder, preferably while engaging in a mutual activity; women prefer face-to-face communication and full attention.

For Clive the best conversations occur while the two of them are driving in the car or lying side by side in bed in the dark. By contrast for his wife, Jean, the most important conversations occur when they are looking at each other, physically close, with no distractions. For Clive such conversations are not perceived as "face-to-face" as much as "in his face."

With a close friend I can discuss my relationship with my wife, my children, my parents, my hopes, dreams, and failures as long as we don't do it face-to-face. When we are both focusing on some external object, there is a connection that is nonthreatening (because either of us can break it off at any time) and because our connection is through the mutual endeavor. There is no notion of let's stop and talk it over—let's go and talk as we work.

2. When a woman describes an unpleasant or difficult event to a confidant, she feels heard when her listener tells of an equal or worse story. When a man is met with a worse story, he may well feel rejected and responsible to "fix" the listener's problem, at the cost of ignoring his own concerns.

When Jean hears that Clive has a stomachache, she may well describe an ache or discomfort of her own. She does this intending to share with him. He *hears* that she is uninterested in him and that he has to address her aches and pains.

3. In describing emotional topics men tend to focus on specific events first, then slowly move to more global reactions; women respond globally before they do specifically.

When Jean asks, "How do you feel about our relationship?" Clive is completely stuck for an answer. He doesn't know how he feels, and he will need to take some time to balance the positives and negatives before producing a final balance sheet. While he is engaging in this lengthy process, she will feel ignored and angry at what she perceives as his lack of caring. In the meantime he will be mystified at her "explosiveness." He will be even more reticent to give a verbal answer in such a dangerous environment. Had she begun with a more specific question (e.g., "Could you clarify what you said last night when I came home from dinner with my sister?"), he would have a ready response.

4. Conversation for women is more focused on context; for men, on content. Women talk to affiliate, men to pass information. Because of this, women are likely to want to speak at greater length, enjoying the connectedness. By contrast men will be prone to listening for the problem

and getting on with solving it. Additional conversation will simply mean more that needs to be fixed. The shorter the conversation, the shorter the list of "to-do's."

When Jean says that she'd like him to clean out the garage, as a way of beginning a conversation about doing more things together, he will hear it as a demand and a threat (*If I don't do it, there will be hell to pay!*). He then tries to close the conversation as quickly as possible to avoid additional requests. She will persist because for her the garage cleaning is secondary to having a conversation about what they could do as a couple.

Thus when a woman says to her husband, "We need to talk," she will be trying to open up a means of affiliating and connecting, whereas he will be bracing himself for a lecture from her on what he's done wrong or what he needs to do. Much of his reaction comes from his interactions with women in his past, when he was chastised or corrected. While his wife may feel that as long as they are talking, they are connected, he may be feeling wary of the drop of the other shoe, reminiscent of mother's discipline when he was "bad" as a little boy, and he may be looking to escape at the earliest possible moment.

Several men also complained that their wives want to talk but don't know what they want to talk about. So they "sit in front of me no matter what I'm doing and just wait for me to begin talking. It's like she decided that it's time to talk and I have to come up with the subject. The damnedest thing is that I know it'll turn into a fight and I'm helpless to stop it."

By contrast, wives often complain that no matter how hard they try to engage their husbands in conversations, all they get in return is a one-word answer.

In *You Just Don't Understand: Women and Men in Conversation*, Deborah Tannen makes a significant point of stereotypical differences between male-sent messages (report) and female-sent messages (rapport).[11] In "rapport talk" the language of conversations is primarily a means of establishing connections and negotiating relationships. Emphasis is placed on displaying similarities and matching experiences. When women talk, it is to affiliate. By contrast men talk to convey information. Tannen concludes that men talk as a means of preserving independence, negotiating, and maintaining status in hierarchical social order. Talking is a way of getting and keeping attention. Men tend to be more comfortable in public speaking and less so in private.

Why is this so? There are two reasons: (1) he has experience of feeling rejected as a little boy; and (2) he is well imbued with a social value that he is a *success object*.

In the course of normal child development, at a very young age little boys experience a sense of being thrust out of the home and world of women. At that time they are supposed to begin connecting more with the world of men. Unfortunately in post–Industrial Revolution society it is unlikely that there is an available world of men with which a boy can comfortably attach. He is on his own, feeling very much alone. Most little boys can identify with Eric: "I grew up in a farming community. . . . I had good parents. . . . They were strict, but not mean and they loved us all. . . . I remember when I was five years old, walking home from kindergarten. I started to think that I would go into the house with mother and my sisters, but then I thought that I could get my milk and cake, and then I'd have to leave and go outside with my brother. . . . There was a true feeling of freedom in that, but it was also so lonely . . . like I really didn't belong anywhere. My father was out tending the animals and mending fences. I figured that when I was older, I'd go out there, too, but now it was just being outside in the yard or barn while the girls were all laughing and hanging around the kitchen with Mother."

As boys we learn that we are outsiders. Any hope we would have of returning to the warm home would only come as a result of some very special accomplishments. Most of us believe that we will only be acceptable if we perform well. I wasn't rewarded or punished for my learning, creativity, or growth in school—it was only my grades that counted. Good grades led to a hope for better grades and comparisons to the hated kid in the neighborhood who had all A's. Bad grades led to groundings, beatings, and endless interrogation. Suggestion that the performance was a reflection of poor teaching, prejudice, or noisy compatriots would induce an escalation of the punishment. Malcolm reflected, "By the time I was in fifth grade, I knew that nobody wanted to hear excuses. They just wanted results. You gave them results or you were dead."

By the time we are adults, we are convinced that our value to other men and women is equivalent to our ability to perform. Problems are not something to be endured, ignored, or discussed. Problems are to be eliminated as soon as possible.

In the work world this attitude normally stands us in very good stead. Success at problem solving is highly valued in most jobs. However, in relationships these same skills may work paradoxically. When it comes to the plumbing in the home, for example, rapid attention to fixing it is highly valued. However, with difficulties in the relationship a "problem solver" may not satisfy the needs of his partner.

So what does a man hear when his wife opens an emotional conversation unexpectedly and in a general way? What do men hear when their wives say, "I want you to be more a part of this family"?

It may come as a surprise to many women that what he hears is *"Be my servant!"* Since he believes that she is reporting (not rapporting), he assumes that she is pointing out something that she does not like about him. Openings like that have led to rejection many times in the past. Because the question is not answerable in clear, specific terms, he has no answer—more grounds for failure and punishment. Finally, because he was not expecting the question, he assumes that he has missed something, hardly appropriate for a good problem solver.

Jim and Pam had been married for thirteen years when the following conversation occurred. It began when he accurately picked up some of her nonverbal behavior and responded.

Noticing that his wife seemed withdrawn, Jim approached her and asked, "What's wrong?" She replied, "Oh, it's nothing," nonverbally indicating that something was truly troubling her. Jim continued.

JIM: Well, it seems like something is upsetting you. Is it something I've done? [*Notice his immediately sensing that he had done something wrong that needed fixing.*]

PAM: It's a lot of things. I just feel like you're not very involved with the children and me.

JIM: [*Fearing he will be unfairly blamed, he jumps to his own defense.*] What do you mean? We spent the whole day together and I'm taking the kids to the park tomorrow.

PAM: It's not that. It's just that I feel like you're not a part of this family.

JIM: So what do you want from me now? [*accurately picking up that she wants something, inaccurately assuming that he could fulfill the need by a behavior change*]

PAM: You just don't seem that involved.

JIM: [*Beginning to fear her withdrawal and emotional abandonment, he tries to convince her that she is wrong.*] I am involved. I've done nothing but work for this family, and on my time off I work around the apartment, and we go out together.

From Jim's perspective her "complaint" about involvement is essentially a negative job-performance evaluation, which precedes a set of instructions for additional work under stricter supervision.

Contrast that with Pam's objective (expressed *only* nonverbally) to become closer and talk about the family.

It is easy to instruct her to be more specific and clear in communication (e.g., "Jim, I'm feeling a little distant. Could we sit together on the couch or go for a walk and talk a bit about getting more closeness in our family life?"). With such a message he will not be thrown into his fears of rejection and he will hear her request as a need for closeness instead of a demand for work.

It is equally easy to tell him to listen to her feelings and respond at that level without adding the rejection or task orientation (e.g., on hearing the words "I don't feel you're involved with the family," he could respond directly to her request: "I'm willing to be involved with you now; let's sit down together and talk").

The sole responsibility for making such adjustments belongs

to neither Pam nor Jim. In fact they both need to recognize the gender-related differences in the way they communicate.

Communication Differences and Power

Every relationship has some disagreements. No matter how loving a couple may be, their method of working out differences of opinion or desire may make or break the relationship. When couples are faced with disagreements, each person will naturally try to get things to go his or her own way. In any such power struggle each will resort to his or her most effective skills to settle the dispute.

In a stereotypical couple the woman is likely to be more accustomed to, and better at, arguing matters using feeling words in order to directly express a wider range of emotions. The male will feel more comfortable and capable with cognitive words that express facts and fairness. She is more practiced in one realm, he in another. If the dispute is to be decided based on who expresses the strongest feelings, she is likely to be the winner. If facts and logic will win the dispute, he will likely prevail. The battle then is not fought over the conscious content itself. It is the unconscious struggle to determine whose language will be used that creates the most difficulty. Once the method is unconsciously determined, the winner will be easy to predict.

If I were engaged in a controversy with Michael Jordan, for example, I would be foolish to have a basketball-shooting contest settle our differences. Similarly if I am better at identifying and expressing feelings, I would want to have decisions based on some measure of emotional response.

Perhaps we could understand better many couple's interactions by examining this unconscious struggle. Consider the following discussion between Fran and Ed. It began when Ed suggested that they visit his father over their Christmas holiday.

FRAN: I can't believe that you refuse to go to my mother's for Christmas. You know her heart is set on spending it with the kids.

[*"This is about my feelings and my mother's feelings, and it involves the children."*]

ED: All I said was I'd like to do something different for a change, and my father offered for us to come down to his place on Christmas Day. [*"This is a discussion about options and choices."*]

FRAN: I could never break my mother's heart that way. I just won't hear of it. [*escalating the feelings involved*]

ED: It isn't that I'm against seeing your mother. We could go over for Christmas Eve and then drive down to my father's place around noon. [*"Let's not get emotional, let's stay with problem solving and choices."*]

FRAN: You want me to desert my mother on Christmas? We *always* go to her house for Christmas. [*Repeat: "This is about feelings and relationships."*]

ED: We always go to your mother's for the holidays. We're going for Thanksgiving too. Besides, maybe she could come with us to my father's. There's plenty of room. [*Repeat: "This is not about feelings. Let's problem-solve."*]

FRAN: My mother would never leave her home on Christmas. Just what are you thinking? [*"I will not try to solve this problem your way. I want to discuss this emotionally and want you to acknowledge my feelings."*]

ED: Why don't you at least ask her? [*"No, I won't get emotional. I want this dispute on a rational level, where I feel more competent."*]

Fran and Ed will probably escalate this into a major argument because neither feels safe on the other person's ground. Subconsciously Fran fears that if she goes along with Ed, she could lose her mother and the Christmas she expected. Ed fears that if he gets into the emotional realm, he will be trapped without any input into family decisions.

To settle this dispute effectively, one of them would have to agree to do it in the way he or she least prefers, or they will mutually have to find some neutral ground. Perhaps Fran will accept the problem-solving approach if Ed will acknowledge how important the feelings are to her.

Without paying attention to the subconscious power struggle as the content, there is no way to know what will resolve the disputes effectively.

How Conversation Is Valued

Men and women seem to value talking quite differently. For women, talking is often a primary form of connecting. For men it is primarily informative. It has often been noted that men interrupt women when they are speaking more frequently than they will interrupt other men. By contrast, women will often wait their turn in a conversation, but will interrupt men when they are doing something other than talking.

Mary Ellen speaks for many women when she said, "Carl is always putting me down. He interrupts me when I'm talking. He just won't hear me out. It's rude and insensitive. I can't believe that he'd be so abusive as to cut me off in the middle of a sentence."

Her husband has a different perspective: "I do listen to her, but she says the same thing ten different ways, or she repeats herself. Once I get the gist of it, I want to move on to bigger and better things. I'm not a dummy. I don't need to be told something ten times. The main reason that I interrupt her is not because I don't respect her. It's because she's always talking. Anytime I speak, it's an interruption."

Carl is listening for the report. Mary Ellen is talking for the rapport. But there's another important component here: the relative value each gives to conversing. For Carl talking is one way to convey information. Often it's not the best way for him. Written words, nonverbal gestures, or telecommunications may get the job done more effectively.

Are men the only interrupters? Many men claim that their wives constantly interrupt them. It is not so much when they are talking. More often it is when they are reading, watching television, paying the bills, or working on a project. For many men these interruptions are by far more disturbing than a conversational one.

It isn't that either men or women are less sensitive than the other; rather they have different sensitivities.

Jay says, "Whenever I begin to work on a project or pick up the evening paper, it's like a signal to my wife that she should talk to me. She has even pushed aside what I'm doing so I would look at her when she's talking. You know, my mother was the same way. No sense that what I was doing was more important than what she wanted. The worst thing is when she starts talking on her way into the room, no care as to what I'm doing, like talking on the phone. She just barges in and starts in the middle of some conversation she's been having with me in her head. Usually it takes me ten minutes just to figure out the topic."

This gender difference can cause some real irritation. My wife will be far more upset if I interrupt her talking. I will be more bothered if she walks into the room in which I'm reading or watching television and begins talking without warning on a subject she has in mind, of which I haven't a clue. It wouldn't be upsetting to me if she interrupted my spoken sentence. I know it doesn't upset her when I want to talk when she's reading or watching TV.

In many situations the gender-centered communication differences are amusing. They provide grounds for better understanding within a gender, as well as a lot of material for stand-up comedians. One of the places where the lack of awareness may be hurtful is in sexual relating.

Sexual Communication

One especially sensitive arena for miscommunication involves sexuality. Research and clinical data indicate that men and women stereotypically show great differences in their approach to sexual relating and in the meaning they give sexuality in a relationship.

As a marital therapist for twenty-five years I have been repeatedly struck by the essential differences between men and women regarding where sexual contact fits into relationships. Jane and Don are a typical example:

JANE: He's just not interested in love and intimacy. All he cares about is sex. And once he's satisfied, that's it. Typical male, no interest in romance, just like all men.

DON: Well, you're never interested in sex. You want to talk it into the ground and then are too tired.

The Sequence of Sex and Intimacy. It has often been noted that for men sex precedes intimacy. Sexual intercourse is commonly the pathway to intimacy for men. For women sexual intercourse is the culmination of intimacy. With that apparent dilemma it is a wonder that any of us have children.

For many men to feel safe with a woman, they need to know that they are accepted by her and will not be rejected. Remember, based on his experience as a youngster, a man anticipates that women will send him out of the home to find his own way to become a man. He feels abandoned and rejected by his prototype woman, his mother. Because of that loss and the social experiences of having to be the initiator of dating and sexuality, he is well acquainted with the feeling of rejection. He will do whatever he can to avoid the hurt of abandonment. This may take the form of a hard, defensive shell that is only rarely penetrated by feelings. It may also take the form of withdrawal; running away when a relationship gets so intimate that its loss would be painful. Finally, he may open up only when he is reasonably certain of love and acceptance. Symbolically, sexual intercourse may be a close approximation to the perfect symbiosis and connectedness he experienced as an infant in the womb.

When a woman takes him into her own body and makes love with him, he feels safer. He is then more likely to be open in other than genital ways. When I am certain that my partner loves me enough to take my body into hers, I feel the arousal of the physical connection and also the sense of full acceptance. In such a context, over time, I will be able to share with her my more intimate parts.

What about for women? Traditionally her dilemma is not as much around rejection as it is around powerlessness or annihilation. For her sexual intercourse means allowing another inside herself. She is unlikely to issue such an invitation unless she is sure of who that person is. She needs to know him in a variety of ways in order to be that vulnerable and open. How does she get to know this man? Her preferred mode is by talking about his feelings. Unfortunately his feelings are locked away until he feels safe. Another battle for home-court advantage is born. Within every relationship there develops a power struggle about who goes first.

It is unreasonable to expect my partner to be sexually ready and available whenever I desire either the physical experience of intercourse and/or the closeness that it permits. On the other hand it is equally unfair that she always determine how and when we are sexual. Negotiations are tricky in this realm. To compromise, each of us has to have the patience and trust that are common only to long relationships. In the early years of a relationship the problem often rears its head over sexual frequency.

Differences in Sexual Frequency. Despite massive social changes, when it comes to initiating sexual intercourse, men are the primary initiators. Social psychological researchers such as Phil Blumstein and Pepper Schwartz clearly elucidate this male role.[12] This goes a long way in explaining the great discrepancies in sexual frequency by couples in different groups. The highest frequency is seen in gay male couples (two men, two initiators); and the lowest, in lesbian couples (two women, no initiator).

There are obvious biological reasons for the difference in desired frequency, but the psychological issue of acceptance is most important to many men. It is clear that women experience the emotional closeness that is a part of sexual relating quite differently.

It is important for me to develop a sensitivity to my wife's feelings. She may be in the position of having to respond to my sexual invitation at a time when she does not desire it because she doesn't feel sufficiently close to me at the moment. It is also important for me to feel comfortable enough and mature enough not to turn that lack of interest into a relationship-threatening rejection. However, it is equally important for me to help her understand what it is like to be turned down when I'm seeking the closeness we are both missing. Lee put it very succinctly: "How do you explain the feeling of having to initiate and getting turned down to someone who is able to have sex whenever she wants? If she desires it, we have it. I doubt that she has ever been rejected in that way in her entire life. Meanwhile I'm the professor of rejection."

The Lightning Rod

It is unreasonable to expect a person who speaks a different stylistic language to automatically understand what we mean. It reminds me of a time when I was in Jakarta, Indonesia. An American tourist walked up to a local resident, asking directions in English. When the fellow nonverbally moved his head from side to side, indicating no comprehension, the questioner asked again, much more slowly and loudly. Of course the answer was the same.

As a male my part in better communication is twofold. I need to learn better the nature of my partner's communication. Second I would do well to translate my language for her, since I know that she hears what I say, or don't say, in a different context.

In at least two situations the failure to understand a partner's communication may be problematic: intimate relating and parenting. It is difficult to provide a consistent, loving, open environment for the children when one parent is looking at the forest and the other parent is looking at the veins of the leaves. Neither is necessarily incorrect; both may be important.

Communication may be the lightning rod that both underscores significant male-female differences and the energy source that exacerbates them. If we learn to interpret each other's language and to communicate clearly, we may then begin to look at differences in parenting with appreciation of the complementarity rather than judgment of correctness.

FATHERING IS DIFFERENT FROM MOTHERING

When men discuss their frustrations in their primary relationships and parenting, they commonly describe their sense of being judged unfairly. Many of us are disheartened by what feels like an omni-present censor. We are constantly being told that we fail to live up to a female standard of parenting. We fail as junior mothers.

The problem is not an inability to be mothers. That should be taken for granted. The discomfort comes from a belief that we *should* parent like mothers, a belief shared by many men and women alike. In fact being a good father is quite different from being a good mother. Any man who sets his goal at being a mother will inevitably be an inadequate one. There are a number of reasons for this.

Before turning to these causes of differences, let's examine a few representative manifestations of parenting differences.

Holding Infants

When a woman picks up an infant, she tends to wrap the baby up into her breasts, providing warmth and security. When a man picks up an infant, he may well hold the child at arm's length and make eye contact, or he will turn the baby around with its back against his chest, or prop the baby up to look back over his shoulder. Each of these "male baby carries" underscores freedom, a sense of sharing a man's world with him. The infant has a need for both exploration and safety. When one parent naturally focuses on one, the other parent can encourage the other.

This doesn't mean that dads promote unrestricted freedom. The way we hold our babies is quite safe. We need to be certain of that. We also want to interrupt the baby's sense that the world revolves completely around him and teach him about the rest of the world.

Play

Men and women naturally play differently with their children. Watch men and women play with youngsters. Women almost auto-matically adopt the child's level of play and join with them at that level. Most mothers seem to retain an invisible emotional umbilical cord that allows them to be aware of the emotional state of their young children. Whether a mom is dueling with her young Robin Hood or baking mud pies at the toy stove, she provides the child with the opportunity to be in charge and direct the play.

By contrast playing with Dad means getting to do what he's doing. Instead of adopting the child's level, Dad becomes teacher of his level. Play can be "Hand me the socket wrench," or "When you throw a ball, use this leg to push." Dads play by teaching children teamwork. We encourage them to try new games, to learn new skills. We invite our children to compete and to push against the limits of their knowledge and skills. If little Billy can be Dad's helper, he can begin to dream about changing the oil or programming the VCR himself.

Discipline

When women discipline children, they use their "invisible emotional umbilical cord" to adjust the discipline moment by moment to the child's current state of mind. Men, lacking any such apparatus, discipline by rules. Women offer the child flexibility and suffer the consequences of continuous bargaining; men offer predictability and suffer the consequences of rigidity.

Neither is necessarily better. Together they produce a balance that aids child development. The "male" method of using rules and clearly defined punishments or restrictions for specific misdeeds allows a child to develop a beginning sense of morality in his or her culture. It also provides a child with consistency, which is particularly comforting.

During the process of separating from the family and becoming independent, our offspring test themselves by pushing against parental limits. When the consequences of their actions are clear, they can begin to make more mature choices. Without those limits they tend to feel unbalanced and intensify their testing.

At sixteen Cindy was a better-than-average student in school. She had just begun to socialize seriously with boys. Her curfew was midnight on Saturday night. From the beginning she was aware that violation of curfew meant grounding. On her second "date" with Chip, a new driver, she returned home at twelve-fifteen A.M. Her father met her at the door, told her she was fifteen minutes late, and that she would not be allowed out the following weekend. He then told her to go to bed.

During the next week he was greeted with tears, begging, sullenness, accusations, and other attempts at persuasion, both at meals and in the evening. At one point her older brother and mother also joined the pleading. Despite the pressure her dad was steadfast.

At the conclusion of her sophomore year at college, she remembered the incident: "I was really mad at Dad that month, but I knew he was right. I did try to see if I could get away with breaking curfew. Partly I was scared being out with Chip. He wasn't that good a driver, and I guess my dad got me out of another date. You know, I could have made it back on time. . . . I never did break curfew again."

Her father recalled the incident also: "Cindy always had me wrapped around her little finger, but something told me I had to draw the line early with her dating. I almost wavered when she said that this boy would never ask her out again and that she'd be humiliated at school, and especially when my wife joined in. But the bottom line was that she had to learn that agreements and rules had to be obeyed. It was also a lesson for her younger sister. Now, that's a child who tested me, but never about curfew."

The father's setting of limits reflects his role as moral tutor and translator of cultural and familial norms. The child needs to incorporate and internalize these norms in order to function well later in life. Slushy or overly flexible rules do not aid a child's creativity; they produce confusion and intensified limit testing. Of course some men go to the opposite extreme. Fathers who are rigid or punitive do not teach values, they generate rebellion. Discipline must be internalized. It is the disciplined adult who has perseverance. Rules need to be fair as well as firm in order to be valuable to a child's learning.

Duty and Responsibility

Closely aligned with discipline is responsibility. For mothers duty and responsibility are commonly more family based; for fathers they are more community oriented. A father's job is to help his children learn how to be functioning adults in the external world. Mothers often focus their attention on a child's belonging in the family. Fathers focus on the child's success in the world. Mothers emphasize the social aspects of life, fathers the functional.

As a father I teach my children about the "have to's" in life: We have to work, we are responsible to our society, we have to help others in need, and so on.

Communication

Because men and women communicate so differently, it stands to reason that fathers and mothers talk differently to their children. Normally mothers use much more emotional language with children. They share more equally with children. They chat a lot more with their children. By contrast fathers teach more and tend to share less of their own current feelings. Rather than converse, they tell stories about there-and-then phenomena. Conversations between fathers and children tend to be much shorter.

All these differences are consistent with male and female communication patterns and with their dissimilar styles of parenting and relating. In the stereotypic family the mother offers the children more closeness, comfort, and a sense of togetherness. Fathers offer the child more of a sense of protection, constancy, and separateness.

As a father I am much more interested in the bottom line before I am ready to listen to all the details of my child's upset. My wife is much more interested in the details of the event, allowing the conclusion to emerge at our child's pace.

When Blake's teenage daughter came home crying from a date, he wanted to know immediately if she was hurt or injured, if anyone else was injured, or if the car was damaged. Then he was prepared to listen to the details of her bad date. By contrast his wife, Marjorie, was comfortable when their daughter began with an account of how she initially was fixed up on the date three weeks ago and a description of her friend's new beau.

I also teach my children how to communicate through work or play. Rather than sitting and "having a talk," I am more prone to discuss matters of import while we are doing a family project, driving in the car, watching a baseball game together, or checking homework.

Finally, being more separate from their children, fathers normally see their children as belonging jointly to themselves and the mother; whereas mothers usually use the terms "my" son or "my" daughter, fathers refer to their offspring with the pronoun "our."

Determining Limits

One of the lessons that men learn by virtue of their role as a family provider and as participants in team sports is how to evaluate situations for reward or danger. As a father I may convey to children the importance of determining whether a particular battle is worth fighting. Where do I put my energy and make a stand? When is discretion the better part of valor?

How may I convey to my child that I cannot take on every conflict with full energy? By my personal actions and reasoning I can show my children how I choose to fight important battles and to avoid fights where the probability of success is very low. How may I help them learn the difference between courage and impulsiveness?

Mothers have far less experience in this realm. They have probably not had the years of team sports. They have usually not been in the marketplace as long or as intensively. In addition, because they are more likely to be emotion rather than logic driven in conflict, mothers tend to fight all battles as if they were equal. There is less gauging of the potential outcome and more focus on the right or wrong in a given situation.

Limitless Possibilities

Finally, fathers have a special role in a child's dreaming about the future. As the representative of the outside world and as the person who most supports freedom in the home, I have the responsibility of encouraging my children to pursue their desires. I am best suited to encourage my daughter and my son to try to realize their dreams. I may do this by pursuing my own aspirations and by encouraging them to try. I also have to pick them up when they fall and encourage them to try again.

A Father's Unique Contributions

A father gives his children a set of values, a more stable environment and worldview, self-discipline, a belief in delayed gratification, guidance, some sense of appropriate social behavior with peers and the opposite sex, and the desire for achievement. To do this successfully, we must gently, yet firmly, confront parental differences. We must risk losing the role of "good guy" in the eyes of our children. We must face the fear of rejection from our wives. We must risk greater amounts of verbal communication.

Generically we do not play with, hold, discipline, teach, or love our children incorrectly. We do it in a masculine manner. The most likely way for us truly to do it wrong is to try to be substitute mothers. When we attempt to be female in our approach to our children, we will become second-class mothers. We fail our children by depriving them of a father's perspective. We also fail ourselves. Many men who feel less adequate or competent either withdraw or express anger, which becomes a self-fulfilling prophecy. In our sullen distance or absence we deprive our children and provide evidence that fathers in fact are second-class parents.

4

PITFALLS AND PERILS: THE INADEQUATE FATHER

The signature of a missing father is the fragile masculine identity of his sons.

—GUY CORNEAU

Knowing how to be the father that I've always wanted to have requires that I explore ideal forms of fathering and successful fathers. It also obliges me to examine those forms of fathering that I would do well to avoid. There is certainly no lack of information available about poor or inadequate fathers. Popular psychology and the media have bombarded us for two decades or more with images of cruel, abusive, absent, foolish, rejecting, scapegoating, alcoholic, unfeeling, and narcissistic fathers.

Calling fathers and masculinity the cause of most social ills represents a profound cultural reversal. In the first half of this century women, particularly mothers, were commonly faulted for any developmental, psychological, or behavioral disorders of their offspring, even after they became adults. Today fathers have become the object of this culpability. Although there is no question that early parenting significantly affects later relationship development and success in many aspects of life, it is obviously shortsighted simply to attribute all the difficulties any adult might encounter in relationships to their interaction with either parent.

However, poor fathering may have serious consequences for children. Both our childhood and later life as adults are influenced by an absent or abusive father. Perhaps your own father was physically or emotionally unavailable. Perhaps he was abusive, threatening, overly dependent, or guilt inducing. What legacy does that leave you? Perhaps, like most of us, you share some of these tendencies. If you are reading this book, you are probably quite dissimilar from the stereotypical dangerous father, yet all of us are potentially susceptible to the pitfalls of poor fathering.

TYPES OF POOR FATHERING

Most writers and clinicians have enumerated ways that fathers can fail their children. In some ways it is a lot easier to recognize the impact of poor fathers than that of good ones. To make this more vivid, I have included several case examples from my psychotherapy practice. As you will see, the problems are not limited to a single generation. A father's missteps are often visited on the son.

Two of the most powerful forms of poor fathering involve absence, be it physical or emotional.

Physical Absence

Many children can develop fears of abandonment by lengthy physical separations from their fathers. A number of men who are today fathers report that they personally did not have any early contact with their own fathers, who were away in the military during World War II or the Korean conflict. Others were abandoned by fathers who truly deserted their families. Some children had fathers who were incarcerated or who spent lengthy time in institutions. Military families, for example, often have to accustom themselves to lengthy or frequent father absences. Sometimes it is the children who are separated from their fathers by family difficulties, war, or illness.

In today's families it is estimated that one half of all children will live in homes without their fathers during their school years. Work responsibilities also frequently create long separations for fathers and children.

Aaron spoke with bitterness about his job when he said, "I have been home only about one week a month for the past year. The rest of the time I'm on the road. It's not by choice at all. Every guy who has tried to get off the road and back to the home office has been riffed. I can't afford that. So I end up supporting my kids . . . but I don't even know them. My wife told me the little one began to talk. I missed his birth and eighty percent of his life so far."

Whatever the causes of the separation, both sons and daughters miss out on some important learning in childhood when their fathers are not present. These deficits seem particularly important in the later development of adult intimate relationships. Sons who were unable to incorporate some sense of adult male role models tend to be overdependent or distant and fearful of intimacy. They look to women for cues on how they should behave. Such men are destined to feel inferior to their partners, not being as adept in female ways of relating. Feeling inadequate in the relationship, these men either withdraw or aggress as a way to feel better about themselves. In place of adult intimacy they emulate media characterizations of men; acting more than feeling.

Daughters with physically absent fathers suffer in different ways. Having no appropriate male role models, they do not learn about how men normally communicate feelings. They have little experience of male limit setting and boundaries. Later in life they frequently find their male partners unreasonable or unfair in relationships. They also expect that their partners will respond more in the way they are accustomed. Having never been validated by men, they may seek approval to their own detriment, giving up their personal standards in efforts to please. Adult daughters of physically absent fathers commonly relent too often in relationships only to subsequently resent and rebel aggressively. Without a father to try out their developing relationship skills, they lack a safe man with whom they may experiment. Thus they are relegated to experimentation with men as adults.

Richard, Lisa, Kevin, and Julius are examples of adults who grew up with physically absent fathers. Each person's story demonstrates the kinds of deficits that father absence is likely to promote.

Richard. The second of four children, Richard grew up in a home with a "scurrilous" father and "sainted" mother. His father, a traveling salesman, was described as a "womanizer," "liar," and "a man's man." As a child and adolescent Richard was "the man of the house" whenever his father was away on a business trip or off "following the ladies." Richard was at the top of his class in high school and went to an Ivy League college, where he also excelled, and then to a major law school before becoming a partner in a prestigious West Coast law firm. His academic successes were matched by athletic exploits.

Although he dated as a young man, he never established a long-term intimate relationship. At the age of thirty he met and married a fellow attorney. They divorced "amicably" after two years. Following the divorce Richard dated "society ladies, movie stars, and models." He was always accompanied by young, attractive women.

Richard prided himself on two things: always "having the best" and "being sure that my mother was well cared for." He possessed a sharp mind and scathing wit and, at age forty, regularly beat much younger men at tennis. In addition to his financial success he was becoming involved in politics and was described in local newspapers as having real potential. Richard was greatly admired by business leaders and by junior members of his firm. Indeed he seemed to make anything he touched successful.

He came into therapy because he felt that all his successes, "the Benz, the house, the collection of art, the trophies, and the money still leave me feeling like something is missing."

Early in therapy the most noticeable characteristic besides his intelligence was his desire to please me. He would talk of exploits, of his devotion to his mother, of his reading my books and other literature in psychology, and of his numerous charitable contributions. He also offered me tickets to sporting events and performances. The more I declined, the more uncomfortable he became, finally asking me if I cared about him at all, since I didn't seem too impressed with his accomplishments or capacity.

When I asked him what would it be like for him if I were not impressed with all his successes, he replied, "Then I'd be a failure." Later he admitted that he couldn't think of a single person whom it would be acceptable to have reject him.

The burden of having to please everyone, and his consequent inability to be in a marital relationship with a partner, was directly related to his early family life. Having pledged himself to his mother, and having no paternal influence to help break that bond, he found all relationships with women wanting by comparison with the intense emotional connection to his mother. His attempt to avoid being like his father in any way left him with only two options: to be loved and admired by (a hero to) everyone, and to avoid the possibility of anyone knowing him well enough to find him lacking. He confessed, "If a woman really got to know me well, she would discover the parts of my father in me."

Because his father was unavailable, Richard never was able to internalize much of the male mode of feeling. The subsequent emotional vacuum was then filled with his childhood sense of what his mother desired from a man, and from cultural images of male heroes. Richard became, as an adult, the kind of man who would please a woman like his mother. Unfortunately that involved a rejection of many of the male aspects of himself. He had to hide any masculine "bad" feelings and lived life entirely on the superficial level. His mother psychologically cooperated by having her son replace the emotional loss of her husband.

Until he could learn to accept the masculine aspects of himself and gain approval for those parts, in this case from a male therapist, he could not allow himself to dig deeper into his feelings, wishes, and desires.[1] He also had to confront his internalized feelings that he was betraying his love for his mother when he became romantically attached to a woman. Two years after entering therapy he was able to develop a loving relationship with a woman, who became his second wife. They are now parents of two children.

The impact of Richard's childhood continues to play itself out in his reactions to his children. As he learns about his own masculinity and about fatherhood, he shifts precipitously between overinvolvement and underinvolvement with his children. As he understands better his personal needs and continues to explore the relationship with another male (his therapist), he is gaining a better sense of how to be himself with his children and to provide a better model of a father for them than he personally experienced. In Richard's words, "Without the therapy I may have got somebody pregnant, but I would never be a father or a decent husband. I would have been as distant as my father."

Lisa. Women do not grow up to be fathers, but the absence of Lisa's father has also been powerful in her personal development. Lisa grew up in a "house full of women"—with her mother, grandmother, and three sisters. Her father, a corporate executive, was described as "a workaholic, who kept putting in an eighty-hour week even after his first heart attack." Her only memory of her father being available was on "one five-day trip to the Finger Lakes. Even then, he spent at least two hours a day checking in to the office."

Lisa and her sisters were all sent to boarding school for their secondary education and on chaperoned trips to Europe. As a senior in high school she got pregnant from a liaison on one such trip and had "the first of my three abortions." Throughout her twenties and early thirties her relationships with men were "passionate, short, and unsuccessful."

Most of the men with whom she became involved were unmotivated, poorly educated by comparison to her master's degree, had a history of failed relationships, or were otherwise inappropriate for her.

Her work life was relatively successful. However, despite a

great deal of talent and collegial respect, something always seemed to impede significant or sustained accomplishment.

Lisa entered therapy in despair over a long-term affair with a married man. It was soon evident that she had great difficulty maintaining a relationship with a man who was her equal and who was also available. She simply didn't know how to interact with a man "who wasn't running away like Dad or a doormat like Mom." In an effort to find a man who was dissimilar to her workaholic father, she was attracted to men who were unlikely to be employed at all. In her ambition to avoid being like her mother, she found men who would need her so much that they wouldn't be able to leave her. Only after a year of intensive psychotherapy was she able to separate love from need, terminate her affair, and begin to date more appropriate suitors.

As part of the therapy Lisa's sisters also came in for a few family sessions. Her two older sisters had followed similar destructive relationship patterns. Only the youngest had been able to form a lasting, positive relationship. It is interesting that right after she finished high school, she undertook the physical caretaking for their father in the last six months of his life.

Having grown up without an appropriate male model, Lisa was in a long-term experimenting phase in relationships. She was unconsciously trying to establish her own identity with males through trial and error.

Kevin. When Kevin was four years old, his father was sent to Cambodia as a member of the military Special Forces. He never returned. From time to time over the years scattered reports indicated that he was a prisoner of war, alive. Kevin relates that his father's disappearance cost him both parents: "My mother keeps a candle in the window, prays every night and still believes that her husband is alive. She spends holidays with families of other POWs and MIAs. I guess I just parented myself for the last twenty years. I don't want to leave her alone, but I just need to get on with my life now. I have a chance for a transfer to the Southwest, and I'll probably take it."

Kevin has convinced himself that his father actually perished many years ago. He doesn't argue with his mother about her faith, but talks openly to his older sister and brother.

Lacking any close sense of parenting in his own home, Kevin found substitutes through his sports prowess and his only girl-friend. While he was in high school he went to live for two years with her family. After high school they went to the same college together and are currently engaged. "Even today I am very depen-dent on Becky. I hate it when we are away from each other. I even worry when she's a few hours late after work. The summer she went to Europe and I had to work was the worst in my life. . . . She worries about my clinging sometimes, but says, 'at least I'm not the jealous type.' I guess that would be worse. I just don't know what I'd do without her."

Kevin's dependence on his fiancée is not unusual for adults who grew up with absent parents. For Kevin the loss of his father was compounded by his mother's complete dedication to retrieving her husband. It was natural that he would attach himself to another loved one with the intensity of a young child's bond to a parent.

Physical Separation by Death. One form of permanent physical separation does not seem to be as devastating as desertion, particu-larly to sons. This is the case when the father has died. In spite of the complete absence of their fathers, these males tend to adapt better than sons whose fathers are absent by choice.

A critical factor here is that the mother may have very positive memories of her husband and will talk a lot about him to her son. This helps create a positive symbolic image of the father that par-tially compensates for his absence. Second she may make earnest attempts to bring other positive male role models into her sons' lives to help make up for the loss without feeling that she is being in some way diminished.

Julius. As the youngest of three children in a poor neighborhood and of a mother who had to work two jobs to provide food and shelter, Julius's early life was more difficult than most. Julius's father died of a congenital heart condition just prior to his son's birth. During his early years he and his family shared apartments with grandparents and other relatives. Concerned that her boys needed a male interest, Julius's mother actively connected them to church groups and encouraged their participation in sports. Julius described a baseball coach as a "real big brother to me and Eddie [Julius's brother]." He continued his association with other coaches and men in his church throughout his high school, military, and college years.

Today Julius is a high school teacher, active in Boy Scouts and Big Brothers. He reports having a sense that "something is missing . . . a birthright . . . a [sense] of being part of a tradition of males." During his wife's first pregnancy he actually dreaded having a son because "I don't know what a father is supposed to be with a son." He also had an unconscious fear that he would not survive his son's birth. After all, his father did not survive his. Julius still struggles with his fears about being the right kind of father to his two school-age sons and baby daughter and is always the first one to ask questions of other dads.

His personal insecurity stemming from his lack of a father is likely to be with him for some time. He is taking all the right steps by recognizing his loss, seeking help from other men, and facing his fears. His behavior as a dad and his intense commitment to his children, as well as to a host of fatherless boys, is a paramount expression of a person overcoming his past personal loss.

Emotional Absence

Far more common than physical absence, and often even more harmful in a family, is a father's emotional absence. Women consistently complain that their husbands, and ex-husbands, were not present or available. These men have overlearned the classic male "strong, silent" traits. Often, emotionally inexpressive fathers are men who are unaware of their own inner life. When asked what they are feeling, they honestly do not know. Trained since boyhood to be out of touch with pain and to respond primarily to duty, these "soldiers" avoid connection with others, living lonely lives even within a family.

The impact on a man's children may be substantial. Many children suffer from growing up in a home where their fathers may be physically present but quite distant emotionally. Their fathers are unresponsive to their needs for attention, affection, and attachment. When these children seek caretaking from their father, they are ignored or punished. This will foster the development of low self-esteem and fears of rejection in the child.

Joseph and Tanya, who grew up in such homes, have suffered both self-esteem and relationship problems.

Joseph. As the oldest son in an immigrant family, Joseph was expected to work hard in the family store, which was located below their living quarters. He described his father as a man "of few words and high expectations." Joseph's childhood was fully intertwined with the family business. "The only time the family was together was for dinner, and the only discussion at dinner was the store." His father presided over these conversations "by virtue of his scowls and glances. Mostly he ignored us kids, gave orders to Mama, and went off to read his [ethnic newspaper]."

A better-than-average student in high school, Joseph says that he never showed his parents his report card. He just forged their signatures and went back to school. He claims he did that because he didn't think his parents would understand the grades or care about them.

He left home for college at age eighteen "on a scholarship and a hell of a lot of dish washing in college." Returning for the summer after his senior year in college, he became incensed when his father was unwilling to listen to his input about the business and his expectation that he would again be a clerk. "That was the last time I ever went back."

Now sixty years old, retired from a successful and lucrative career, and launching the youngest of his own children, he still worries excessively about how others will view him. When he meets other retirees in "the business," he is plagued with concerns that he will not impress them or that they won't like him. Tears come readily to his eyes when discussing his father. His insecurity around other men in particular brings to mind the depressing memory that his father never told him "I love you."

Tanya. Now thirty, single, and successful in her career as a fashion consultant, Tanya reflects on her upbringing: "My father was the classic example of why I don't want to get married. Whenever I think of him, I picture the TV, beer, potato chips, and either orders for us kids to be quiet or his loud snoring in his chair. I think when they thought up Homer Simpson, they used my dad for the model. It was just like he never cared about Mom, us kids, or anything. He only cared about his beer and TV. I lived in that house for eighteen years and I don't think I ever got to know who he was at all. . . . Well, Mom's fate will not happen to me. No guy is gonna get me to be their servant and mother."

As Tanya spoke, her bitterness about her father and men in general expanded. She engaged in male-bashing rhetoric, claiming that "the only halfway decent guys are gay. All the straight ones don't know how to talk to a girl. They just grunt."

However, in the same conversation she claimed to want to have children and a good family life, saying, "I guess I wouldn't know a good relationship if it hit me in the head."

Her immature perceptions about male-female relationships reflect a lack of opportunity to learn by experimenting with her dad. She maintains a childlike categorizing of men by polarization.

Joseph and Tanya both grew up in homes where their father's body was far more evident than his consciousness or involvement. Neither of them felt nurtured by a male; neither received a full sense of masculine feeling. In both cases Father was distant, contained, and unavailable. Such an experience is bound to have a long-term impact on the relationships they seek and develop as adults.

Their stories are far from unique. Many of the men I've interviewed have little sense of their father's hopes, dreams, or desires. Many of these men also have considerable difficulty talking about their own inner life with their children. To some extent everybody gets a bit tongue-tied talking about those most important matters. Perhaps this is something you want to improve in your own life. Perhaps, like Joseph, you don't really know much about how your father felt about you. In Part II of this book we will explore these issues in depth. For now it is valuable to consider that emotional distance in your own fathering may not be all-or-none. There may be subtle deficiencies, imperfections that can be corrected with insight, practice, and a few good models.

Absence involves something that a father does passively. The following forms of poor fathering involve actions that directly harm children: verbal threats, physical abuse, and scapegoating. Each of these involves extreme forms of punishment. Men who frequently engage in them have somehow lost sight of a crucial boundary between discipline and punitiveness, teaching and coercion. Far more significantly, they seem oblivious of their children as people and have begun to treat them as objects.

Verbal Threats

Discipline or punishment that involves threats of a father's leaving the family, killing himself or others, or withdrawing love will be damaging over time. Coercion through such threats may produce a short-term compliance but long-term deficits.

Attempts to control children's behavior by threatening to give them away or doing away with them may well also be exceptionally deleterious. The following quotations represent clear memories that many men recall from their youth:

"If you don't knock off that behavior, I'm sending you off to 'the home.'"
"I brought you into this world and I can damn well take you out of it."

It is unlikely that their fathers ever truly considered following through with those threats, yet men who recalled such fears as boys often report continuing insecurity and fears of abandonment in adult relationships. It is not uncommon to find these men being excessively security conscious or willing to accept outrageous behavior from their partners.

Martin. At age forty-one Martin is a charming, extroverted marketing executive who has been married twice and is now supporting four children from those marriages. He has occasional limited personal contact with his children. By his own admission, Martin is the "master seducer," having had sexual relationships with well over a hundred partners. He tries to "charm" every woman he encounters, including a meter maid who gave him a parking ticket and the receptionist in the therapy office on the day of his first appointment. He was particularly fond of "hitting on" mature women who were older than himself. He described both of his wives as "warm, caring, and good mothers."

Martin was the product of a home in which he was very close to his mother and oldest sister and distant from his father, an immigrant who "never quite mastered the new language." He describes his father as very cold and rejecting. A regular family drama involved Martin's father becoming upset with his behavior and threatening to send him away to "the old country" to learn proper discipline, whereupon Martin's mother would swoop in to save her son, telling her husband that he would go before her son went.

As an adult Martin looked for women to satisfy his needs for love, affection, and unconditional acceptance. Unfortunately no matter how much he received, he feared that rejection and abandonment were imminent. A common tactic was constantly to push the limits of relationships until the rejection finally came. In both of his marriages he developed intense romantic relationships with other women. When his wife at the time accepted the affair, he intensified it. When she gave him an ultimatum, he experienced the expected rejection.

For Martin, rejection would always be a part of his relationships because the seeds of his abandonment were not in the women but in himself. Having incorporated the disapproving father as part of himself, he had a "fatal attraction" to such rejection. This connection regularly emerged in his dreams.

In one of his recurrent dreams he experienced himself being a little boy who was banished from his home by a conqueror. He is saved by three sisters, who take him in and protect him. However, when he is caught in the act of copulating with the eldest sister, he is turned over to the enemy for execution. Both consciously and in his dreams, for Martin, relationships were tests of acceptance.

Martin's father may not have meant his threats to return his son to Sicily for discipline, but Martin believed the threat enough to internalize a sense that ultimately he would face abandonment. Of course the threats alone were insufficient to create such a powerful consequence. There was nothing else in his relationship with his father to counteract that threat.

Martin's father never did actually send him away. Saul, on the other hand, experienced exile from his home when he was four years old.

Saul. When his mother was hospitalized with polio during his childhood, his father sent him to live with an aunt, a widow with four children of her own. Saul described her as "a good person who had too many children to take care of." He reports that he really missed his mother and his sister, who was living with other relatives.

When his mother returned home, he and his sister were reunited with the family, but "it just was never the same. She [his mother] was weak, and we had to act like adults. Plus, there was the constant threat that if her condition worsened, we'd be banished again."

He laughs ironically when he relates that his mother outlived his father. Reflecting on his father's life, he says, "He never knew his own parents, so he just didn't understand what I needed as a kid. It was like he got frustrated by his life and he lashed out by pushing everyone else away. He was very unhappy, never made friends. I don't even know if he liked my mother. I'm sure that all those years of caring for an invalid made him frustrated."

As a teenager and adult, relationships came hard for Saul. He describes himself as "accidentally promiscuous." Fearing rejection from women in his life and having little understanding of adult male roles, Saul was particularly attracted to women who were unlikely to provide for those needs. If a woman was warm, loving, and open to him, he became anxious that she would leave him and ultimately set in motion ways of ending the relationship. He felt safer with a woman who seemed to have little capacity for loving. If he could get such a woman to change her basic ways, to convert herself for him, then and only then could he be sure of being loved unconditionally and wouldn't fear the loss. Of course such a conversion was highly improbable.

One of his longest relationships, an on-and-off affair with a cold, reserved, sometimes depressed woman, exemplified his pattern. He struggled to win her over, to bring out her gentleness and tenderness. It was almost as if her being truly loving to him would symbolically replace the love he yearned for from his father.

Saul was also exceptionally cautious about money. His need for security was projected into a belief that the protection offered by financial security would serve him in two ways: make him attractive to "quality women" and keep him from a life of despair and loss.

The threat of abandonment to a child is particularly frightening. Once internalized, this fear operates unconsciously in later intimate relationships. Sons and daughters who subconsciously fear abandonment will have great difficulty trusting others.

The other great fear of young children is of being annihilated.

Abuse

Any parent who has had an inconsolable, screaming infant, a "mouthy" teenager, or a child who habitually disobeys family rules can understand the *impulse* for abuse. Many parents believe that certain (particularly dangerous) behaviors call for a swat on the backside or nonaggressive spanking. However, actual abuse of children is in many ways the ultimate violation of parental authority. When children are beaten, they will be psychologically damaged. In some instances they may also be harmed physically. Such experiences may take years to overcome fully. It breaks the sacred covenant of parents to protect their children.

Some fathers who lose control of their anger or frustration take it out on the child. Many adults today remember being beaten as children: cutting the switch to be whipped; being on the ladder and being beaten with a brush, hanger, or belt; or simply being punched and assaulted. Today there is mounting evidence that physical and sexual abuse of children by fathers is far more widespread than was earlier reported. News coverage of children who were beaten to death has appeared on national media. Whatever the actual incidence of such abuse, even a single case is excessive. Parents who use their size and strength or employ terror as a method of child raising will likely produce offspring who will have low self-esteem, low pride, and be bullies with their peers. As adults they will be more prone to perpetuating the cycle by abusing their own children.

Were you abused as a child? Was physical beating considered "normal" in your upbringing? Have you regretted losing your temper and striking your own child? Many of us would answer those questions affirmatively. Many of us regret the potential harm to our child. I can recall spanking my own son when he was about two and a half years old. At the time I felt it was justified. For almost a year afterward, whenever he saw me angry, he would say in a plaintive voice, "Don't spank me, Daddy." It broke my heart to see him so frightened of me. I do not consider that single swat on the behind abusive, but his reaction made me realize how scary it was for him. Incidentally that turned out to be the primary outcome. He may have been fearful of another spanking, but his behavior did not change.

Neither my son nor I was physically abused. George and Alicia were.

George. A forty-four-year-old former Marine and Vietnam veteran, George is the divorced and distant father of four children. He has little contact with any of the three younger children, claiming that he barely got to know them before "she dumped me and got everything in the divorce." He says that he meets with his twenty-two-year-old daughter and that they attend Alcoholics Anonymous together almost weekly.

George's father is described as a brutal and cruel man who would "get loaded every Friday after work and beat the hell out of any of us who got in the way." As a child he was twice hospitalized after being beaten by his father, once after trying to protect his mother and once when he discovered his father molesting his ten-year-old younger sister. At age seventeen he dropped out of high school and ran away from home, ultimately "ending up at Parris Island and then in Nam."

Wounded twice in Vietnam, he returned to Minneapolis, "left the Corps with no job prospects and addicted to dope and booze." His first marriage followed, and ended two months later when he struck his wife "because she was flirting with someone." He married again, to a "drinking crony." When that short marriage ended, he ended up in a VetCenter detoxification program. During this time he managed to complete his high school education and enter a trade school.

His third marriage "was problematic from day one, but it lasted ten years and we had four children." However, he began drinking again and became verbally and physically abusive to his wife and children. After one of these episodes his wife ordered him out and obtained a divorce and restraining order to keep him away from her and the children.

Although George has been sober for the past three years and continues to make amends for his past, he still struggles to limit the aggressive feelings he has had since he was a little boy. He describes feeling "guilty for leaving my mother and sister with that monster and deserting my wife and children." What is particularly interesting about George is that he takes one aspect of fathering quite seriously. Although he has little interest in trying to meet with the three younger children, he has been conscientious about his financial responsibilities; he has never missed a child-support payment. It is an aspect of fathering that he well understands and takes very seriously. For him the financial responsibility is the total responsibility.

Alicia. As the youngest of five children, Alicia described her childhood as growing up in a "house of hypocrites, putting up a good front for the neighbors but rotten inside." She describes being beaten with a wire hanger and belts by her father and also of being sexually abused by him and two of his friends, whom he invited to join the molestation.

She recalled her only dating experience in high school: "I guess in retrospect it was a date rape. I didn't say no, I just froze, and he had his way with me." After being with the same fellow for eight months, she became pregnant. "When he begged me to marry him and have the baby, I split, and my mom arranged for one of those back-alley abortions."

Despite some success as a saleswoman, her sexual relationships have remained problematic. She has been in several "abusive" relationships and has terminated three unwanted pregnancies. She also describes sexual intercourse as "no fun for me, but it's what they want so I go along." At least two of her "lovers" have also robbed her on leaving, one time abandoning her in a foreign country without her passport or any money.

She claims to be close to her mother and one sister, who was also sexually abused by her father and "who finally turned him in to the cops." She limits contact with them because she is also quite angry with both of them for not protecting her when she was young.

There is reason to doubt that Alicia will ever fully recover from the childhood abuse. It would certainly take long-term therapy and a lot of motivation on her part.

Finally there is the example of a forty-five-year-old man who appeared on *The Oprah Winfrey Show* on February 19, 1992, whose response to his childhood abuse was to have a vasectomy at age twenty-eight to make sure that he would never abuse a child.

Scapegoating

Men who are frustrated by their own failures and inadequacies may well turn to blaming others in an attempt to relieve their own internal distress. By "projecting" the fault externally they experience a greater sense of personal safety. When the child becomes the object of the blame, it is often problematic.

"Everything was fine until you came along."
"If you had been better, I wouldn't be in this fix now (your mother wouldn't be drinking again, etc.)."
"We had the auto accident because you kids kept distracting me."

From a psychological perspective, blaming one's deficits and defeats on others has the short-term advantage of preserving one's personal feelings of worth. Many men who become fathers are physically ready for the job long before they are psychologically mature enough to handle fatherhood. For such a man, blaming the children for his own failings is a common part of daily experience.

What becomes of a child who is regularly led to believe that he or she is the cause of all the family discomfort or failures? How will such a child grow up?

As a culture we Americans tend to believe that we have unlimited potential. Therefore anything less than excellence must be the fault of someone or something. Rather than examine our own lack of ability or motivation, it is sometimes easier to hold the child(ren) responsible.

Nadine. "I was only thirteen years old, but I remember it like it was yesterday," recalls this thirty-five-year-old CPA. "My father was defeated in a local political election for school board, and he walked in the door and said he lost because there were rumors about me and boys at the school."

She was so unsettled by these false and inappropriate accusations that "I decided right then that I could never tell him or Mom anything ever again." Nadine became increasingly reclusive throughout her high school and college years, "and was working on my master's degree in accounting before I really dated anyone seriously. I always thought that if I ever got close to anyone, I'd let them down and they'd destroy me."

It is clear that the single incident all by itself could not have caused so much of her social avoidance. However, it is symbolic of a childhood in which "I was the reason that everything went wrong. If the toilet backed up, he'd immediately say it was that I used too much paper or 'feminine products.' If the electric bill was high, it was my radio."

Claude. The son of an influential attorney and writer, Claude grew up as the wealthiest child in a small town. "I remember other kids looking at our house. It was really big for that community. Despite the wealth and privilege, or because of it, I never belonged with my friends at school. But my father was a part of that. One time when my one friend was over, he told me he thought Mike had stolen something. He was always acting like the D.A. at home. Dinner was the time when my sister and I would be grilled about what we did all day."

When his father was himself indicted for tax fraud, a charge that was ultimately dropped, he continually blamed Claude for "talking to others outside the family about our finances."

Claude recalls that he always felt as if he was on the witness stand, accused of a heinous crime. Even today whenever someone asks him a simple question, "I tend to get paranoid." As evidence of this, in response to a questionnaire he agreed to complete regarding his experiences as an expectant father, he declined to answer more than half the questions, claiming that he didn't know exactly what I was after. He also "corrected the language of the questionnaire to reduce some of the ambiguities."

At age twenty-nine Claude has a "long history of being with women that nobody could satisfy." He finds himself attracted to very critical women, but cannot tolerate when they turn their critical eye on him, especially sexually. In "protection against being left," Claude always seems to be lining up his next relationship while he is involved and has rarely been monogamous. It may not be coincidental that his father had a mistress for almost twenty years because his "mother apparently had a very low sexual drive."

In addition to identifying with his father sexually, he shares another of his father's traits. As much as he hates even the hint of being blamed for anything, he is openly and consistently critical of others.

There are other, less punitive ways in which a father may harm his children or stifle their development. These involve weakness and manipulation. When adults fail to parent, the children are left with the burden of growing themselves, and sometimes their parents, up. Two prominent ways that parents abdicate their responsibility is with excessive guilt, and dependency. They control their children through their apparent weakness.

Guilt Induction

Similar to blaming, parenting that induces guilt promotes overresponsibility and impossible demands on children. Some fathers assert that the child's behavior is or will be responsible for the unhappiness, illness, or death of one of the parents. ("Your poor grades are killing your mother!")

A child who grows up in a guilt-inducing home is at risk for low self-esteem and consequent relationship problems later in life. Whether a child feels guilty for a lack of accomplishment or for some transgression, the effect can be devastating. Some fathers who themselves feel guilty employ the power of guilt to control their children. Although the short-term benefit is there, long-term what the child incorporates into his or her psyche is a sense of not being adequate, competent, or acceptable.

Jason. When he was in his twenties, Jason fell in love for the first time with Kristina, a woman who was not acceptable to his traditional Jewish parents. Despite his strong feelings, his father's admonition that such a marriage would cause his mother to have a second heart attack was sufficient for Jason to break off the relationship. Two years later he became engaged to a woman who was not only of a different religion but of a different race as well. Despite support from friends, his two sisters, and his fiancée, he was unable to get over the sense that he was harming his parents, potentially killing them by such a marriage. Nevertheless he did marry Tomiko. They had two children and what most observers would call a better-than-average marriage, but he continued to feel that somehow he would be responsible for harm coming to his parents.

Ultimately this feeling created a wedge between him and his wife. He also sought out his earlier love for a brief affair. In marriage therapy he began to explore his personal sense of having no birthright, of not being acceptable the way he was, of always having to perform to get what others received simply by being.

This feeling pervaded his entire life. When his three-year-old daughter became angry with him for restricting her candy eating, she told him that he was uninvited to her birthday party. He felt horribly guilty and "tried to do anything to change her mind." At work a casual comment by his boss will send him into a "frenzy of worrying and fear." As a marketing executive, his fear of failing causes him to be overly perfectionistic, hence less productive than he should be. He feels guilty both about sending out an inferior product and about not getting something out on time, a prescription for immobility. Jason has internalized his parents' lack of acceptance as an excessively rigid conscience. He is very hard on himself and is prone to guilt feelings on almost any occasion. It is important to recognize that this doesn't necessarily inhibit his behavior. He just feels terrible no matter what he does or doesn't do.

Marilyn. The second of three daughters, Marilyn grew up in a puritanical, fundamentalist home where any behavior was potentially cause for repentance. Her father, a self-styled lay minister of their small church, believed that even slight transgressions from a very narrow path "were surefire pathways to eternal damnation." During her early school years she was very frightened that she would do something that would not only disgrace her family but send her to hell.

Puberty was very difficult for Marilyn and her father. She was the first of her classmates to develop breasts and to menstruate. Sexuality was a forbidden subject in the home. She remembers one night when he found her "necking with this boy in the field behind the school. He and I stayed up all night with him praying for my soul and me on my knees, hands clasped, crying for hours. When dawn broke, he sent me off to school without breakfast and with the admonition that another such incident would surely destroy me and the family forever."

In Marilyn's terms, she decided that she "might as well be damned for a sinner as a saint." That decision and her early maturity led to her reputation as the "easy" girl at her high school. She recalls, "I was no virgin, but the extent of my reputation was amazing. I didn't try to change it. I probably wouldn't have known how, but I think I wanted to embarrass him by it."

Throughout the seventies she was sexually active, experienced scores of one-night stands, and "never felt that anyone would want to be in a relationship with me." As a result her first two marriages were to men who were far inferior to her intellectually and occupationally.

Today the owner of a small, successful business, she "occasionally get[s] the feeling that he is watching me from heaven and grimacing at everything I do." Although she claims that she has given up any hope of living up to her father's impossible standards, she has yet "to shake the guilt feelings that come along from time to time."

Her fear of being found out stays with her. To avoid being found wrong, she will "deny no matter how overwhelming the evidence. I also frequently tell these white lies, just so nobody ever thinks that I messed up. I just can't stand the thought of that. I know I need to be more responsible. The lying has ruined more than one relationship."

When asked how she might do that, she replied, "I guess I need to stop lying to my therapist and tell her the truth." Her legacy from childhood interferes even in her attempts to get help.

It is important to recognize that encouraging your children to be sensitive to the needs of others, both within and outside the family, is quite valuable. We are right to teach compassion. It is excessive compassion that becomes guilt. Caring for others is among the most noble of human emotions; feeling responsible for another is dangerous to one's personal mental health.

Dependency

Fathers may reverse the parent-child roles by hanging on to the child. Often an alcoholic father must be cared for by a young child. These children may be cheated out of their childhood years, become "parentified" at tender years, and have difficulty in adult intimate relationships that require equality.

Dennis. As a forty-six-year-old man who has worked in the helping professions all his life, Dennis is a study in contrasts. He grew up in a home where, as the late-arriving "accidental" youngest child, he spent most of his early years caring for his alcoholic parents. When his mother died while he was in the eighth grade, he took care of the family finances and the daily care of his father until he died eleven years later, of cirrhosis of the liver.

Dennis's reaction was to avoid "marrying or getting close." His longer personal relationships have all replicated the caretaking role. "I've lived with two women who were real sick until they died, and with a drug addict whom I finally had to leave." He has also spent his adult life as a worker in residential homes for mentally disturbed and severely retarded individuals. He related, "I do fine with the patients, but I don't really know how to deal with the staff much."

Dennis's past simply didn't prepare him to relate on an equal level with other adults. Well trained in the role of caretaker, he cannot let others care for him.

Sandra. When her parents divorced, all of her brothers and sisters remained with her mother. "My dad was so pitiful. Someone just had to stay with him. I was the youngest, so I kinda got volunteered. . . . Mostly it was okay. I still went to the same school and had the same friends, but Dad never was too keen on my going out with guys. He was always afraid that I'd leave him like my mom did."

Never remarrying, her father treated her more like a wife than a daughter. She was his homemaker, launderer, and cook. After her graduation from high school she was his escort on business trips. "The life was actually exciting, but I never got to live my own life during those years. Then when I met Ricardo, my dad was very jealous. He did everything he could to break up that relationship. I know it wasn't on purpose, but he was afraid to be alone. Eventually that's what happened. When Bradley and I got married, Dad was pretty messed up. I went back to take care of his business, etc., twice, until Bradley put his foot down. . . . He still depends on me a lot."

A SPECIAL FORM OF DEPENDENCE: CHILD AS SAVIOR. Sometimes the demands are for the child to make up for the inadequacies of the father. The father who couldn't quite make it to the major leagues as a baseball player might try to relive his own life with a different ending by pushing his son to be the ball player (violinist, scholar, or money-maker) that he couldn't be. These fathers depend on their children to fulfill the father's wishes.

One such example was the story of Jimmy Piersall, the multi-talented but emotionally unstable outfielder with the Boston Red Sox and Cleveland Indians in the 1950s. In the book, and the subsequent film, *Fear Strikes Out,* we can see how the intense pressure to perform by a father helped land his son into the major leagues, but without the emotional maturity to handle the life there. Jimmy Piersall had to leave baseball for a time for psychological treatment. Although this book and film were hardly classics, they struck a nerve in many "tennis moms," "Little League dads," and other parents who try to live out their personal dreams through their children's successes.

Patrick. The eldest of eleven in an Irish Catholic family, Patrick lived each day as a child trying to "be perfect." His schoolwork and athletics as a boy were exemplary, "but not quite good enough for my father. I remember one day being called into a conference with him and Sister Regina because I had an A-minus in Effort, the only blemish on my otherwise perfect all-A report card. He was so upset by that grade because he said it meant that I wasn't trying hard enough and that I would bring shame to the whole family and the Church."

Patrick's reactions to such events were to strive mightily to be perfect in all aspects of life. He entered the seminary at fourteen and was ultimately ordained as a priest. Even that was insufficient for his father's standards. He remembers, "Somehow, no matter what I did, I was always compared negatively with the saints. My father was particularly fond of bringing up the dedication of Father Damian, and not very subtly suggesting that my own parish was the easy way to do it."

In his twenties and early thirties Patrick's attempts to please his father came into direct conflict with his increasing sense of his sexuality. A brief nonsexual but very personal relationship with a parishioner was very discomforting. In addition he had a growing feeling of attraction to another priest. By age thirty he was "certain I was homosexual, and struggling daily to suppress all urges and thoughts."

Such attempts to suppress, paradoxically, brought the subject to greater awareness. "After two years of hell I got involved with a man on a trip. I was filled with a feeling that I was finally in the right place for the first time in my life, and also filled with a sense of shame and guilt."

At the time of this writing he is "on leave" from the Church, is living with a male lover, and has confided only in one of his sisters, who "came out [of the closet as a lesbian] herself a long time ago." Patrick confided, "I know that I will never be able to tell my father. Even the hint of it would kill him."

When asked how his father responded to his sister's public announcement, he replied with a laugh. "He was angry and told her he didn't want to see her again, but he relented and didn't die; but I couldn't—it'd be different."

Patrick's life was dedicated to taking care of his father's needs. He has only now begun to consider what his personal needs and life agenda might be. The need to be a savior for his father was so deeply instilled in his mind as a child that he could not consider taking care of himself.

When a parent is dependent on a child, the child loses out on many opportunities to experience childhood and to grow through the developmental stages. These "parentified" children act like adults, but often fail to internalize the growth of relationship skills necessary to be a fully functioning adult.

IF YOUR CHILDREN'S MOTHER FAILS

It is important to note that mothers err in all the same ways that fathers do. Perhaps your partner's mistakes with the children are far more visible to you than your own. If so, she may see yours more clearly. We have a lot to share with our female counterparts about parenting. We may also have to complement some of her deficits by offering our children what our partner cannot.

The most important thing to remember is that children need firm, fair parenting. They need to experience an ongoing emotional relationship with their fathers to learn about reciprocity in relationships and a spirit of community and teamwork. When children do not receive that, they yearn for what they're missing without quite knowing what it might be.

FATHER HUNGER: THE IMPACT OF POOR FATHERING

Whatever the form of the poor fathering, both the child and grand-children are likely to suffer. Among the symptoms common to children with absent, abusive, distant, threatening, guilt-inducing, or dependent fathers are low self-confidence, timidity, and inflexibility. Sons especially will often remain immature and overly dependent, more susceptible to psychological and psychosomatic ailments such as anxiety, depression, obsessive thinking, compulsive or ritualistic behavior, phobias, allergies, and intestinal problems as teenagers and adults.

Without a positive model of masculine emotional strength, a son will be less sure of what he is feeling. He may seriously repress his anger and his unfilled need for love. As an adolescent he may demonstrate extreme gestures to attain some of the love for which he yearns, such as halfhearted attempts at suicide, running away from home, malingering, telling exaggerated stories, and manipulations.

In the past decade a few pioneers have been studying the effects of a lack of fathering on children.

James Herzog, a psychoanalyst, coined the term "father hunger" to describe the psychological damage in young children who were deprived of their fathers through separation, divorce, or death. He concluded that these children were likely to have more trouble controlling their aggressive impulses. In addition he suggested that in the long term, "father hunger appears to be a critical motivational variable in matters as diverse as caretaking, sexual orientation, oral development, and achievement."[2]

Author Stephen Shapiro expanded the list of potential damage to sons: (1) adoption of feminine types of behavior and concomitant confusion about sexual identity; (2) an unsteady or shaky sense of self-esteem, which makes them excessively conscious of security needs; less self-affirmation, ambition, and inquisitiveness; (3) sexual inhibition; (4) learning problems; (5) less faith in and respect for moral values; (6) more trouble accepting responsibilities; little sense of obligation or duty toward others.[3]

Focusing primarily on absent fathers, Guy Corneau speculated that sons who have not had the opportunity to internalize a set of firm, fair limits are particularly reticent to trust legitimate authority figures or to develop a sense of their own authority. Without the support of the incorporated paternal structure they tend to be disorganized, less motivated, and ineffective. He concludes that these sons demonstrate a greater incidence of psychological problems, substance abuse, and antisocial behavior.[4]

Journalist Andrew Merton defines *"father hunger"* as a "subconscious yearning for an ideal father that results in behavior ranging from self-pity to hypermasculinity and frustrates attempts to achieve intimacy."[5]

Sons are not alone in their "father hunger," writes Victoria Secunda in her recent book, *Women and Their Fathers*. For daughters,

> the most painful legacy is reflected in their love lives. . . . [Most women] try to deal with their father hunger by recapitulating their childhoods, along gender lines, in their relationships. . . . It is fathers more than mothers, who determine what it means to be a "girl" and how comfortable she is—or is not—in her sexual skin. Fathers have the more profound impact on a woman's sexual and romantic choices and relationships, whether Dad was a full time parent, divorced from Mother, or gone.
>
> The father-daughter relationship is the proving ground for a daughter's romantic attachments, her dress rehearsal for heterosexual love.[6]

Psychologist and psychoanalyst Dr. Michael Diamond suggests that girls who lack a father with whom they can identify remain out of touch with their desire or ambition. Some daughters become Mom's emotional substitute for a distant husband. Since they've been overly close to Mom, their expectations for an intimate partner are for someone who will also hold on too tightly. In such relationships there is no room for individuation or growth.

Other women may simply learn to expect that men will be absent or unreliable when it comes to emotional support. That being the case, they will passively seek and find a man who is unavailable, thereby replicating their parents' relationship, or they may never learn how to deal with a man who is present, becoming the distancer themselves.

As great as the dangers are, experts will attest that poor or inadequate fathering alone is no guarantee that our sons and daughters will be severely damaged. Many successful adults lacked optimal parenting. Some overcame it by idealizing an absent or weak parent. The idealized father replaces the real father in the child's psyche. This idealized father is then used by the child to self-parent internally. One danger of this is that the child may so idealize the internalized male that he demeans or debases women who are present and real.

Other children find acceptable father substitutes to replace the father that fails them. If this stepfather, uncle, teacher, "big brother," or coach is not idealized, this may be the best solution.

Although poor fathering does not inexorably produce emotionally disturbed offspring, there is little question that fathers who exhibit the traits examined in this chapter make their children's lives far more difficult. As adults these children tend to pass on the negative examples to their own children.

TURNING IT AROUND

This list of the many ways we may mess up our children's lives may seem either overwhelming or overdone. Most of us are not ogres. For us the deficiencies may be quite subtle. A little too much coercion here, too little acknowledgment there, a brief insensitivity to how enormous a particular problem feels to a child. It is impossible to avoid completely all the pitfalls and perils of poor fathering. What is important is that we are all aware of the hazards and of our own missteps. We also need to be aware of the deficits from our own fathering and of the considerable social pressures to emulate popular male stereotypes, caricatures that detract from the job of fathering well.

Many of us have simply had insufficient role models to know what will help our children. Many of us have insufficiently looked internally to find out who we are and what is truly important to us as fathers and as men. This is hardly a single accomplishment that we can attain and relish. There is an ongoing process of knowing what our children need. To truly know, understand, and avoid the biggest pitfalls, we have to engage in an ongoing discipline of self-examination and awareness. We need to explore our changing personal need for security and freedom. Most of all we will need to do this without encouragement or permission. We may help one another by openly sharing our personal trials and failures. Our spouses may be able to recognize our struggle, but they will not be able to empathize with it. I alone can ultimately face me and my fathering.

Learning to avoid the negatives will go a long way toward minimizing harming my children. That's only a beginning. If I want my children to flourish, to grow into happy, healthy adults, I have to give them a whole lot more. To be a truly good father, I must be involved with my children in positive, effective ways. It is to those qualities that we now turn.

5

THE GOOD FATHER

*The "good father" is there to be loved, imitated
and introjected, and makes himself available as
a model for the boy's developing gender
identity.*

—JOHN MUNDER ROSS

Susan described her father as "the perfect dad. No matter how
busy he was or how hard he worked, he always made some time
and space for me. We went on a lot of excursions together, and I
really got to know what he loved and thought about things. I loved
going to the baseball games with him. He just loved being there,
and it was one of those times when I could eat all the junk food I
wanted. It wasn't like he was talkative. Mom did most of the talking. He just quietly stayed in the background, but you could count
on him to say what he thought. He was the strict one too. As much
as I hated his rules and groundings as a teenager, I knew he was
right. . . . Until I met Jay [her husband], I thought I'd never find
anyone as good. I knew how perfect it was when he and Dad met
and they instantly liked each other."

Ali also remembers his father as the most important influence
in his life: "He gave me his wisdom, although I'm not sure I ever
got it all, and his patience and time. He was a cabinetmaker, an
environmentalist when it was not the popular thing to do. He never

finished high school, but was the smartest person I knew as a kid. He always respected my mother. What was so different about him is that he took the time to do things right, never rushed a job: 'The tree grew for fifty years, should I make a drawer in a day?' I wish I had as much patience. My family would be better for it. My dad even died properly. He made sure he talked with each of us kids and the grandkids and then drifted off in his sleep. I think he's probably teaching God a thing or two now."

Wouldn't we all want to be remembered this way? It is easy to believe that the influence of these fathers was far-reaching and that their children benefited from their parenting. What distinguishes such men?

The good father is available for his children. He is able to show them his interest, love, and caring. He teaches them values by words and by actions. He understands their needs from a child's perspective, yet he maintains his protective parental role. The good father encourages his children to experiment within proper limits. He allows his children to know him well enough that they may incorporate him into their personal psychological selves. He shares with them his pride at their accomplishments and his own. He is always available in times of crisis.

How may men give these gifts to their children?

The answer lies in two realms. The first is personal awareness. This crucial factor is examined in depth in Part II of this book. The other basic factor is involvement with one's children. In the current chapter two components of this involvement are explored: (1) direct contact and (2) understanding and playing a role in child development.

FATHER'S DIRECT INVOLVEMENT

In the last chapter we explored how a father can plant the seeds for his children's psychological damage by his physical or emotional absence. It is reasonable to assume that father involvement with children would have an opposite effect. If you were closer and more involved with your own children, would it truly make a difference? Fathers, mothers, and children all believe so.

Of the over eight hundred fathers I interviewed, an overwhelming majority reported feeling guilty about their limited contact with their children. They truly "regretted" the loss of that time. Their wives agreed. Many believed that the children often suffered from a "daddy deficit."

I asked a group of school-age children what they would most like to be different in their relationships with their fathers. Over 60 percent of the elementary and high schoolers said that they wanted more time with their fathers. College undergraduates also reflected this desire; 77 percent reportedly wished that their fathers were more active in their lives and that of their siblings.

Experts concur. John Munder Ross wrote, "It is closeness with the father and trust in him which ideally allow a boy to temper the aggressivity of both his curiosity and his assertiveness.... More secure in these ways because he experiences his father's care and because his father does indeed help him become masterly and manly, a boy may be further freed to fulfill creative wishes."[1]

Dr. Lora Tessman demonstrated that involved fathers encourage or stimulate a daughter's curiosity, exploration, and independent judgment. "He involves her in joint endeavors, shows trust in her growing capacities, and enjoys being playful with her."[2]

Los Angeles psychotherapist Dr. Michael Diamond stresses the importance of good fathering on a daughter's ability to practice relationships with male figures and subsequent ability to develop mature adult relationships.

In addition, a host of clinical and research materials underscore the importance of a father's involvement with his children on their proper gender identification in later life.

The evidence is in. Fathers and their children need more time together. Everybody seems to want it, yet increased father involvement somehow remains elusive. Why doesn't it just happen? Somehow desire, acknowledgment, and yearning are insufficient for implementation.

There are some hints from clinical studies and research. Many factors influence the connection between fathers and children. If we want more involvement with our children, we may need to understand what holds us back.

Factors Affecting Father Involvement

In my research I have uncovered ten factors that influence the level of a modern father's dedication to child care and parenting. These factors are complex and intertwined. Some of them may pertain directly to you as an individual; some may be irrelevant. The three most salient involve the father's desire, the mother's cooperation, and the nature of the relationship with his partner. These are considered first.

A Father's Level of Desire for Involvement. Some men are very interested in maintaining a close connection with their children. Others prefer more distance. Each of us needs to find our personal desired level with our children. This usually fluctuates as the children grow. Some men feel more comfortable around school-age children than infants, for example. These men become increasingly involved with their children as they mature. Others find intense connection right from birth.

Connie, a mother of three, described her husband's desire to be with his children: "Nick is really a good father—a great one once the kids can talk and reason. I thought he was uninterested in them in the early years, but as soon as Jessica became four, they were inseparable. He relates best to school-age kids, not to infants or toddlers. It works out well, because I love the little ones."

Ross is a stay-at-home father who provides the primary care for his infant daughter. His desire for involvement is very high. Although he experiences loneliness and "a need to talk to other fathers who are in a similar situation," he prefers being with the baby to being at work outside the home.

Lars, by contrast, feels "fumbly, bumbly, and inept around the baby. The truth is I spend more time at the office now than I did before. Mostly it's because I worry about the money side of things, but also because I'm all thumbs around her. . . . I think I'm most touched by the baby when she's asleep and I can watch her in the crib late at night."

Lars changes diapers and bottle-feeds his daughter as a job rather than as a loved pursuit.

The Mother's Willingness and Desire to Share the Childrearing. Even when a man has a deep wish to be involved, he may not find it easy to achieve unless his wife relinquishes some of her own primary connectedness to the child.

Janice is the mother of a six-month-old daughter. She confessed, "I'm embarrassed to say this, but when I'm with Megan, I feel like John is an intruder. I mean me and the baby have this perfect little love affair going, and then he comes home and wants to break in. I know it's crazy and unfair, but it's such a strong feeling. Sometimes, you know what I do? When he comes in the door, I find a way to pick a fight, and then when he gets angry, I pick up Megan and march off to my bedroom . . . where we can be alone."

Although most women want more relief and help with household tasks, they are not always willing to yield control over the nature and form of that relief. Many men complain that their wives ask for more partnership but reserve the right to assign them jobs. If she wants help, but remains in the role of boss, neither partner will feel good about the result.

Many men feel angry that their efforts to be with the children are blocked. Charlie commented, "It doesn't matter that I am working with Alicia or Timothy, she'll just come up in the middle and tell them to make their bed or clean the bathroom or something. It isn't that these jobs don't need to be done, it's the interruption with my time with the kids. It's like she can't stand to see us having fun without her. The only way I ever get any time with Alicia is when we physically leave the house. Otherwise she and Jill will get into a fight and I'm left to pick up the pieces. . . . I don't get that much time with them anyhow. I just want our family time to be good time."

If either my partner or I believe that she is the more informed parent because of her gender, my involvement with my children will be automatically mediated through her. She is the gatekeeper between the father and the children, a role that began during the pregnancy. Many fathers report that they have to make an extra effort just to have quiet time with their children.

Carter reported that he is unwilling to accept an arrangement in which his wife assigns him the chores as a way of keeping the children to herself. He elaborated: "I love to spend time with the kids, but she interrupts with jobs she wants done. There is no way that I'm going to do the dishes instead of read to the kids. I'd rather do them later, but she wants them done before the story, not after. To my mind, if she wants 'em done, then she's got to do them. I just don't get but two hours a day with the kids, and I won't give them up for chores. . . . So sometimes she picks a fight by saying I'm not interested in helping out the family. . . . Well, that's what my father did. He worked all the time for the family, and I never got to spend any time with him. . . . So the long and short of it is that the wife and I holler at each other a lot and fight about who does what and when."

Carter and Karen have an ongoing battle in their relationship. The essence of their power struggle as well as potential resolutions for any couple with similar problems will be explored in a later chapter. What is significant now is that problems in the couple's relationship detract from the father's relationship with the children.

The Couple's Relationship. No single factor in childrearing is as powerful as the relationship between the parents themselves. It is a common domestic tragedy that children are drawn into conflicts between spouses. Too often they become the pawns in a parental struggle. This is especially problematic in families in which the parents, unhappy with the marriage, "only stay together for the children."

Children have the (apparently unfortunate) tendency to emulate parental behavior rather than parental directions. What children learn in a home with warring or noncommunicating parents is how to become inept at relationships themselves. A family therapist once commented that it was fortunate that George and Martha's child in Albee's play *Who's Afraid of Virginia Woolf?* was imaginary. A real child in such an environment would have been in psychological jeopardy and so would the grandchildren.

A summary cliché about couples becoming parents is that the arrival of the first child makes all that's good in a marriage better and all that's bad in a marriage worse. Equally true is that a good marriage makes all that's good in the child's life better; a bad marriage makes all that's bad in the child's life worse. Mutual caring and understanding and a loving relationship can be modeled and internalized. This will foster a child's growth and development. By contrast, children who live with combative, self-centered parents will tend to become more suspicious and mistrusting. In addition at least one child in such families will be thrust into the role of referee. Later, as adults, these children are at risk for sacrificing their own identities in their intimate relationships.

When the marital relationship is troubled, it is easy for the father to be distracted from involvement with his children. A man may avoid his kids to avoid or punish his wife. By contrast he may give them the affection he withholds from her. Neither is very healthy for the children. Most commonly he will make his time at home as short as possible.

In addition to the impact of these personal influences, external factors, such as work, child care, support, and domestic problems, may affect a father's level of involvement and time with his children.

Economic Factors. Just as for his father before him, financial concerns often dominate a man's thinking about what it means to be a father. For most men, providing financially is imperative. A father who needs to support his family may well do so at the expense of time with the children.

Socioeconomic forces that oppress women by offering lesser

pay for equivalent work, or closing off opportunities for higher-paying jobs to women also greatly impact married men. If my wife is able to make only seventy-four cents to my dollar,[3] it seems obvious that I will have to put in extra hours outside the home.

When economic demands require two incomes, a mother's ability to be with the children is necessarily limited. Fathers are therefore called upon to increase their involvement with the children while maintaining a full-time job outside the home. In such families something has to go. Usually it is couple-time or alone-time.

Joan and Steve were so concerned about child care that they resolved the problem by working different shifts. He was home with the children until three P.M. while she worked at the factory. When she came home and assumed child-care responsibilities, he went to work on the late shift, arriving home after midnight. They sacrificed their social and couple time for the children and their financial needs.

Many couples can successfully carry out such an arrangement for a period of time. Long-term, however, the "split shift" marital arrangement tends to wear down both partners. They become emotionally depleted, a state that may actually produce poor parenting.

Most men do not have this kind of marital arrangement. We simply work longer and harder to keep up with the family's needs. We also suffer emotionally from the fear that we will not be sufficient providers. The unfortunate corollary to our extra work and financial worry is reduced time with our children. Many of our own fathers traded involvement with us in order to provide financially.

The balancing act between work and family is a difficult one for most men. We would rather be at the Little League game than the late meeting with the boss, but we know that missing the meetings may have dire consequences.

James Levine, former director of New York's Fatherhood Project, and frequent lecturer on the subject of fathers in the workplace, has poignantly shown that changes in the workplace to accommodate fathers and their families are progressing at a glacier's pace. For example, paternal leave, when it is available, may not be a reality for a man who wants to move up in a company. Despite social changes fathers remain as the primary economic provider in most families. Even when we do not bring home the lion's share of the income, we carry the emotional responsibility of providing for the family. This makes time with our children a trade-off. Do we accept a lesser standard of living for them in exchange for a closer family life? Each of us must make very hard choices about that balance in our lives.

Career Aspirations and Family. Some career fields are quite demanding, particularly in the early years, which often coincide with young children in the home. Many men are torn between fear of losing competitive ground at work and desire to be with their children. In some career fields the "fast track" requires seventy- to eighty-hour work weeks. There is simply little time left for children when getting ahead on the job or personal advancement takes precedence.

When his first child was born, Tim, at age twenty-eight, was moving quickly through the middle-manager ranks at a Silicon Valley company. He would often stay at work until eight or nine P.M. in order to get ahead. Two nights a week he pursued a master's degree in business administration. "When Rory was born, it worked out well because it was just before Memorial Day weekend. I only had to miss two days at work and then had the long weekend. So I didn't miss much. The truth is that I'm much less efficient at work now because Sandra needs me home by six P.M. or so. . . . I know that sometime soon I'll have to make a decision about whether I can stay on the managerial fast track or switch to the 'daddy track' and give up some of my dreams of a vice presidency."

Whatever Tim's choice, he will face a loss. He will have to forgo, at least temporarily, either time with his new son or his career dreams.

Your Partner's Work Outside the Home. If a woman is a full-time homemaker and mother, it is expected that she will have the greater time involvement with the children. By contrast, if she works outside the home for equal hours, the household and child-rearing tasks must be redivided. Of course every couple must work out the details of who does what and when.

In her recent book, *Second Shift,* sociologist Arlie Hochschild claims that women automatically pick up the extra duty when both parents work outside the home. Clinical data and reports of research where both men's and women's work were observed suggest that the discrepancy is overstated for many intact families.[4] When the amount of time men and women work at home and on the job is objectively calculated, the totals often exceed eighty hours per week for both wives and husbands. Such an exorbitant number of work hours usually precipitates a power struggle over different perceptions regarding what is to be considered "work" and who is to be responsible. Because both parties feel overworked and underappreciated, this struggle takes years to resolve.

As a father it is critically important for you to participate in the division of labor and allocation of work and child care. If you abdicate that responsibility, your wife will probably assume the role of supervisor and assign duties. You will probably not like the arrangement. Alex described his home situation with frustration: "She claims all the time with the kids and gives me the dinner preparation and cleanup. Then I get sent to the garage to listen for 'the funny sound' in her car. So it's ten at night when I finally turn on the TV and she yells from the bedroom to turn it off because she's trying to sleep. Then in the morning she tells me I'm not interested in being with the kids, because she's the only parent who spends any time with them."

I asked Alex if he wanted to be with his children more after work. He replied that he did. When I asked how his wife got to be the one who assigned the chores, he said, "I never really thought about it."

For a father a wife's work outside the home may afford extra time with the children. If you want that extra time, it can be quite rewarding. It may also be an extra burden that creates increasing fatigue and resentment. The best antidote for most of us is to determine what we want and to negotiate with our partners; it sure beats initial acquiescence and subsequent griping.

Although it is an uncommon solution, if you want to be the homemaker and child-care person, you would not be the first or only man to do so.

Availability of Additional Helpers. Quality time with children is distraction-free time. Being with children while your mind is preoccupied with the next meal, household chores, or work pressure is both difficult and unsatisfying. The availability of others who can do chores, or take the children for some time while you do the chores, often makes your time together much better. In much of modern American society the nuclear family has replaced the traditional extended-family living arrangement. Couples who are fortunate enough to have supportive family members available, and close by, are increasingly in the minority. Without the availability of grandparents, aunts, brothers, or sisters, parents have to increase their own child-care load and form cooperative arrangements or hire help.

The major difference with such help is that it feels less secure than relying on relatives and is therefore more of an emotional burden. Hiring help often creates a necessity for extra income, which in turn means extended hours of work away from home for the parents.

Carla, a mother of two preschoolers, remarked, "It's been a nightmare. First we went the route of a mother's co-op, but because there were only three moms in the co-op, and one of them wouldn't take the kids when anyone was sick, it only worked out occasionally. Plus we could get a call at six A.M. and find out that it wouldn't work that day, so the scramble began. We tried live-ins for a while, but they were unreliable, and the young ones were needing as much parenting as the children. And they were always leaving without notice. I just don't know if my working is worth it financially or emotionally."

For Carla the chance to be out in the work force "with adults to talk to" was worth the upset. Most parents who hire help feel worried about their children's safety, frustrated by the inconsistency, and guilty about leaving their children. In my own home we somewhat humorously referred to the succession of live-in child-care workers as Nanny Wars. However, as for Carla and her husband, we accepted the trade-offs as the best solution we had. Among the compromises we had to face were unreliability of child-care workers, unpleasant disciplinary styles, and an almost constant run of family illnesses generated by preschool contact with other children. At one point we were certain that every Thursday the snack du jour was milk, cookies, and a virus of the week. On the positive side some of the child-care providers were superb, offering welcome support for our parenting. Some preschools and child care furnish education as well as support for children and parents.

When relatives and natural (neighborhood) supports are unavailable or inconsistent, the father's role in child care will often increase proportionally. When he is also called upon to work harder outside the home to provide financially, major compromises must be made. Many of us prefer to pay someone else to do the chores, saving time for us to be with the children.

The Father's Legal Status. Hiring help or balancing work and family time offer opportunities for hard choices. Some men, by virtue of their legal status, have far fewer options. The high incidence of divorce, separation, remarriage, and out-of-wedlock pregnancies in our society virtually guarantees that a large number of parents will not live with their biological children throughout their growing years. The vast majority of divorced fathers do not have custody of their minor children. It is therefore not surprising that involvement will fluctuate for men who are not living with their children or who are not allowed access to their children.

Noncustodial parents have limited access to their children. Their time together is often characterized by intense involvement alternating with complete absence. Many divorced parents experience their life with their children as a constant series of hellos and good-byes, without time for a natural daily environment.

The growing number of single fathers also face difficulties.

When a man is alone with his children, he will likely face a number of changes in his lifestyle. He must establish new priorities for work, child care, nurturance, and personal time. Just as for single mothers, his juggling act will never be uncomplicated. Feeling exhausted and depleted, he may lose some of his ability and desire for involved parenting.

Stepfathers and stepchildren will not feel the same way toward each other as they feel toward their biological or adoptive family. A stepfather has fewer rights with stepchildren. He may not be allowed to discipline them. He may have to compete psychologically with the biological father. He is not an equal parent with the biological mother.

For many men separation from their children is the most painful experience in their lives. Some spend years struggling with ex-wives and a normally insensitive legal system just to gain the right to have a reasonable amount of time with their own sons and daughters. Those who prevail, gaining the additional contact they seek, report that the battle was worthwhile. If you are a father whose connection with your children is blocked, you will need to assess how much you truly want to have more time with them and then take appropriate action.

The Father's Personal Values. Some men have strong beliefs about their level of involvement and time with their children. If this is a priority in a father's life, he will do everything in his power to be present and available for them. Other men firmly believe that direct involvement with children is for women or others. Their fathering is more attuned to providing and protecting from a distance.

Raymond described himself as "heartsick every night when I'd come home and Teddy was already in bed. I'd just go into the bedroom and sit by the crib and hold imaginary conversations with him."

He was so committed to a close relationship with his son that he quit his higher-paying job and took a lesser position to be close to home and available during his son's waking hours. This meant that his wife also had to work part-time outside the home and also support Raymond's time with the baby. According to him, she was delighted to do so.

By contrast Keith believed that "babies and little children are women's work. I love my kids, don't get me wrong, but I don't relate that well to their constant needs. I know that the best thing I can do for them is to earn a good living, give them the advantages I didn't have, and stay out of Regina's way when she's taking care of them."

Keith and Raymond clearly have different kinds of involvement with their children. Perhaps you feel different than either of them. What long-term impact will your personal preferences have on your children? Raymond's children will not have the financial wherewithal that they might desire, but they will have a close relationship with their father. Keith's children will probably be better off economically, but may suffer the pangs of father hunger. Whatever your beliefs, it is crucial that your partner understand what she can count on.

The Father's Personal History. Men who grew up without a close connection with their own father may be prone to replicating that low level of involvement. Or if that experience was particularly painful to them, they may do just the opposite. Certainly if you were abused or abandoned as a child, you will have more to overcome in order to be close to your own children. Similarly, men whose own psyche is damaged and those who suffer from low self-esteem may have more trouble being involved fathers.

One man who has a very close connection to his children describes his own history: "Thirty-five years of training. From the time I was four or five, I wanted to grow up to be just like my dad. He was the best father, and he trained us boys well. Way before it was fashionable, I knew that men did dishes and laundry, made beds, listened patiently to their wife and children. My big problem was finding a woman who also wanted to have a family and didn't mind a sensitive man around. In my twenties I was just a wimp when it came to the ladies, but now, without changing anything in myself, I'm the 'good example.' I just knew my whole life that what I wanted was to be a father. I was in Big Brothers, Scouts, and the PAL. I even umpired and managed Little League when I was single."

Your personal history as a son has set examples and challenges for you as a father. Your abilities to tolerate ambiguity, to express your emotions, to be patient, and to be empathic will influence your fathering. Wishing to be a certain kind of dad is a good start. Knowing how you were fathered and how you have developed as a man will constitute a next step.

Going Beyond the Factors Influencing Involvement

With all these influences there is hardly any typical modern father. Each father must negotiate and renegotiate the level of involvement that is right for him. The right amount of right style depends on individual predilection and your children's needs. Whatever level of connection you choose will demand trade-offs. If you want to be closer to your children, you will have to give time, psychological energy, and emotion, reduce some career aspirations, and negotiate with the mother.

Even if you choose greater involvement, it is only the beginning. Time with children and interest in their lives is necessary, but hardly sufficient for good fathering. To grow fully and properly, children need a great deal more from their fathers. To foster growth and development of his child(ren), a good father must know how to connect and how to let go. He must provide limits, a masculine role model, a male mode of feeling, and an alternative to mothering. A good father must develop positive paternal attributes, skills, and traditional roles. All of these skills are predicated on a father's understanding of his children's development and the significance of his input at each stage of their growth and maturation.

THE FATHER'S ROLE IN CHILD DEVELOPMENT

The Child's Work

As a species we humans have an extensive maturation period before we are able to take our place as functioning members of society. We have to survive until our teenage years in order to be able to reproduce. In complex modern society it takes a good many additional years before we are capable of effectively thriving ourselves or nurturing our offspring.

From birth we are faced with the task of *individuating:* being able to function independently and effectively as mature individuals. To become fully functioning adults, we have to master a series of developmental-growth stages. Each of these stages represents increasing separation from others and decreasing dependence on parents for emotional and physical needs. As the child conquers a developmental task (eating solid food, talking, walking, relating to friends, going to school, leaving home, etc.), the separation between child and parent increases, allowing for progressively greater independence.

Children who separate prematurely may leave physically and/or psychologically before they have received enough psychological support or nurturance. Their internal sense of self will be incomplete. The cost of leaving the nest too early may be an incomplete person, lacking empathy or a clear sense of how to relate effectively. They become "pseudoadults," more capable of mimicking adult behavior than of feeling adult emotion.

The child who cannot separate psychologically from parents remains a child, dependent on parents for crucial support. Such an adult child will have difficulty in adult relationships and may never be truly prepared to become a parent. The necessary separation need not involve physical distance. What is crucial is that the psychological boundary between parent and child become progressively clear with maturity. As an infant I do not have to know where my care giver ends and I begin. As an older child I may experience others' emotions as my own. For example when my mother cries,

I may also. As an adult I must be able to separate myself from others. It is only when I am clear about my own personal, psychological boundaries that I may successfully merge with another.

As parents our prime goals are to keep our children safe and foster their independence in age-appropriate ways. It's a job that requires patience and timing. Many parents experience their children's growing independence as a personal rejection. If they react by clutching the child, they will interfere with the child's growth. Of course, if they welcome the child's individuation too readily, the child may feel rejected.

The Father's Role in Children's Independence

If the major developmental task for a child is separation, it stands to reason that a father is a very influential figure. In traditional families, where the mother does more of the homemaking and hands-on parenting, she represents the home and the world of children and nurturance. Such security and nurturance are the foundation from which a child can safely begin to explore the external world. Formation of a healthy adult identity requires a sense of security, which comes from this foundation. The child needs to know that returning to the safety of home is always an available option.

Security alone is insufficient for a child to develop a healthy adult personality. There is an equivalent need for freedom. In the traditional family this is where the father comes in. By his representation of the outside world the father is the force through which the child begins to interact with the external world, confront it, and internalize it. The father provides children with the opportuntiy to test themselves against objective standards, to experience success and failure through competition with others, to learn about options that are not available in the family of origin. When children confront the often unloving or unfair demands of the outside world, they develop a fuller sense of themselves, become aware of their relative skills, and understand better that the world does not revolve around them personally. Adult development requires that the child internalize both a sensitivity to self and personal security needs, and a sensitivity to the needs and behaviors of others. By his ability to thrive in the world, and his encouraging his children to share in that world, a father represents both a sense of personal security and fosters a child's experimentation.

In the words of Stephen Shapiro, "Acts of fatherhood are acts that balance support and care against the need to set limits for childish dependency."[5]

Single parents have a particularly difficult job. They must support both freedom and security. As a single father you need to represent the home as well as the outside. Most successful single parents seek and utilize community resources. Joseph, a single father of three girls, commented, "I was usually on top of helping the girls by listening to their needs. Then when my first started puberty, she didn't want to talk to me about it. I didn't feel slighted about that. Maybe I was uncomfortable too. I got my sister to spend some time with her, and a woman friend at work was real good talking to the kids."

Nontraditional families are explored in depth in Part III of this book.

Mothers and Babies

It is easy to understand how the mother comes to represent the inner, more subjective reality. Because the child was created in and born from the mother's womb, there is an especially strong bond between the infant and mother.

Psychologically the infant cannot distinguish between self and other. To the baby, Mother and her breast are all part of himself.[6] Even when the infant begins to recognize where he ends and his mother begins, the emotional bond remains powerful. To some extent this connection is reciprocal. For many women their personal boundaries include their children. Once a child has been part of a mother's body, she may feel a more or less permanent emotional interconnection. Mothers can love children as a part of themselves in a particularly nonjudgmental way.

Father and Child

Fathers cannot attach to children in the same way that mothers do. Fathers may well love and connect to their children fully as much as mothers, but the connection is different. The biological (umbilical) link simply does not exist.

The father is usually the first significant other that the child meets outside his mother's womb. He is the first representation of whatever is not part of the infant-mother expanded self.

As the nonself the father becomes the prototype of the first triangle relationship. He introduces the primary elements of separation between the mother and the child. By his separate yet loving presence he triggers the process of differentiation wherein the baby becomes autonomous from the mother.

The Triangle

As the adult companion to Mother, a father serves as an initial wedge in the intense mother-child interconnection. As the infant becomes aware of the couple relationship, and of the relationship of parents to other siblings, the child begins the process of recognizing his own aloneness and separateness in the world. Over years and through a host of developmental challenges this process promotes maturity and the formation of a separate adult identity. The mother's willingness to forgo the symbiotic state and to reconnect with her adult partner is an integral part of this growth. Sometimes, when the mother-child link is too intense, the father has to persist firmly in his efforts to reestablish the primacy of the couple relationship. The child can then learn about adult intimacy: intense connection with feelings of security and clear separation of the individuals (freedom).

The father who does not have a clear sense of himself as a person and of his mission may feel excessively jealous of the mother-infant bond and may force a confrontation between himself and the infant. He may demand that his wife choose between himself and the child. Lem, for example, insisted that his physical needs take precedence over those of his one-year-old son. Mario, another new father, began drinking to excess, pressuring his wife to extend the same kind of care to him that she paid to their baby. Ellen reported that her husband began to express so much anger at her "withdrawal, rejection, and inattention" that she acquiesced "against my better judgment."

Whatever form it takes, any such confrontation is one that the father will inevitably lose. His partner will resent his neediness and the interruption of her own intimate connection with her child. Furthermore, in a paradoxical way his excessive demands will normally increase, rather than decrease, her bond with the child. Sensing a threat to that relationship, the mother may well rededicate herself to keeping the emotional umbilical connection strong. In such families both mother and father lose. Unfortunately the long-term loser is his baby. An infant who is forced to fight for Mom's attention with such a large, childlike, and ominous opponent has no counterbalancing attachment model for the mother's symbiotic love.

The child in such a situation may find it more difficult to separate from a mother whose predominant need is to maintain the protective cocoon around herself and her child, keeping her husband on the outside.

This is not to suggest that any jealousy an expectant or recent father might experience is inappropriate. In fact, a sense of loss of the spouse's affection and of being replaced is almost universal. It is also an important observation to share with the mother. The father is the person best suited to inform his partner of the loss of balance in the family, and to help her recapture the family equilibrium wherein all members give and receive affection as separate, interdependent beings. The child's perception of the amorous desire between mother and father along with the warmth and security for himself provides a healthy model for later relationships.

How Fathers Foster Effective Separation

A good father must help his children individuate. He accomplishes this by modeling and by being the agent of socialization.

The father is clearly separate from the child. He is not p the same physical-emotional symbiosis. In the family he is c nected and a major figure, yet he is also autonomous. Having model who both belongs to, and is independent in, the family helps the child experience the possibility of becoming interdependent. Psychologically the child can use the father's role to develop an internal psychological representation of a separate self-and-other. This internal structure facilitates a child's recognition of himself as an individual.

Once children recognize their separateness from others, they are able to develop the ability to understand through abstraction and to experience empathy. They can also channel their innate aggressiveness into self-defense, self-affirmation, a capacity for exploration of both self and other, as well as sexuality.

As the physical and emotional family representative of the external world, the father helps his children make the transition from the household to the realities of the culture and society into which they are born. Children can practice safely with Dad the behaviors that will develop self-confidence for their dealing with playmates, school, career, and adult relationships. Often children will challenge Dad to games of skill or power wherein they may test their emerging skills without risk of being annihilated or embarrassed.

Of course in modern Western cultures the mother also plays this role for children. Working outside the home, she, too, brings the external world into the family. However, the father has a special position even when Mother works outside the home, because he is not part of the initial symbiotic mother-baby bond.

Although a father's love for his children is usually as unconditional as a mother's, his expression of acknowledgment and approbation have traditionally been more conditional. This is consistent with male expectations and training in our culture that rewards will be based on success. We expect to receive just rewards for what we do. As a male I do not expect to be honored or prized for my feelings. The way I understand my world and my role as a teacher is to focus on action. It seems natural and comfortable to treat my own children the same way.

ntly the parent to reward accomplishments
leges. This contingent quality helps the
of responsibility and a willingness to test
u to be more experimental in action. This bur-
e of freedom must be balanced by a father's setting
of safety and stressing good judgment. By recognizing a father's ability to face reasonable risks, by recognizing established regulations and authority, and by respecting firm guidelines, the child learns freedom within security: two essential traits for adult success in career and relationships.

There's often a delicate balance here. Many fathers overdo their competency-based rewarding, becoming conditional in the expression of their love for their children.

Stanley, a sixty-one-year-old man, remembers his father that way: "He was a stickler for detail . . . and never satisfied. I did everything I could do to please him . . . football star . . . scholar . . . good worker. In high school I'd go in every day after school and weekends to help out in the shop. All he ever did was criticize. I remember one football game. I was really racked up, fumbled, carried off the field. All he said to me was that the team lost. I found out from my sister that he waited at the hospital the whole time I was there. He died never telling me he loved me and never telling me that I was good enough in his eyes."

There are also many fathers who act like harsh authority figures with their children, teaching rules and respect for authority without helping the child to feel loved or to develop the ability to recognize when to be experimental.

Such fathers only understood part of the equation, particularly with boys. Firm to a fault, they underscore their son's separateness without paying attention to the importance of a son's need for nurturance.

Independence and Gender

Traditionally fathers have been considered more supportive of their children's independence and mothers more supportive of their security. The results of my surveys suggest that the relation-ship may be more gender related. In general fathers seemed more supportive of their son's independence and less supportive of their daughter's. Mothers by contrast supported their daughter's separa-tion more than they did their son's.

This corresponds to gender differences in discipline and play. Fathers tend to play more roughly with sons and more gently with daughters than their partners do. Parents also tend to be stricter with children of the same gender.

It probably relates to a parent's sense of better understanding the risks to, and limits of, a person of the same gender. In addition our same-sex children are our personal replacements. We may be tougher on them out of a personal need for them to represent us better. Lynn expressed this thought: "I love my daughter as much as my son, but it's different. My son will carry my name and survive me. When I'm gone, he's the only one who can continue my life in this world."

GOOD-ENOUGH FATHERING

It is clear that being a good father involves a host of complex skills and psychological stability. It is easy to believe that we have to be perfect, or we will hurt our children. Clearly none of us will ever attain perfection as a parent. What we need to do is to keep devel-oping as men and to do the job of fathering as well as we can. The goal is not to be a perfect father, it is to be a good-enough father. That involves quantity and quality time.

Time: The Currency of the Nineties

To be able to provide a balance of firmness, fairness, and love, a father needs to give his children a considerable amount of time; a commodity that is frequently in short supply. Many studies indicate that school-age children often get as little as ten minutes a day with their fathers. Ten minutes from a tired person at the conclusion of a grueling workday is insufficient.

"Good-enough" fathering entails being involved with your children's experience of the world: their hopes, their cares, their relationships, their fears, and so on. Part of being a father requires a man to hold in his mind his seven-year-old daughter's rejection by her newest "best" friend, his son's worry about running as fast as the other preschoolers, the date of the upcoming Home and School Day for parents, what food is currently "hated," the importance of playing a board game with his preteen, or his adolescent's need to make him wrong.

Availability for, and genuine interest in, the children's projects, friendships, trials, and tribulations require full attention and substantial time. With this time children have a clear sense of Father as an active part of the family. They experience his excitement and his limits, his strengths and his weaknesses, and learn to accept those traits in themselves. Then he is not viewed solely as an authoritarian impediment, a "cash cow," or a person of limited import compared with a mother.

By seeing their father's imperfections and his reaction to them, children begin to recognize a real world in which perfection is not always expected. He shows his children that "the exercise of power does not have to be humiliating, that healthy competition and emulation do not always lead to stomach ulcers, and that ability can be a source of joy, not of alienation."[7]

Solo Time

When we take responsibility for our children's basic needs, as we listen and interact with them, it becomes important that we do these both alone and in the presence of our partner. Often, when the mother is present, the father gets assigned a background role, with the mother as the primary parent. Children, particularly male children, need to experience their father's competence in their care in order to feel safe with him and to more readily emulate him as a role model. When the mother or an older sibling is present, the intensity of direct father-child interaction, the father's responsibility for child care, and his availability may be diminished. As eleven-year-old Philip put it, "I like it best when me and my dad go out in his car [a two-seater]. Then we can talk about the [baseball] Giants. Mom always wants me to tell him about school. We both like to talk about the Giants. When we go to the baseball game, it's just the two of us—no girls allowed."

If the mother, sibling, or a friend is also present, the father and child may be much less aware of, and attentive to, each other. One aspect of family life that is enhanced by greater involvement of mothers in the work force is the increased potential for solo time for fathers with their children. The quality of time alone with children is more focused, more intense, and more intimate than time when mom is also available.

One of my sister's fondest memories during her high school years is of the evening meals she and our father shared while I was away at college and our mother was working. During those times the two of them would talk freely and further develop their relationship.

Many mothers, considering themselves the primary parent, have a difficult time watching their husbands parent differently from themselves, and take over to "do it right." If you are an active father, you will have your own way of parenting. It is likely to be just as "right" as a mother's way and quite different. You may have to listen to your partner's preferences and discuss your own. If you allow her to determine how children are to be fathered, your family may well end up with a second junior mother and no father.

It is important for fathers to recognize how their partner may encourage or limit their access to the children. Some women continue the gatekeeper role, necessary during pregnancy, long after the child is born. Others actively encourage solo interaction between father and children. The father who wants to maintain an important role in his children's lives by being available, interactive, and responsible may well have to confront and negotiate with his wife to keep his connection with his children active.

Recently, on a national talk show, a guest was complaining

about her husband's "refusal" to spend any time with the family. Yet the facts emerged that she made all the decisions for the children's schooling and activities, had moved him out of "her" bedroom into the guest room, and kept the family in severe credit-card debt, necessitating his taking on a second job. Neither the hostess of the program nor the expert of the day suggested that perhaps his biggest deficit was his failure to confront her and insist on compromises.

Another national news-magazine program, which aired in May 1992, showed a similar orientation.[8] Dedicated to examining family life in the nineties, the program highlighted interactions between a husband and wife. The husband was viewed as passive, ineffective, and noncompliant in his household duties. He was portrayed as an example of the typical male noncontributor around the home. Nobody seemed to notice that the wife was perfectionistic, gave orders in a harsh tone, and spent most of her time complaining about how he didn't do enough. It is not surprising that he "moved at a snail's pace" rather than jump to the tasks and standards she set out. Nobody questioned her right to be the boss.

These may seem like extreme examples, but they represent commonly held negative views of fathers. Unless a father insists on being active as a parent, he may either be assigned to the worst parenting duties or be ousted from his children's lives by his partner. As men we cannot fault the woman who takes such control. She honestly believes she is doing the best for her children. We must look to our own responsibility for taking and accepting the active role if we desire it.

Rather than interfere, some wives will greatly encourage our efforts. Joseph calls his wife "the greatest fan of my relationship with the kids. Whenever there's an opportunity for me to have time with them, she actively supports it. Last year, just before my son's birthday, my boss dumped a load of photocopying in my lap just before closing. When I told Rhonda that I'd be stuck at the office for at least two hours, she just asked if I'd rather spend the time with Ben and his friend. Within like twenty minutes she drove the boys up to my office, took over the xeroxing and sent us out. I'm a lucky guy, I'll tell you."

When I asked him if he would have done the same for her in similar circumstances, he said, "Yeah. I do those kinds of things all the time, but I'm the problem-solver type. You know I always end up with the technical problems. That's why it was such a gift. . . . I did make it up to her in a way, I arranged to take off for a few days last winter and had the kids alone so she could go skiing with her sister."

When I commented that it sounded like they were both lucky, his eyes teared up and he said, "That'd be the highest honor in this life to feel that I was worthy of her and the kids."

Peggy, a mother of three sons and a childbirth educator, commented,

It was hard for me to accept Daniel as an equal parent . . . some of my early training and working with pregnant and new mothers, I guess. . . . The truth is that he's a terrific dad, and he does best when I leave him and the boys alone. He gives them so much that I would never think of. The other day, Jimmy got a cut above the eye and I was rushing to be the nurse. I was getting nervous, Jimmy was crying, and the other boys were getting uptight also. Daniel just quietly said to me, "Why don't you take the other two boys out for a few minutes and leave me and Jimmy alone?" We came back in five minutes, and Jimmy was not crying. He was smiling and bursting with pride when he ran up to me and said, "Daddy let me wash my face and I put the bandage on all by myself." It's great to realize that there's so much I can learn from my husband about parenting.

Two typical outcomes of father-child alone-time are that the children perceive their fathers as more interested in them and view their fathers more favorably. The more active and interactive the involvement, the greater the impact on the child's relationship-skill-building. Often the two most common weekday father-child activities are helping with homework and watching television.

Alone-time with Father is more than just time without Mother. Dad is not simply a substitute when she is tired or unavailable. Many adults remember fondly their time spent with their fathers while they were growing up. When a child is alone with Dad, there is a special opportunity to experiment with certain forms of behavior.

When Glenn is with his father, "we get to do things outside." Sixteen-year-old Avram reports that the "thing I get to do with Dad is me and Bobby and him go fishing. We just sit out there in the boat . . . sometimes we talk . . . mostly he tells stories about how his dad took him fishing and the day they caught the biggest bass ever. . . . He really loves to fish and to be with us boys." Eleven-year-old Sara says that when she and her "daddy get alone, he lets me do things on his computer."

Natasha, my ten-year-old daughter, is particularly fond of playing intellectual and word games with me. We both enjoy how our minds solve the problems we set for each other. She also asks and argues about politics more with me than with her mom.

Whatever children do uniquely with their fathers can be valuable. Children are very good at intuiting what any adult has to offer and of learning those things from him. It is also good for men to be a buddy (albeit a responsible one) to a child. Fathers have the opportunity to grow emotionally as much as children in the interaction.

Do Boys and Girls Experience Father Involvement Differently?

A father's role in the socialization of children may vary depending on his attitudes about gender roles. Many men treat boys and girls quite differently.

In general, girls will feel closer to their dads with greater one-to-one interaction. For boys the experience is more complex. Feeling close carries with it a sense of belonging to the male world.

Thus, for boys, fathers feel a need to provide a strong male role model that involves displaying more emotional control, competitiveness, discipline, and other characteristics typically identified with masculinity.

Family constellation plays a significant role in how much time fathers tend to spend with different children. Fathers who are the sole wage earners in the family typically spend much more time with sons than daughters, whereas fathers in dual-earner families spend about equal time with sons and daughters. This is consistent with family gender-role values and a response to the extra needs boys may have in a household that has a more female quality. In addition mothers in more traditional, single-earner families are more likely to play the "gatekeeper," engaging daughters in domestic activities in which fathers are seldom involved.

Gender-related differences are consistently observed in all parents. Mothers and fathers tend to be rougher and tougher with children of the same gender as themselves. There is more to teach them and a better sense of the limits to which a child of the same sex can be pushed. With fewer gender-typed constraints, father-daughter involvement may be more relaxed, more pleasurable, more accepting, and less critical, thereby enhancing the relationship for both fathers and daughters, at least prior to puberty and adolescence.

It may be important to recognize these gender-related differences in your own background. Were there different rules for sons and daughters in your family of origin? Were there different privileges? Was either sex favored by Dad? By Mom? As fathers we may consider expanding our repertoire with both our sons and our daughters, rather than trying to change it or make it equal for everyone.

OF MANHOOD AND FATHERING

A father is a powerful model for his children. In addition to his love and caring, a man's personal self-esteem is repeatedly conveyed to his children through his behavior over time.

Claire said that the most impressive thing about her father was that he always seemed to know where he was going. "It wasn't that he didn't make mistakes or find himself in strange situations. It was that he never seemed to lose his way in life. He always had the big picture in mind. He was balanced in a way that few people are. For my father, family came first. Work was to be done well, and he loved the Red Sox. No matter how much any of those three let him down, he always was optimistic about the future."

Kevin remembers his father as "not real book smart, but he was confident that he could find out any information he needed. . . . He was a problem solver who used limited resources very well . . . and he knew someone who could do anything."

Children seeking security in a large, confusing, and sometimes hostile world need a strong parental figure who can protect them, answer their questions, and above all, a person who can take care of himself.

Strong, self-assured, knowledgeable, protective, fair, worthy of respect, willing to take appropriate risks—these are all descriptive of traditional fathering. They remain a cornerstone of good fathering. To these must be added nurturance, sensitivity to children's age-appropriate needs, effective listening, access to and expression of emotions, humor, willingness to work on the marital relationship, self-awareness, and increased time with the family.

Children with such a father may expand their sense of manhood to include many traits that are often considered exclusively maternal. Such an expanded notion of gender roles allows both sons and daughters greater freedom in developing their own unique ways in their world.

To be a good-enough father, I obviously need to be a good-enough man. I need to know more of who I am, where I am going, and what I want for my children. I need to be dedicated to leaving this world a little better off for my presence. The primary place for this contribution is my children. If they can be better people than I, and my grandchildren better still, I will certainly have served the purpose of my generation.

That's a tall order. Just to make the challenge greater for my children, I want to improve myself as I go. I want to be a good-enough father. To do that I need to be aware of the pitfalls of poor fathering as well as the challenges of good fathering. Most of all I need to get to know myself better and to make adjustments that are consistent with my hopes and values.

Before taking personal stock of ourselves and our legacy for fathering, it is important to set forth a road map for our journey. As fathers we must not accede to definitions of good-enough fathering that come entirely from without. We need to declare what constitutes fatherhood from a deeply personal male perspective. The "Declaration" that follows represents the ideas, yearnings, and feelings of over eight hundred of our brothers.

6

A DECLARATION OF INTERDEPENDENCE

I. It is crucial that I do **not try to become another mother.** That is my wife's job—she's better at it than I am. Men and women must offer their children something different.

I do need to **educate women about fathering.** I cannot blame them for thinking that mothering is proper parenting and that men should emulate it. I need to talk to my wife and children about how it is to be a man and to demonstrate my appreciation and enjoyment of male ways. I need to counteract, by my person, the superficial linking of masculinity with aggression, war, and destruction. I must resist the omnipresent, simplistic psychobabble that characterizes all women as victims and all men as scum.

II. As a man I am genetically and culturally patterned to **protect my family.** In modern society the primary form this takes is to provide financially and emotionally for the family. Whatever men's excesses in this realm, we are absolutely unready to let go of it. Indeed we men need to regain our pride as providers, without falling into the trap of all work and no play.

III. I want to demonstrate **courage** for my children. I must let them know how I am courageous. Whether I am a soldier, a fireman, an engineer, a stockbroker, a teacher, a mechanic, or a salesman, I face challenges every day. I need to identify the fear within myself and to share with my family my angst and my battles with those fears.

IV. I need to be **encouraging and supportive.** I don't want to compete with my child. I don't want my son to fear his dad, and I definitely do not want to fear him.

V. I want to give my children **trust** that a dad will put their safety and needs before his own. I will respect the rights and boundaries of my children. Children need to know that their father will support them and encourage their independence. With so much talk about men molesting children and abusing them, I will stand as a strong counterexample to my children and my culture.

VI. I want to demonstrate **male compassion and warmth as men express it**—working in concert, sharing brief eye contact, a slap on the rear or a hug communicate just as well as words. My father has it, my friends have it, my father-in-law and grandfather had it. It is not the same as women's expression, but very much as valuable. When my daughter was a toddler, my mother extolled her feelings and my daughter's "intelligence" to anyone who would listen. At the same time my father was on the floor quietly playing with his granddaughter.

VII. I want to be **flexible.** Solutions that worked when I was eight, eighteen, or twenty-eight may fail when I'm thirty-eight, forty-eight, or fifty-eight. I need to show that there are many paths to a goal, not simply one inexorable route that must be followed.

VIII. I want to teach **discipline and "stick-to-it-iveness."** My kids want to know that Dad endured hardships at work and persevered. They need to see me working through problems, learning from my errors, and coming back to try again. It's important for them to know that Dad stayed up all night trying to solve a problem on the computer, finish a project in my workshop, or program the VCR, and why I did it.

IX. I want to be aware of, and when appropriate, to share

my **fear** of rejection by my wife, my parents, other women, and men. Most importantly I need to reveal to my children the nature of my struggle against these fears and how I handle them.

X. I want to prepare my children to be part of a **team.** Men bond by doing things together, not by talking at length, face-to-face, about our loves, problems, and fears. Often, as we engage in some physically exerting work or play, most often facing in the same direction, we will speak in a cryptic, elliptical, often symbolic manner.

XI. I want to teach my children of the primacy of **physicality** in connecting with others. I want them to feel close to me when we run, playfully wrestle, and exert ourselves together. As a man I trust better when I have sweated with, or competed with, another person. *Whereas for women, physical connection is often the culmination of intimacy, men commonly seek physical connection as a doorway to being emotionally intimate.* I need to assert that my way is different, not wrong.

XII. I need to know the **limits** of how to share my experience. While I need to help my children learn how I approach life, I need to offer them content in age-appropriate ways. When my three-year-old asks, "Where do I come from?" I must answer in a very different way than when my ten-year-old asks the same question.

XIII. I must be cautious in my role as **problem solver.** Just because someone indicates that there is something wrong doesn't mean that I have to take on the problem and fix it. I must be alert to playing a part in solutions, but I must also combat my culturally induced impulses to get to the bottom line as quickly as possible. Often others bring us problems as a way of beginning a conversation, rather than generating action.

XIV. I must be willing to **confront** my partner. I cannot always take the easy path of acquiescence when my wife and I disagree. I need to listen to her, stand up to her, face the force of her conviction, and keep myself in the discussion even in the face of an onrush of verbal assurance that she knows that her way is best.

XV. *The biggest task of all!* I need to **face myself** and my own history. I must explore my feelings about my father, recognize and relish what I love about him, appreciate what I don't like about him, and forgive him for being who he was. I need to face my fears of the unknown, apologize to, and forgive my son for how he will react to my limitations.

MY FATHER, MY SELF

OUR FATHERS: THE IMPORTANCE OF A MAN'S OWN FATHER ON HIS PARENTING

*Sons need to ask questions
about their fathers' lives
and truly listen to the answers.*
—SAMUEL OSHERSON

Robert Bly, the poet and symbol of the Mythopoetic Men's Movement, draws heavily from psychodynamic writers like Sam Osherson[1] and Carol Gilligan[2] when he underscores the imperative male need to connect with their own fathers: "If a son does not understand clearly, physically, what his father is doing during the year and during the day, a hole will appear in the son's perception of his father."[3] Contemplating his own relationship with his parents, Bly reflected, "For the first time I began to think of my father in a different way. I began to think of him not as someone who had deprived me of love and attention or companionship, but as someone who himself had been deprived, by his mother or by the culture."

Bly asserts that until a man connects with his father's feelings of rejection and grief, he cannot face and resolve his own feelings of banishment from the family.

For many of us our father remains a distant, unexpressive person, somebody we know mostly from deeds rather than words and feelings. How do we get to know our fathers? Just who is this man, "my father"? How will I be a father if I don't know what mine was like?

Family therapist Frank Pittman wrote,

Even though I knew I wanted to be a father when I grew up, I didn't know exactly what skills were required. I needed a model of a father, a real live one who could talk to me about what the profession was really like, and how it might differ from my mother's fantasies (and remembrances of her own father). That should not have been too difficult a job. My mother had thoughtfully provided me with a fine father, and it would seem natural for me to have talked to him. But that wasn't the way it worked out—for me, for my friends, or for just about any other man growing up in my generation.

We of the 40's and 50's grew up with fathers who were off at war or at work and who weren't part of the family even when they were at home. We are essentially fatherless. When we had children, we became fatherless fathers. We either had no concept of what fathers were for, or some glorified fantasy of the paternal role. Lost and confused, we waited for somebody to tell us what we were supposed to do. Some of us assumed that our wives knew what fathers were about, forgetting that our wives hadn't had fathers either.[4]

Dr. Pittman argues that fatherless men, lacking a male model of fathering, may go through life in a "childlike" way. Men raised exclusively by women naturally expect that both they and their children will be cared for by their wives. They may have no real idea of what is expected of an adult man in return. "Men who have been raised without fathers can't help but be amateur parents, and may even be amateur human beings."

Many men who lacked adequate fathering truly do seem to relate in a childlike way. They seek self-definition from their wives.

They expect their wives to "mother" them as they try to replicate the only intimate relationship they have previously experienced. These men often compete for affection with their own children.

Of course not all men raised without fathers turn out this way. Some men more fully identify with their caretaking mothers. Dr. Larry Peltz suggests that such men may become excellent caregivers as adults. "They develop a female or androgenous mode of being. Often they provide the majority of caretaking in both their families of origin and procreation. They frequently are found in the helping professions. Yet they lack a significant part of their psychology: a male sense of being."

Santayana's dictum, "Those who cannot remember the past are condemned to repeat it," is particularly salient in a man's personal life. If a son cannot benefit from the lessons learned from his father, he is destined to copy his father's actions blindly, to do the opposite of what he considers were his father's blunders, or to reinvent the wheel.

How may I learn from my own personal history? The story begins with my birth and extends backward in time to my father's and grandfathers' lives. How much of my own father's personal history do I know?

The recent popularization of John Bradshaw's "inner child" workshops and books, the blossoming of the whole field of "adult children" counseling generated by the addiction work of Stephanie Brown, Claudia Black, and others, and an increasing sensitivity to the scope and implications of childhood abuse is providing a new social awareness of the importance of our family history in our adult lives. Any man who is unaware of the important influences in his own father's history is likely to carry around emotional baggage that serves him poorly. Until he understands the source of such emotional reactions, he will be inordinately controlled by them. Bradshaw believes that such a man will feel lost, incompetent, or at loose ends in relationships.

When Penny and Paul came into marital counseling, they were on the brink of divorce. The reason they both cited was constant arguing over money. She described him as "cheap," "penny pinching," and "controlling." Of course he saw her as "a spend-thrift" and "a compulsive spender, who never saw a boutique she didn't need to enter."

Their perceptions of each other were colored more by their own personal history than by objective reality. Paul's father grew up during the Great Depression of the 1930s. He was actually given to a foster home by Paul's grandparents, when they could no longer provide him with food and shelter. After three years the family reunited, but his father remained withdrawn and depressed. Since that time Paul had carried an unconscious message: "When you don't have money, you fail, and you lose your family." Whenever Penny spent money, Paul unconsciously winced in preparation for the presumably inevitable rejection.

Penny grew up in a very different environment. Her paternal grandfather was a traveling salesman. He was rarely home, and his homecomings meant gifts and good times for the kids. Her father followed that tradition, showing his affection for his wife and children by showering them with presents. To Penny, spending money meant feeling loved. When Paul refused her desires, he "threw a wet blanket on my fun." Unconsciously it also meant that he no longer loved her.

Both Penny and Paul were not only reacting to the real budget issues common to most marriages, but they were also responding emotionally to unconscious fears of rejection. Until they were aware of these unconscious fears, the fights escalated because each saw their partner's behavior as unreasonable and threatening. Once they had some insight into their own and their partner's feelings, they could begin to resolve the objective budgetary issues.

Penny and Paul are not unique. Our adult lives are deeply affected by the kind of parenting we received as young children. We are just beginning to understand that fathers may have a far more important and unique role in child development than was earlier believed. A successful father is not simply "Mr. Mom," manifesting skills learned from mothers. As I become a father, the impact of how I was fathered emerges.

As a father I will pass on to my children the influence of my own upbringing. If I truly want to be a better father, I need to know a great deal about my own father. Our sons learn from us in two ways. At one level they imitate our behavior. At a deeper level they identify with us and internalize us at a very young age. In a sense, the young child takes in his parents psychologically just as he takes in food biologically. That internalization then resides in his unconscious mind, ready to be activated when he gets involved in relationships and when he becomes a father.

We will first examine the real fathers with whom we grew up. In the next chapter we explore our internal psychological fathers.

KNOWING MY FATHER

The following questions are intended as guidelines to better under-stand who our biological or adoptive fathers were. I encourage you to take the time to answer each question personally. Discovering answers to some of these questions may take considerable time or effort. You may be surprised to discover how much, or how little, you know about your family history. In addition to sample answers provided by other fathers, I have included small examples of my own family history as a guideline and as a consistent thread.

1. What can you learn about your father's family life when he was a boy?
2. Who was your father as a boy, an adolescent, a young man?
3. What was the legacy he received from his own father? How was he taught fathering?
4. How did he feel about your birth and early childhood?
5. How were you a joy and a threat to him personally?
6. What do you know about his relationship with your mother?
7. Is your father the same father that your siblings experi-enced?

> **8.** What substitute role models did you have?
> **9.** What is it like to have a healthy relationship with one's father? Which parts of your father-son relationship were healthy?

1. What can you learn about your father's family life when he was a boy?

If the way I was treated as a child by my parents influences the kind of father I will become, it is reasonable to assume that my father's early life also had an impact on how he fathered me. It is likely that I have been a passive recipient of what he learned from my grandfather.

If my father grew up in a loving home with an involved father, he was exposed to many of the parenting skills he will later want to express with his own children. As a child I will benefit from these talents. If he grew up in an alcoholic home, with an unavailable father, he is also likely to automatically pass some of that on to me as well.

When I understand what it was like for my father, I may gain some understanding of why I was treated the way I was as a child. As the son of a father who was orphaned, for example, I, too, may have to learn much about parenting on my own.

Franklin's grandfather was a steelworker in Pittsburgh who worked long, arduous hours to support his family of ten children. Franklin's father, William, the youngest of his siblings, faced poverty and essentially grew up in the streets. At age sixteen he ran away and joined the military with a fake ID. On his discharge twelve years later he set out for Texas with his wife and daughter. Franklin was born a year later. Like his father he was the youngest child. Unlike his father he was under constant surveillance by both parents. He was pushed to excel in academics and graduated from an excellent college and graduate school.

It is interesting to speculate on the impact William's history had on Franklin's parenting. He was far more involved than his own father. He held high expectations for his son's behavior. Franklin himself became a father for the first time in 1990. He "dotes" on his new daughter, but "worries constantly about supporting her and the other children I want, on a teacher's salary."

David's father had a quite different path. As the son of a Jewish professor in 1940 Germany, he was interred in a Nazi concentration camp. Escaping twice, he reunited with his remaining family and found his way to the United States through China and Argentina. His primary devotion in life was to his family and to the state of Israel, which he visited several times with David. On one of those trips, after his wife's death, he met and married another Holocaust survivor.

The only child in his family, David lived a very sheltered life in the small New England university town where his father was a professor of Modern Languages. The familial value of intellect and education carried him through medical school.

At age forty-two, a successful physician, David has been engaged to the same woman, a Christian, for nine years. His palpable "fear of commitment" relates directly to his father's experience. To marry this woman, whom he loves, means symbolically to "let Hitler win by eliminating the Jews." To decide to marry also means that he is more vulnerable emotionally to loss, just as his father and stepmother who lost family in the Holocaust were.

Gary is the middle child, and oldest son, in a family with seven children. His father and mother are both the youngest of six children in their families of origin. Among the family, Gary was the "loner." His three oldest sisters tended to group together, and the three years between him and the next youngest brother also created a gap. Like both his parents, Gary felt neglected as a child. Gary's paternal grandfather deserted his family just prior to his father's birth. There was never any expectation that a child needed much besides food and shelter in any of these families.

Gary is now considering separating from his wife and two children and leaving his fourth job in the past three years.

My own father was born during the First World War. He grew

up in a "ghetto" community in Boston. The youngest child of a poor immigrant family during the Depression, he followed the proper path of work immediately after high school. His father, my grandfather, came to America during the great immigration period from Eastern Europe, in the first decade of this century. He was Old World in many ways—foreign speaking, autocratic, and demanding obedience. As the youngest child my father was cared for by his parents and older siblings. His early life seems hard by today's standards, with little in the way of finances, emotional support, or guidance. He was expected to follow traditional work roles, stay out of trouble, contribute to the family, and honor his father. Despite their distance my father's connection to his father was quite strong. Although not a very religious man, my father faithfully went to worship services every day for a year following his father's death.

2. Who was your father as a boy, an adolescent, a young man?

Where did he grow up? What do you know about the living conditions? Where was he among his siblings? Who was he close to? Did he have pets? Friends? What were his joys and disappointments as a boy?

If we want to better understand why our natural tendencies seem to follow certain trends, we may find clues in our own fathers' boyhoods. Did your father grow up in poverty? Was that a reason for his overemphasis on work and financial security? If he grew up deeply connected to a large extended family, what impact did that play in his later life? Was he always more connected to his family of origin than his family of procreation? Did he become frustrated by his children's separations from him?

Wes's father ran the only general store in a small Kansas town. He remembers as a child being embarrassed and feeling different because they had the best house and the most money in the town. The store was a family operation. Wesley senior took over the same store when his father retired. As a child his entire life outside of school was spent in one building. The store occupied the bottom floor, and the family lived upstairs. "My grandfather did not take a vacation out of the county until he retired. Then he and Gram went to St. Louis and Chicago by train. From that day forward, Dad was in charge of the store. For him, keeping the store running was his duty. . . . Nothing else ever mattered. Oh, he and my mother went to church and socials, and us kids went to school, but Dad was always in the store from the time he was seven years old. . . . My grandmother died in the store, literally, not even upstairs in the family quarters."

In a "history repeating itself" scenario, Wesley senior took his first real vacation, a two-week trip to Hawaii, when Wes became manager of the store.

Eli's father, Isaac, had quite a different life. Growing up in a series of orphanages and foster homes in the early 1930s in New York City, he claimed no particular location as home. When Isaac was sixteen, he was accepted at NYU, worked nights and weekends, and had his bachelor's degree by the time he was nineteen. He then began a lifelong pattern of traveling, working in a new place and then moving on. Eli claims that he was "conceived on a plane between Hong Kong and Thailand, born in Switzerland and brought to Toronto before I was six weeks old to get the best [Canadian] citizenship papers." Like his father, Eli developed poor skills for lasting friendships. He claims that his "preeminent legacy" was to be "able to get the most out of one-night stands." Isaac's only "mentor or hero was Jack Kerouac and a hobo or two along the way." Although he apparently had two sisters, he never connected with them. Eli grew up with an intact family, but, like his father, no permanent dwelling.

My own father was the youngest of five surviving children. His early years were spent in severe economic times. From the stories he told us as children, his friends were long lasting, made from among his teammates on baseball and hockey teams. As an adolescent he was expected to work hard, and when he returned with his paycheck, all money was immediately handed over to his father, who would then return "almost enough carfare to take the street car to work the next week." Like most of the kids in his neighborhood, hitching rides by jumping on the back of the street-cars on Blue Hill Avenue was the way to get around. He greatly admired an older brother who was apparently tougher than most kids in the neighborhood, someone who got into enough trouble during school years that he served as a formidable protector. My father grew up with two great loves as a boy: his cat Johny and baseball; the latter he passed on to his son. From stories, I gather that most of the caring and affection he received came from those realms and from his music. As a youngster my father developed a great ear and love for music. By the time he met my mother, he could readily play the piano, "just hum a few bars," and he would entertain.

3. What was the legacy he received from his own father? How was he taught fathering?

Was his father close, warm, and loving, or was he distant and cold? Did he even get to know his father? Was his father born in the same country or environment? What did he learn from his father? Have they pursued similar jobs or trades?

If your father was required to follow in the family trade, he grew up with an extra modicum of security at the price of his free-dom. If he was very different from his own father, he may have had a difficult and lonely childhood. Perhaps your father came from an immigrant family. As a part of that generation his role was to bring the family into the new culture. He probably had to traverse two different cultures and possibly two languages. What influences did the role of cultural translator have on his later parenting? As a member of the second generation born in the new country, you grew up with very different cultural expectations. What lessons from his childhood could your father use when he became a father to a generation with quite different values?

Jamal's father, Willy, had to learn fathering on his own. His grandfather disappeared when Willy was a toddler and returned infrequently throughout his youth, usually drunk. His grandmother would "put up with him for two or three days [two of his sisters were the result of those stays] and then boot him out again. You know, until I went through my own divorce, I just assumed that Grandpa was a brute and that she was a good-hearted soul who was charitable. . . . In retrospect maybe she only wanted him around to sire children. Granny never got along with adults, but was great with us kids. . . . Anyhow he just never had a father. There were no men in Grandma's house for any length of time. The only positive memory about the man were that he always arrived with a beat-up guitar and could play the blues. The neighbors all used to tell Dad he could be in Chicago or New Orleans."

As a boy and adolescent Willy was "the man of the house." There was little time for play, friends, or after-school fun. He had jobs to do, chores at home, and schoolwork. For Willy and his siblings the two ways to initiate their mom's wrath was to mess up in school or in church. His only male models were the music teacher at school and two or three guys from the church. To this day, according to Jamal, his dad is very uncomfortable in conversation and in expressing or receiving any physical affection. "The only time he ever seems to be not at work at something is when he plays the piano. Then Willy is in a different world. I'm sure it's why I became a musician."

As limited a contact as Willy had with his father, he received one particular inheritance—the love of and ability for music. The best of his father was also passed on to his son.

Barry also received a family legacy, one far less benign than music. His grandfather spent a good portion of his life "in bars and behind them." Barry's father grew up in an alcoholic home with his mother and "a series of uncles." He was a loner who turned to alcohol and drugs as a teen. His adult life has included psychiatric and substance-abuse hospitalizations. Expelled from school in the eighth grade for drunkenness, he was involved in petty crimes and the street scene. In a sad case of history repeating itself, Barry's grandfather was in prison when his father was born; his father was in a psychiatric hospital and didn't learn of Barry's birth until he was three months old.

John is a minister. "My father, Father's father, and many before that were also ministers. There has never been any meaningful distinction between home, church and community. It is just the way it is. The Porter boys are the local ministry."

His father, Matthew, grew up in the church, literally and symbolically. Life was dedicated to service and sacrifice, but there was never any sense of privation. John's grandfather was a stern "old-time preacher type." His children knew him as the community knew him. He was a very private man and seemed no different at home than he was elsewhere. Matthew grew up in a home where moral values were stressed, punishment was swift and frequent, and rules were not to be broken. He married his childhood sweetheart as soon as he graduated from the seminary. According to John his mother was just like his father. She was reserved and respected in the home and in the community.

During his father's childhood and adolescence he was taught duty above all else. He was well behaved and got adequate grades in school. He was never encouraged to be creative or to explore new ideas. John remembers that his father had a "crisis of faith" at one point, but the potential disruption of their lives and his own father's counsel was enough to bring that to a swift halt.

Feeling rejected as a youth, my own father did not follow in his father's footsteps. My grandfather was personally distant and inflexible, expected and received deference from his wife and children, and was a tailor by trade. He was catered to at home. My father was warm, personally close, and deferred to others most of his childhood and adult life. Growing up in a patriarchal home, he learned to cater to his father. Later in life he continued to elevate others' needs above his own. Not identifying with his father personally, he also went into quite different work.

4. How did he feel about your birth and early childhood?

As hard as it is to imagine, it may be very valuable to examine the impact of your birth and childhood on your father's life. The birth of a child is often a signal event in a man's life. What reaction did your father have to your birth? What were his feelings about you as an infant, toddler, youth, adolescent, and adult? Was your birth a negative event in his life? A positive? Did it mean harder work, more hours on the job or a rewarding trip home? Was it a celebration of the marriage with your mother, an accident, a requirement that they marry?

Jean-Claude, the oldest son of a university professor, describes what he knows about his arrival:

> I was definitely a wanted child. My parents "tried" for ten years before I was born. They finally got it right with me, though, because my three sisters came in the next three years. I was always the pride in my father's eye. He took me to the college as early as I could walk. He took it upon himself to make me "a civilized person," planned for me to go to the Sorbonne when I was eight years old. He was my master teacher, instructor in History, French, and Athletics. He claimed that he was only doing what his father had done for him. When my son, Pierre, was born, I was there and wondered for months whether I'd be able to dedicate my life to similar pursuits, but you know what my dad said? He said that he couldn't imagine being there for my birth—he said it was too biological. Makes you wonder.

Tosh said that his birth was a particular burden on his father: "I was the 'surprise' child. My next youngest sister was thirteen when my mother got pregnant with me. I guess they thought that her menopause was complete or, as I prefer to think of it, unrestrained passion. I also think my mother wanted a reason to stay home. My father was fifty-four when I was born and ready to retire from his work for the county. So when I came along, he had to work another ten years. He never complained and gave me all that he could, but it made his life much more complicated and delayed his gardening dreams. Both my parents were involved in my life. Last chance, you know. My sisters were gone, and I had them all to myself. I know that my dad always wanted a son, so maybe it balanced out."

When Erik asked his father about his birth, he was more than surprised. After hours of questioning he finally heard quite a story. Reportedly his mother was having a child out of wedlock. She delayed too long getting to the hospital and actually delivered Erik in the backseat of a police car. The officer who delivered him ultimately became his father. What he had never been told was that his parents met for the first time while he was being born. "My father was always close to me. He said his life was going nowhere until he, Mom, and I met that day. He quit the force soon after, because it wasn't safe for a family man, and started his business. I guess I could say that my birth changed his life completely."

It's been very hard getting much information from my own father about the impact of my birth. It is clear that I was wanted and that they were trying to have a child. I do know that he was proud to have a son, and I've never really doubted his love for me, but he hasn't talked much about my birth or the changes in his life and in his relationship with my mother. He may not remember his reactions from half a century ago. He may have simply gone through them as something he was supposed to do. He has described great excitement and joy when, as a toddler, I would become very excited and race toward him calling "Daddy" as he stepped off the streetcar returning from work at the Navy Yard.

5. How were you a joy and a threat to him personally?

Was he pleased to have a son? Did you bring him pride? Were you a disappointment? Did your presence cause stress or a rift between him and your mother? Was the birth of a son a particular psychological threat?

Answers to questions about one's own impact are always elusive. It is not easy to be objective when the subject is oneself. Most men are also unclear about what their fathers liked or disliked about them personally. Many of our fathers only commented on our successes or failures. Your father may have never talked directly about what he appreciated or liked. I usually learned from others when my father was proud of my accomplishments.

Kirk described "knowing at an early age that my father was very threatened by my relationship with Mother. In her way, she left him to be with me when I was born. My older sisters also resented that a lot. She used to call me her little man. She was obsessed with my needs. My father never complained, that I know of, but that was about the time he started having this long affair. I think now that he sought out Betty because he needed to know that someone found him attractive and desirable. Mother was terrified of anything sexual. I think a little boy was the perfect love for her. The biggest disappointment was that I never had any relationship with my father, and a poor one with my sisters."

Paul had the opposite experience. He was the oldest of four children. He states that he knew that he was "the apple of Dad's eye. From the time I could walk, he was always taking me with him. He used to show me off to his friends and co-workers. I was his companion for many years. I especially enjoyed going to work with him. He was a printer. I loved the big old presses and the smells of ink and grease and metal. Sometimes, when I was about ten, he let me run some small jobs. I remember one time when I printed everything upside down. He wasn't angry or anything. He treated it like an initiation. He showed off the error to others and then talked about how he had made the same kind of mistakes when he was young. Pretty soon all the men in the shop were joking with both of us and telling of their own and each other's blunders with the presses."

Cedric's father thought it would "spoil" him if he showed too much positive regard for him or his "doings." He related his deep sadness that his dad never quite made it to a Little League, high school, or college baseball game or his debating-team events. "He was quick to let me know when I screwed up, but had little praise for me."

Cedric believed that his dad always favored his sister. He spent many years as a boy feeling like "the result of birth-control failure." Reflecting on his dad's life, he recalled that he didn't remember seeing his dad joyful about anything. He was dedicated to work and Mother. "Us kids were just there, I thought." After his death in 1984 I heard from my mother and an uncle that he had been ecstatic at my birth. I wish he had told me.

Most of the time my father seemed pleased to have a child and son. He seemed genuinely to enjoy being with me and sharing his interests and life with me as a youngster. I think at times my endless questions bored him. Mostly he seemed more interested when I would join him. He was unaccustomed to coming to my games and performances, something he got from his father.

He also had expectations that I would surpass his achievements and pressured me to succeed. I wonder whether there was at times a conflict about that also. I do know that the guiding principle for him and many men of his generation was for their children's lives to be better than their own. I know that as a child and adolescent one of my disappointments was that he wouldn't take my side in my mammoth battles with my mother. Occasionally he would mediate, but usually took her side. That always felt rejecting.

Many men grew up feeling that their early life doomed their father to a position of family supporter or outsider. Was that true of your father? Or was it a joy and privilege for him to have a son whom he could support?

Other men said that they don't think their fathers ever cared because they left them or didn't protect them from their mothers or from the community.

6. *What do you know about his relationship with your mother?*

Was he your mother's silent wage earner, a tyrant in his home, or a shadowy unknown? Was their marriage a love marriage, a marriage of convenience, a disaster?

Happiness in the marital relationship may be insufficient to guarantee good parenting, but it sure helps. A father who feels loved and accepted will probably have a lot more emotional and physical energy to pass along to his children. By contrast a stormy, painful marriage may make any time in the home unpleasant. In that kind of home a man will be distracted from parenting, on guard in his emotional life, and well defended. If your father felt rejected in the family home, he will most likely not have been able to overcome the marital disconnection enough to be close with you or your brothers and sisters. If he did, he may have tried to compensate for the marital losses by overly close relationships with the children.

Lindy describes his parents' relationship as "stormy. The only reason why they didn't get divorced was that they were Catholic, and they wanted to be sure that the other one was always being tortured. My father was always angry with her for spending money. He also couldn't stand his mother-in-law always being in the apartment. She and my mother would badmouth him all day, and then when he came home, the fights would start. My brother and I would hide in our bedroom or turn up the radio so we wouldn't have to listen. Sometimes when he got too frustrated, he'd take it out on us. I hated that."

When Trent was young, his father was "a tyrant."

He drank too much, what you'd call an alcoholic today. And when he drank, he was mean. He always expected to give orders and have Mom and Stephanie and me just jump up and do it. If he thought we delayed, he'd come after us menacingly. He was just never the kind of person who should have had kids. I know Mom was sometimes hard to live with, but I think she was reacting to him a lot. He would boss her around, and she would just do what he told her, but then she'd get sick [depressed] and be unable to do anything, or she'd spend all her time with her brother and his single friends to get even with him. One time when I was about twenty-two, he took me out to his favorite bar and, after too many drinks for both of us, he started to get weepy and talk about how frustrated he was with the marriage. He told me a lot of things I just didn't want to hear about their sex life (or lack of one). He also said that he knew she was unfaithful. His life with her was pretty miserable by my way of thinking.

Theo had a very different kind of father. He called him the "ultimate wimp." He'd work all day, come home, and then after dinner start doing most of the housework. Theo described his mother as "a tennis bum." His dad would work to please her, without success. In Theo's recollection his dad put everyone in the family before himself, especially his wife. "It was essentially an extension of his relationship with his mother. He served her until she died and married the same kind of woman. My grandfather was killed in World War II, so Dad pretty much grew up with no father himself."

Theo didn't think his parents' relationship was a good model for him, but he believed that it worked for them. His father never complained. His mother "loved" him. He did think that they had an active romantic life, "from the late-night giggles and sounds of bedsprings." He also remembers his father being as affectionate with his mother as he was devoted to her. Theo remembers his embarrassment at his parents' "public displays of affection" when he was a teenager.

It seemed that Quentin's parents "had the ideal marriage." He didn't think they were the best parents, but they were very close and happy with each other. He remembers that his parents' bedroom was "off-limits" to the four children. He confessed that he once sneaked into their private domain and found a love note under his mother's pillow.

Doug, an unmarried father of three, told the interviewer that he planned to stay with his partner of eleven years and mother of his children, but he would never marry. His parents' marriages and divorces were so traumatic to him, and apparently painful to them, that he swore that he would never get into a similar situation himself. He claims that his parents married right out of high school. "They fought from day one. Screaming, yelling, hitting each other. They never grew up. They divorced each other impulsively and then remarried the same way. I never knew which one I'd be living with. Mostly I hung out at my grandmother's house when they were losing it."

Finally, Kim describes the relationship between her parents as very solid. "They married later in life, and it was a second marriage for each of them. I always had the sense that they were very sexual with each other. They seemed like equals and they always made big decisions together. . . . Sometimes they'd fight over things, especially money and Mom's shopping, but they always agreed on policies for me. I don't talk much about my parents because people look at you strangely when you say you had great parents who loved each other and you. I once told my girlfriend that I wanted to marry a guy just like my dad and be just like my mom, and she just kinda looked at me like I was from another planet."

My own parents have always supported and depended heavily on each other. They love each other in a way that would not work for me, but it has lasted for over fifty years. I think their relationship was more supportive than passionate. The big fight was always over loyalty and whom Mother put first—the children, her family of origin, or my dad. She always came first for him.

The enmeshed closeness of my parents' relationship and the loyalty conflicts always seemed potentially dangerous to me. One of the ways that I unconsciously escaped from emotionally replicating their form of intimacy was to maintain a considerable geographical distance, spending most of my adult life to date almost six thousand miles away from their home.

7. Is your father the same father that your siblings experienced?

What do you know about the way your siblings experienced your father? Was he seen as acting the same toward everyone? In some families oldest and youngest children separated by many years have vastly different experiences of a father. Have you talked at length with your brothers and sisters about how they saw Dad? What new information might be available from them?

Faustino Bernadett, my father-in-law, had four sons and three daughters. His relationship with his oldest and youngest sons was quite influential, but very different. As a struggling family doctor beginning his career, he was more of a model to his oldest son. By the time the youngest was growing up, his career was established. There was a lot more time for personal contact. Dan got to know his father much more as a person with hobbies and interests outside of work. Both of these men now reflect very positive traits and memories of their father, but they carry him in different ways.

In my own family of origin my sister and I are only four years apart, yet we also had different "special time" with our father. When I was the only child at home, I was predominantly with my mother as an infant and preschooler. By contrast my sister was in high school when I left for college. She and Dad had a lot of very special times and conversations when Mom was working evenings and just the two of them were at home.

As a family therapist I have been amazed at the different fathers siblings experienced. In the Sullivan family, for example, Patrick, aged sixteen, saw his father as "brutal, cruel, and crude." His sister, Kathleen, ten months his junior, described the very same man as her best friend, "a shield from Mother's moods."

What can explain such differences? To some extent parents treat children of the opposite sex differently. There are also built-in genetic differences between children that fathers relate to dissimilarly. In the Sullivan family Patrick was described as "just like Mom." Kathleen resembled and emulated her aunt, who had been a second mother to her father.

Jon said that he never could relate to his father the way his older brothers did because they were all "jocks" and he was the family intellectual. "They were all Navy, just like Dad. They were all football and track and wrestling. I was the reader. Dad used to view me with evident distaste when I reluctantly tried to play tag football with them and my cousins. God, I was uncoordinated. Soon I'd retreat to the sidelines with my books. I was the classic last kid picked on any team. The final break came when my brothers were both in Southeast Asia during Vietnam, and I was running a draft evaders' refuge."

Ethan remembered his father as always being on his side and never on his brother's. "Allen could do no right in my father's eyes. Maybe because I was the firstborn, maybe because Allen and Father were so much alike, but they fought from day one till the day Father died. He was quite unfair. Allen's art was criticized while my scribbles were praised."

According to many sons and daughters, their fathers "mellowed" or "got worn out" over time. Younger siblings often felt that their father was more easygoing or permissive. Scott is twelve years older than his youngest sister, Amanda. They spoke about the differences in their dad's rules and understanding. For Scott his father was authoritarian and restrictive. He remembered that he always had the earliest curfew and was the last to get a car in his group. His father "was not someone you would talk to or reason with. He was the lawgiver." By contrast Amanda "can't remember ever even having a curfew. Dad and Mom were always asleep by the time I got home. . . . Of course they knew I didn't need one. I was always home on time, not like my sister Cathy. Dad was also a listener. I could talk to him about school or trouble with my boyfriend. He got uncomfortable, I think, but he was available."

8. *What substitute role models did you have?*

Were there any other men besides your father who played a significant role in your life? Was there a big brother, scoutmaster, coach, or teacher who took you under his wing? What special qualities did he have? Many men today were greatly influenced by father figures who were not biological relatives. Often these unsung heroes provided crucial male nurturance to youngsters at critical times. Teachers, coaches, big brothers, mentors—all may render the missing ingredients.

Cliff's "calabash uncle" was a baseball coach in high school.

To Cliff's way of thinking he was the sole difference between a respectable life and one "as a beach bum." Coach Kam encouraged him to stay in school to play baseball, and to play baseball as a way of staying in school. He gave Cliff (as well as many others on the team) his time, encouragement, and place to do the homework. Cliff said that he respected Kam so much, he wanted to be a coach just like him. That meant staying in school and hanging out with the kids who did.

Miguel reports that his priest took a real interest in him and gave him a place to stay when home became too chaotic. A family friend for three generations, this substitute grandfather helped him get into the parochial school on scholarship and followed his progress on a regular basis. Miguel so identified with him, he decided to pursue the priesthood. When he later became disenchanted with that path, it was again Father Javier who encouraged his evolution. Miguel recalls, "The first time I ever cried as an adult was at Father's funeral. I named my son after him."

My own high school years were rocky. The school was more of an ordeal than a place for learning. Much of my time was spent at the guidance counselor's office, while he and I puzzled over why I was such a problem person. The one bright light in those years was the military-drill instructor, Major Kelly. For reasons unknown to me he took me under his wing, encouraged me to be on the trick drill team, and was generally available. Hanging out with him, practicing maneuvers, and generally feeling understood, went a long way to helping me survive the rigors of Boston Latin School.

Teachers who turn adolescents lives around by virtue of their presence, caring, and strength have long been celebrated. In the recent film *Stand and Deliver,* Edward James Olmos, playing the role of real-life teacher Jaime Escalante, a Hispanic math teacher, dramatically demonstrated how previously underachieving students could respond to such encouragement.

Substitute male models can provide fathering to children that is for some reason missing or incomplete. Desmond recalled his math teacher in the tenth grade, who broke up a fight on the playground, then:

took me aside and read me the riot act. He wouldn't listen to any of my jive. He just stuck on me like a bee on honey. By the time he was through giving me a talk and detention, I had the feeling that if I didn't shape up, this dude would do me worse than the Greens and Oranges [gangs at school]. Then the next day he sees me in the yard before school, and he says to me if I light up on school grounds, I'm meat. I thought the guy had powers, man. How'd he know Eddie scored a joint for us? I followed him in, and he started to talk about how he grew up. Then the next day he told me more. Next thing I knew, he's a friend and I don't want to mess him up by getting in trouble. He introduced me to this senior, who he helped, and the guy just said, "This dude is the best way to go at the school." So when I graduate, he shows up at my parents' house with a friend of his from the community college and they say I'm going to work there this summer to pay my tuition for fall. Man, my parents and me never even thought about it before. So the rest is history.

Five years later Desmond was the first member of his family ever to graduate from college. He was tenured in the mathematics department at a major university when he was interviewed.

Not only potential delinquents or troubled youngsters have such male role models. A number of men recalled being inspired or favorably challenged by positive male role models. For Brent it was a minister, for Sam an older brother, for others, uncles or family friends.

9. *What is it like to have a healthy relationship with one's father? Which parts of your father-son relationship were healthy?*

If we are to visit common images of fathers, we are hard-pressed to find positive examples. Yet they do exist, quietly, and in decent numbers.

Many men who remember an otherwise unhappy childhood recall certain events that they shared in some special way with their fathers. Perhaps there are special memories of these times. Some men can identify exactly which ways their fathers were available or involved. Did you have to be doing something in which he had an interest? Perhaps your father was more available during certain years than others. If the relationship fell apart during the adolescent years, there is a solid foundation established earlier. Some boys remember their father's deep involvement with them during or until some family event occurred or until they reached a certain age. These times of involved parenting provide a solid basis for subsequent reconciliation with our fathers and for promoting our own best efforts to be good fathers.

Some men and women have primarily fond recollections of their fathering. At age thirty-seven Corinne remembers her relationship with her late father as "perfect." He was a stay-at-home dad who cared for the home and the children. She says, "Both my parents were affectionate and caring. I never thought about how any fathers might not be that way. When I had trouble in school, he went and talked to me and talked to the school. He also respected my judgment. From the time I was ten years old, he always asked for my opinion if something would affect the family or me."

Carlos calls his father "my best friend. He's a wise man and a strong man. My dream is to be like him, respected by others, loved by my family. . . . I think what made him that way is that he respects everyone else, especially his children."

Marty had a very realistic response to this question. He thoughtfully related, "I don't think you can just have a 'good' relationship. It changes over the years. When my father was young, he was pretty self-centered. I don't think he really got to know me until I was about five or six. Then, when I was playing sports, he got real involved and interested in me even though he was no athlete. When I rebelled in college, he was about the only father who didn't make a big thing of my long hair. He just kept asking what I was trying to prove, and was I achieving my goals? I didn't feel close to him then, actually until my kids were born, but I always respected him. Now overall I'd say it's good."

Some of the characteristics of a positive relationship are mutual respect, affection, strength, good listening skills, time with children, honesty, humor, and self-enjoyment.

For most of us the relationships with Dad were mixed. The good parts were not a constant. My relationship with my father went through many stages, marked by a combination of love, respect, and frustration. At various times each of those feelings was more dominant than the others. In general I've always felt close to my father, but I was frustrated by the barriers he seemed to set between us. He never did allow me to fulfill my unconscious mission of making him happy. His concern for my mother's feelings sometimes blocked my access. His difficulty expressing some feelings or of hearing mine were stumbling blocks. Yet when I ask myself, overall, did I have a good relationship with my dad, the answer is quite affirmative.

I know that my relationship with my father was not unique. For most men the relationship contains both healthy and unhealthy components. Wally, for example, said that he was so angry at his father for so long that he couldn't appreciate anything about their relationship. After reconciling with his father at age forty-two he finds much to relish about his current and past relationship.

Even men whose relationship with their fathers has historically been more positive than negative may need to work on that relationship. The first step involves some detective work into the nature of your father's life.

If you want to discover who you are as a father and as a man, you may find a number of clues in your father's life. As you learn some of the details of his history, you may have a far better understanding of why he fathered the way that he did. Knowing what was happening in my father's life when I was young may give me insight into some of the deep emotions I experience with my own children. Why do I respond so "instinctively" to some of their behaviors and not so to others? Some of the answers lie in my imitation of his behaviors. Far more involve who he was as a person on the inside, that is, the father with whom I identified as a boy and whom I carry around in my psyche today.

The nine questions in this chapter are meant as a general guideline, a beginning of your own more personal inquiry. If you would like to know your father better as a path to your own fathering, or if you hope to be closer to him, the questions are worth answering privately. However, a word of warning: Finding answers or access to information may be frustrating. The following hints may be helpful.

HINTS FOR GAINING INFORMATION ON YOUR FATHER

1. If your father is still alive, try to get him to reminisce about your boyhood in general. Don't pose specific questions until you need specific answers. He may find it easier to remember time periods or events rather than the nature of the relationship. *Try to do this alone with him.*

2. Before you ask specific questions, think them through carefully. Plan your approach.

3. Pick a time and place that will make him feel most comfortable. It may be doing something together, driving, sitting across from each other at a table, or on the phone. Be careful to choose a situation that will allow him the most freedom to reminisce.

4. If your father is not alive or is unavailable, seek out relatives and neighbors. Ask them what they know about his life and your relationship. Your father's siblings may be particularly good resources. This may take real detective work. Some men have found great resources in unlikely places.

5. Watch for areas that remain undiscussed. They might be family secrets. Some of these secrets might be important for you.

6. One strategy that has been successful for many men is to explore their roots with a family tree. Complete as much as you can. Then ask for help from your father or others. As ancestors are identified, try to get your helpers to chat about them. Several people have been successful, when they asked their parents to help, because it was a class assignment.

7. Another strategy is to go over old photographs with your family members and ask for stories about the pictures.

8. It is best if you ask your mother and father the same questions separately. When they are together, one will be the spokesperson. You'll get the official story instead of the raw one.

9. Some families have artifacts such as biographies or old news clippings available.

10. In addition to the questions posed in the chapter, consider some of the following:

- Which of your father's dreams were fulfilled? Which went unfulfilled?
- What did he want in his life that he did not receive? What does he regret?
- What feelings did he allow you to see? Which ones were hidden?
- What were his passions?
- How was he strong? How was he weak?
- Why did he have you? What did it mean for him to have a son?
- What have you always wanted to ask but haven't yet?

THE FATHER WITHIN

*I've long since retired, my son's moved away
I called him up just the other day
I said, I'd like to see you if you don't mind
He said, I'd love to dad if I could find the time
You see, my new job's a hassle and the
kids got the flu
but it's sure nice talking to you
And as I hung up the phone, it occurred to me
He'd grown up just like me
My boy was just like me.*

—HARRY CHAPIN

The discovery of my actual father, described in the last chapter, is only the beginning of my quest for understanding. Whatever the reality of my father's life and experience, I carry within me an *internalized* version of him that reflects my childhood experiences, fantasies, and creations. It is this internalized father that generates my unconscious emotional reactions and automatic behaviors when I become a father.

Sara Maitland wrote,

I have two fathers. I have a material, biological father. His name was Adam Maitland; he was born in 1913. . . . I have another father. This one is alive and well and rampaging inside. He never goes away, although sometimes he is silent; he is never ill, never weakened, never leaves me alone. He lurks about under other names—God, Husband, Companion—and all those relationships are made possible (which is nice) and impossibly difficult and conflicting because of the father who is in and under and through them all. In my late teens I fled my father's house; it has taken me a long time to realize that I carried with me the Father from whom I could not escape by escaping childhood, from whom I have not yet escaped, and from whom I have had, and still have, to wrest my loves, my voice, my feminism, and my freedom. It is this Father that I have hated loving and loved hating.[1]

Whatever my investigative efforts, some aspects of my actual father's life, motivations, and feelings will always be something of a mystery. Discovering the father influences that I acquired as a youngster and carry in my unconscious is a venture of another order. It may be a more important one. Those parts of my unconscious father, of which I am unaware, are bound to have an inordinate impact on my relationships, my psychological state, and my emotions.

As children many of us vowed never to do to our children what our fathers had done to us. If we are vigilant, we may be successful for the most part. It then comes as a surprise when we hear our father's words coming out of our own mouths. Sometimes we find ourselves doing exactly what he did, exactly those things we were sure we wouldn't do.

How does this occur? What programming kicks in to recapitulate history? A lot has to do with our childhood experiences and how we internalized our fathers when we were children. Some of what we learned about fathering happened at a subconscious level. As we identified with our fathers, we incorporated our images of "father" comparably to the way we took in food. Just as the food was broken down and transformed to our physical growth, these images were converted to become part of our own psyches. As a part of our being, existing at "cellular" levels, these images remain in our unconscious mind, ready to emerge when we become fathers.

Each of us carries around with us, at an unconscious level, imprints of our parents' values, ways of being, fears, and abilities. As much as we try to avoid being like our parents, there are unconscious drives to do so.

Some of these replications are amusing and harmless. My wife has four brothers. They are very different in many ways, yet they share two characteristics that are amazingly evident when they are together. They all speak in the same measured way, with a characteristic spacing, that perfectly emulates the speech patterns of their late father. They also walk in a way that is exceptionally reminiscent of their dad. None of them is aware of these characteristics. As boys they somehow internalized how a man walks and talks from exposure to the way their father walked and talked. Later in life they reproduced his manner.

Almost two decades ago I shared a house with three other people. One morning one of my thirty-year-old housemates appeared for breakfast looking stunned and worried. In response to our queries, ashen-faced, he slowly replied, "When I got out of bed just now, I made my father's sound."

In recent years I have personally become aware of laughing exactly the way my own father did when he was younger. I am sure I never made a conscious attempt to do so.

None of these transmitted traits is likely to be of psychological concern. Other unconscious paternal traits may have a bigger impact.

Harvey described his actual father as a distant, sullen man who had little time for his wife or children. As the owner of a small store in downtown Oakland, California, his work hours were long, and family vacations nonexistent. With evident sadness Harvey reiterated his disappointment that the business always had higher precedence than family. "Other men coached Little League, went to their kids' Christmas plays, and took their sons fishing and hunting." When his father died of a coronary, Harvey dropped out of college to take over the store, but "by then it was a lost cause. I liquidated what I could—enough for my mom's rent and food— and finally went back to school. The worst part was that when I cleaned out the store, I found all my old high school football clippings in a book with his old keepsakes. Why couldn't he just tell me he cared, or come to a game?"

Harvey entered therapy with his fiancée (of six years). He said that he couldn't commit to marriage, but "I think I love her, and am not interested in anyone else." Aside from the commitment issue, the relationship was described as "good."

As he talked about their life together, his "commitment phobia" became more clear. For Harvey and Melinda marriage meant children. Underlying his misgivings about marriage was a personal fear that he might have a son who would go unknown, "the way I was unknown. . . . I just don't know how to talk to kids. I feel uncomfortable around them. Besides, I don't have the time. My career is just taking off. I need to work twelve hours a day just to keep up."

Despite his conscious efforts to avoid it, Harvey was unconsciously replicating his father's life: He was work focused, would not allow himself to get closer to loved ones, and avoided children. His feelings about his own inadequacies kept him from facing his fears of verbally acknowledging connection. Somehow his internalized father's pain was also driving Harvey's life.

There are situations where the "like father, like son" phenomenon may be quite debilitating. Many men go through life as if in the grip of some powerful subliminal paternal legacy. One form this takes is a multigenerational motif of addiction or antisocial behavior. Patterns of child abuse, alcoholism, and some forms of emotional disorders have been shown to visit the sons, and grandsons, of men with these problems. Some of this transmission could well be genetic, but even if the genes provide susceptibility, we acquire a great deal from the behavior we observe, the meaning it has for us, and our feelings at the time.

Mack was the son of an alcoholic, abusive father. As a small boy he learned to make himself scarce whenever his father had been drinking. As much as he hated the effects of his father's alcoholism, he, too, began drinking in high school. In the army he "lost stripes almost as fast as I got them" for being drunk and disorderly. His first marriage ended when he struck his wife after being out drinking with his buddies. His drinking with his friends diminished after his second marriage, but he typically had a six-pack every night after he came home and fell asleep in front of the television.

Mack was referred to therapy by Child Protective Services. He had discovered his thirteen-year-old son using drugs and had beat the boy until the neighbors called the police. The three-generation pattern of substance abuse and violence is commonly seen by social-service and mental-health practitioners.

As a child Mack swore that he would not turn out like his father. Yet despite his repugnance about growing up in such a home, he somehow ended up replicating the same horrors with his family of procreation.

As most parents are painfully aware, our children tend to imitate our behavior far more than they follow our "sage" advice. Patterns in our families of origin commonly find their way into our families of procreation. Like Mack we are convinced that we will *never* do what our parents did to us. Yet somehow we do often repeat history. How does this come to be? Why are we so programmed to be just like our own parents?

HOW CHILDREN LEARN

Children are born with a host of genetic predispositions for growth, traits, and abilities. They are also born without any knowledge of society or acceptable behavior patterns. The most prominent ways that they learn social mores are imitation and trial and error. Their home environment deeply impacts both. Children will learn to imitate the adults with whom they live. Patterns of speech, posture, movements, and gestures will all be copied to some extent. Similarly, trial-and-error exploration will be limited by the values and mores of the society in which they live.

Unconscious Learning

Children and adults learn differently in a number of important ways. For adults new learning is affected by all previous knowledge. We experience new phenomena by virtue of the explanations made possible by what we have already learned. The dramatic amount of learning common for children in the early years takes place without preconceptions.

Children take in new information as they experience it in the moment. Lacking an existing frame of reference, they do not have the ability to evaluate, compare, or understand new things in context. Learning that occurs this way is particularly powerful. Children do not examine their parents' actions, compare it with social norms and their own experience, and make informed decisions taking these multiple factors into account. They simply identify and internalize the ways their parents (and others) do things, and imitate them.

Furthermore early learning is qualitatively different from later learning. Child-development experts have shown that until children reach a certain stage of development, their way of thinking is actually different from adult thought patterns. Younger children's learning is more egocentric, more dominated by perceptions, with facts and fantasy little separated. Young children learn and remember more through association than through reason. Two things that occur together are accepted by children as having a causal relationship. Thus for a child "the moon comes up at night because I need to see in the dark." This type of egocentric, symbolic, associative learning is characteristic of unconscious processing.

Children do not separate the emotions they feel during an event from the facts. In their unconscious minds the event and the emotions are stored together as memories as they occurred to the child's level of understanding at the time. Often events that are associated with certain emotions in childhood retain their emotional value in our unconscious mind well into adulthood, long after our conscious mind dismisses the connection between the two. As adults we may subconsciously react with strong feelings to events or images that activate the connections we made as children, before we were capable of causal thinking.

Parental Incorporation

As young children our parents, or caretakers, are the most important individuals in our lives. They must provide us with nurturance, safety, and stimulation, or we do not thrive. Because they are so important for our very existence, and because they dominate our environment, we incorporate images of our parents into our subconscious mind. Created by a child's mind, our internalized images of our parents are emotional, powerful, larger than life, and primitive. As we grow and learn more about society in conscious ways, these early images are covered over by successive layers of adult "reality." However, our feelings and internal sense of our parents that we internalized at very young ages remain with us, out of conscious awareness, in the primitive form and level of understanding in which they were first acquired.

These unconscious images evoke strong emotions and inhibitions, often at surprising times. As part of our mind they influence us in a number of ways, most commonly through our feelings—producing fears, attractions, comfort, or warnings.

Because our parents dominated our relationships as young children, and because there was little separation between emotions and actions, our internal images are likely to have a particularly strong unconscious influence in our adult romantic attractions and parenting. To a certain extent, whom we choose as a partner and how we feel and behave as parents reflect these incorporated childish images of our parents. Thus, how I, as a youngster, experienced my own father, powerfully influences the way I will father my children.

When Father Is Absent

For many boys early incorporation of their father is problematic because he is physically or emotionally unavailable. What kind of images can the young boy assimilate if his father is inaccessible? With what does he fill this vacuum? It seems likely that he either has to learn how to be a man from someone besides his father or make it up himself. In either case he is likely to incorporate a model that is somewhat magical or ill suited to him.

Many a young boy whose father is unavailable learns about fathering from his mother or from other women. His "male" identification and internalization are necessarily filtered through her feelings about his father or males in general. A negative internal sense of father, or men, may well be created and then carried throughout life. Later in life this can turn into self-denigration or be projected onto potential partners as misogyny.

Gary is a suitable example of a man who never knew his father. He grew up "in a household of women: my mom, grandma, and three sisters." He remembers that his father and all men were "bad-mouthed all my life." Lacking self-confidence, he married a "strong-willed, independent woman." Feeling that she was the competent parent, and feeling inadequate as a male, Gary saw little that he could offer his two sons. Physically present, he was emotionally distant from both of them. His emotional withdrawal replicated his own father's absence. In this way another generation of boys in this family went unfathered.

A young child with an absent father has to make up for it on his own. He will likely create a father image from mythical images of fathers. Some boys, lacking a real father to internalize, seek out external father figures to follow. This is often a prescription for membership in gangs, political movements, or cults—an attraction to rigid guidelines for living. They also have a greater propensity toward substance abuse.

The abandoned son will have to find some way to explain to himself why his father left. His personal explanations of the abandonment may involve magical feelings of omnipotence (e.g., "I drove him away because I was too bad, too powerful," etc.) or impotence (e.g., "he left because I was a disappointment").

Both the omnipotent and impotent feelings come from the childlike (superstitious) thinking of overresponsibility. Once internalized, the feeling of having caused the father's absence can become the source of two divergent feelings in later life: (1) deep loneliness, disconnection, and sense of isolation and (2) guilt (at having caused the absence).

Each of these may have dramatic impact on later personal self-esteem and on intimate relationships. A son without an internalized sense of a real father will try to explain the absence to himself. There is fertile ground for fabrication. Commonly these sons either idealize or degrade the father, identify with the fantasy, and then struggle with the shame or guilt. As an adult he may well fear another abandonment to the point of being afraid of relationships, avoiding showing vulnerable feelings, or becoming overly dependent on a woman to avoid rejection.

Bruce's father deserted the family when Bruce was four years old. At first, as an only child, he enjoyed the extra attention from his mother and his new position as the only man in the home. As a preteen, however, and later as a teenager, he had constant difficulties with the law and school authorities. He once told a high school counselor that his father was a great man, a success in all walks of life, and said it with assuredness. By comparison he saw himself as a failure who could "never live up to the family heritage."

Kenny's father's absence was purportedly because of work pressure. He took only one week's vacation during Kenny's entire school years. As a forty-five-year-old man sorting through his own divorce, Kenny said,

> I never knew much about him. I have these sayings of his that run around in my mind. "A penny saved," "Money doesn't grow on trees," and so on. But I always wondered why he never wanted to be with us. I felt like it must have been my medical costs that he had to work so hard. He sent me to expensive private schools and college. I was always feeling like I was getting things from him, but I didn't ever seem to feel like I was getting anything of him. My wife, I mean ex-wife, was like that also. She was withdrawn and depressed her whole life. No matter what I did, it was always the same. No matter what I got from her, I felt lonely and wrong. Of course she criticized everything I did. Father wasn't overtly critical. . . . He just wasn't positive. . . . He just wasn't there. . . . I may have some of him in me. I'm definitely a workaholic. Even though my kids live with me now, I don't see them much.

Kenny's father was not present for him as a young boy. Yet he was important enough to be emulated.

An example of the search men make to compensate for their absent fathers can be found in this quotation from Mark Twain: "At age of twelve a boy starts imitating a man and he goes on doing that for the rest of his life." We know now that it begins much earlier, more like twelve months than twelve years.

Separation and Individuation

To become a functioning adult in our culture, a child goes through a series of steps that promote progressive independence. From the earliest stages of childhood it is the child's job to separate from the symbiotic connection in the womb to autonomy, and it is the parents' job to promote this developing independence. These stages are always disruptive and difficult for children and for parents.

The first major separation-individuation crisis occurs between eighteen and thirty months on the average. The *terrible twos* is a term customarily applied to the youngster's expressions of independence, most often punctuated by an increased frequency in utterance of the word *no!* by every member of the household. A similar process occurs during adolescence.

When girls separate from Mother, they reconnect by virtue of their shared gender. Boys, however, need to separate more permanently from Mother and identify with their fathers, their own gender model.

Sam Osherson, author of *Finding Our Fathers,* points out that both the psychological separation from Mother and the identification and bonding with Father are problematic for boys.[2]

According to Dr. Osherson, because the organization of family and structure of parenting make caretaking a female activity, Mother represents closeness, tactile connection, holding, feeding, and caregiving. Father is more amorphous, someone the child knows from a distance. Even if he is warm, he may be remote. For young boys there is terror, great sense of loss, and fear of abandonment in recognition that as a male he must leave the world of women. He questions if he can exist without, or be different from, Mother.

Many two-year-old boys enjoy dressing up in women's clothes, affirming that they are going to be mommies when they grow up. Not much later, accepting the fact that they will not be mommies, they determine that they will marry Mommy.

For some boys the only way fully to relinquish the woman's domain is to denigrate feminine, softer, more sensitive sides of themselves. They repress their needs to be taken care of longer. Such boys lack the opportunity to grieve over the loss of their intense closeness with Mother or to master their own wishes to be female and to continue to be cared for by adults. As they grow up, they retain the feeling that only women can fill them up, help them feel complete. This creates difficulties with intimate relationships later in life. Relationships in which they do not feel that they get enough will produce resentment. In addition, as men they might prematurely leave relationships on their own, replicating their experience of leaving or feeling forced from the nest too early.

Osherson, Robert Bly,[3] Lilian Rubin,[4] and others all point out that many adult men carry around an internal burden of vulnerability, dependency, or emptiness, still grieving their loss of the emotional mother-son connection. They relive, on an emotional level, the time when going to Mother for help was inappropriate and they wouldn't or couldn't go to Father with the confusion, hurt, anger, or sadness they felt. When men are put in touch with this pain as adults, they respond ambivalently—with rage, sadness, fear, shame, and bravado, as well as with curiosity, hope, and a desire to heal the wound they feel.

Popular caricatures of modern men reflect the behavior, but not the feelings, of these wounded males. Some of these men see women as rejecting, and they compensate by objectifying women first. Others expect any woman to replace the mother they wanted and they look for caretaking in adult relationships, playing little boy to the competent mother. There are also men who, anticipating rejection when they are needy, cannot request help from a partner.

Instead they take care of everything on their own and subsequently resent women for playing little girl to their role of father.

Internally and emotionally all are responding to their childhood experiences of separating and individuating. Such unconscious reactions often shape what we expect from women and men in ways that influence how we respond to work and family pressures of modern times.

The antidote to such wounded feelings is to experience male nurturance, beginning with Father and culminating from ourselves as men. Each time a life crisis emerges or a personal loss occurs, there is the potential for rekindling ancient experiences of unresolved separation and loss that occurred when we were growing up. At the core of these feelings are our own vulnerability and dependency as men, the needs for security, and the fear of rejection. Without a firm internal sense of maleness, men will be stuck with extreme reactions: either rejecting women or paying an exorbitant price to feel secure. Lee, a fifty-five-year-old professor, is a good example of this: "My father achieved a sense of security at a very high cost. He did it by giving up his will to my mother. Unfortunately when she dominated him, she also dominated me. I've suffered all my adult life with a need to please a woman, at any cost, for fear of her displeasure or rejection . . . and resenting it."

Lee's pain, and that of other men of this era, has been exacerbated by the social changes that have dominated relationship dynamics over the past two decades. As a result of the women's movement and the concurrent increasing expectation for men to be more involved in pregnancy, childbirth, and early parenting, modern fathers lose the division-of-labor buffer that characterized men of their father's generation.

As we become more involved with our young children, our own father hunger reemerges. We become aware of the personal hurts and rejections from our own childhood, as well as our lack of a model for fathering. When we relinquish that shelter of detachment, we are thrown back in touch with those feelings of helplessness and powerlessness that were insufficiently mastered in boyhood.

The Child Is Father to the Man

Lee claims that his adult relationships have been colored by his father's relationship with his mother and the model of male acquiescence that he experienced as a child. Some men talk of a lifelong quest to get their father to stand up for himself, to be the man who can intercede for them with Mother. Still others realize that the only lesson they learned about relationships in their families of origin was silent avoidance. A model of father acquiescence does influence future relationships and choices, but an equally powerful influence is the relationship that existed between themselves and their father.

It is important to recognize that attraction to others as adults does not completely reflect logic and adult motivation. To a great extent we are attracted to people who somehow communicate that they will meet some unfulfilled need of childhood, a person who will make our life happy forever after. It is commonly thought that boys marry Mom ("I want a girl just like the girl that married dear old Dad"); and girls marry Dad. It is more complex than that. It isn't the person as much as the *relationship* that draws us.

For most adults there is a strong tendency to replicate the relationship we had with our same-sex parent. These unconscious attractors are particularly problematic for boys who have absent or missing fathers. They will tend to marry, or be attracted to, people who will allow them to repeat the relationship with that absent dad. It may be that the woman is cold and withdrawn like Dad was; it may be that he will become his dad and be the withdrawn one. In either case the relationship carries into another generation, and he will have a host of unmet intimacy needs.

Whether your actual father, father substitute, or imagined father was close, involved, abusive, distant, or absent, your unconscious internalized images of your father may be the result of several sources, including actual experiences, stories, and feelings of others; cultural input; and personal needs and desires.

It is important to remember that the internalizations begin when a child is very young and incapable of evaluation or censorship. The images are then carried unconsciously along with all other childhood experiences and memories. They function, later in life, as they were instilled—in a childlike and precognitive way. Unconscious visions and expectations of fathers thus seem somewhat larger than life.

SOME FORMS OF INTERNALIZED FATHER

Commonly held father images include hero, wimp, secretly vulnerable, wounded, and angry man.

My Father the Hero

To many young boys, a father may be a hero in many realms. Less frequently available than Mother, his appearance and presence may be more novel and exciting. His world of work may seem much more exotic and exciting from afar. If he travels, he may have stories to tell of strange, distant places, which seem romantic to the young child. A father who is involved with struggles against authority or who is honored by others may also be seen as heroic. In fact absence often stimulates a larger, more mythical sense of father, concurrent with feelings of insecurity and abandonment in the son.

The son who carries a "heroic" internal father may well feel a need to live up to the image in order to be a man and father himself. To the extent that it motivates him to expand his limits, it may be quite positive. However, if the internalized image is of mythic proportions, the son will always fall short of his expectations of what a man really is. This will commonly produce feelings of inadequacy by comparison with the image.

Living up to an image is never easy. As Homer said in *The Odyssey,* "For rarely are sons similar to their fathers: most are worse, and a few are better than their fathers."

A combination of the image and the reality may also be a stumbling block for the son. Ben Jonson, in an oft-quoted passage, reminds us, "Greatness of name in the father oft-times overwhelms the son; they stand too near one another. The shadow kills the growth: so much, that we see the grandchild come more and oftener to be heir to the first."[5]

A contemporary of mine is such a man. The son of an "intellectual superstar," he often hid his own brilliance, finding innumerable ways to avoid publishing his own scientific discoveries and theories. In relationships he married four women who were all inferior to him intellectually. Each time the relationship ended for failing to meet his unconscious expectation that his wife and children would hold him in the esteem his mother and the world at large accorded his father. His twenty-eight-year-old daughter recently published a biography of her grandfather to rave reviews.

The son of a father who was adored in the family of origin may expect the same adoration in his own family of procreation. Yet as he becomes more involved with his family, he will find that he is not given the status he believed his father had. He may feel disappointed and angry at the "lack of respect" he experiences. It is valuable to remember the old cliché, "No man is a hero in his own community."

Brad is a minister, the son and grandson of ministers. His father is revered as a great teacher and innovator. Brad's early life was punctuated with frequent moves and stories of the admiration, respect, and awe with which "everyone" held his father. Following in the family tradition, Brad went to an excellent college and a highly regarded seminary, where he received his doctorate of divinity.

Deciding against using his father's influence, he and his bride went on a mission, then took a position at a local church in a poorer neighborhood. He has remained with that congregation for fifteen years. Despite his longevity and obvious caring from his parishioners, Brad has always felt like a failure. He feels inferior to most men in influence, fame, and finances. Internally he is constantly competing with his father and losing. He recently stated, "When my father was my age, he had already built the biggest church in Michigan and began consulting with the National Church. . . . We never questioned or thought about money as kids, but my four children go without and unless they get scholarships, the only way they'll be able to go to college is Grandfather."

By virtue of such inner comparisons between the image of the father and the personal reality of the son, the heroic internalization can be particularly problematic. Any such comparisons are destined to leave the son feeling inferior.

My Father the Wimp

At the slightest hint of conflict, some men may cave in to their boss, their friends, their parents, or strangers. However, because of the salience of the home environment for children, and because of their need for balanced male and female energy, it is particularly problematic for sons when a father essentially gives up to his wife's will. Regardless of what goes on in their father's work life, these sons may grow up seeing him as dependent and helpless.

The son of a "henpecked" father often internalizes a sense of a man as servant to women. He will be excessively dependent on a woman's praise or reactions and will end up so fearful of rejection that he will do anything to keep a woman happy.

Marty's father was a quiet, passive fellow. He seemed to live in the home only by permission of his wife. According to Marty, "He was the ultimate servant to Mother's wishes. His goal in life was to get her a cold drink from the fridge before she asked for it. He was like that at work too—he ran around to please the headwaiter, was apologetic to customers, gave up the best stations to others . . . he just would not let anyone get mad at him."

Sensing the lack of male strength in their family of origin, some sons unconsciously take on the responsibility of being "the man of the house." They carry with them a need to fight Dad's battles with Mom, often feeling hurt when she prevails and Dad fails to defend them.

Many sons who were battered as children were stuck in such roles. Nicholas Groth's study of "power rapists"[6] included many men whose boyhood was dominated by an aggressive mother and a passive father. When I met Don, he was twenty-nine and incarcerated for the third time for assault. Despite his record and tough exterior, he responded very well to firm, caring treatment. He came to understand that most of his attacks on men, who were physically much larger than himself, reflected a need for male limit setting and strength. His father was battered by his mother and her sisters. He and his brother were also beaten as children by his mother and neighborhood bullies. Each time he "prayed for my father to save me, but all he ever did was tell me to stay out of her way, or learn how to avoid fights."

A corollary of this is the need by many sons to make their father's life better. This is another form of dependency, because as long as Dad stays ineffective and impotent, the son is trapped in his quest to create a powerful adult male model.

Lee's father was always dedicated to his family and subservient to his wife. When asked what he wanted to do, he would always reply, "Ask your mother." As he was growing up, Lee always evaluated important events in his life by estimating how much he could share it with his father. With his first paycheck he bought two tickets for a Broadway play his father always talked about. His father declined because he was worried about the repercussions of leaving Mother home alone. When his job took him to England, Lee thought long and hard about how he could share his impressions of Europe with his father. Lee's need to make his father's life fulfilling carried over to his marriage. His wife was a woman of very low self-esteem, an avoider, who believed that others always had more right to anything pleasant. Prior to their divorce, Lee "did a song and dance just to try and get her to smile. I would turn myself inside-out to make her happy, and nothing did . . . it was just like being back trying to better Dad's life."

Many men whose internal image of their father is dependent or weak may spend most of their adult life fighting off personal feelings of helplessness or unworthiness. Such men will excessively try to please others as a way of avoiding conflict or, conversely, overcompensate by always being tough, aggressive, and provocative.

Wimp or Superhero? One of the great stories that was told in my neighborhood while I was growing up was the story of Bert and Estelle. Bert was the characteristic "nice guy" who lived with a bitter, complaining, "kvetching" wife. She would constantly berate him in public for minor faults. Of course Bert played along, consistently failing to do things up to some standard. Estelle was fearsome to the neighborhood children as well as to her husband. We would run past her house for fear of her shrill, critical voice. Their own children were cautious, overly polite, and frequently "grounded."

One week a story spread like wildfire among the adults in the neighborhood. As children eavesdropping on our mothers' excited phone conversations, we heard of some "shameful" thing Bert had done to Estelle. Finally their son, my classmate, told the story. Apparently they were coming home from a long shopping trip. The traffic was heavy. It was a hot summer day, and Estelle was very critical of Bert's driving and of his getting them into the traffic jam. Finally he snapped at her, saying it wasn't his fault. Offended by his insolence, she pursued the criticism with extra vehemence. After a few moments the big event occurred. Bert stopped the car in the middle of traffic, shut off the engine, pocketed the key, and left Estelle and the auto right there. A nondriver, she had to get the car towed home. Bert may have been a pariah to our mothers as they discussed his shameful desertion, but to the little boys, and many of the men, in the neighborhood Bert's heroic walk was the equivalent of the exploits of Robin Hood and the Lone Ranger.

Bert was not the only father who impressed his children by uncharacteristically standing up to his wife. Charles recalled the day that he felt that his father

> showed me that I didn't have to turn the other cheek. It was Easter and we were at my [maternal] grandparents' house for Easter dinner. Well, as usual when she got anxious, my mother was really on us kids for getting grass stains up our new clothes. Finally after about an hour he said quietly to her, "Let them alone. They're just being kids. We'll get the grass stains

out when we get home." Somehow that was like gasoline on a fire. She just started in on him in front of everyone. Then he asked her to talk privately in the other room—more gasoline. . . . Finally he just said, in front of everybody *at Easter dinner,* "Shut up, Grace!" You could have heard the silence at the table for what seemed like hours. Later they both apologized to each other and to my grandparents. My grandpa privately told my dad that he said the same thing to her when she was growing up—and it worked.

Protesting in an insulting or harmful way is hardly optimal. It is far better to avoid being so acquiescent that one's partner does not have to be in such absolute control. What a child needs to experience is a strong male presence, firm and fair, a father who can be counted on for safety and limits.

Men are not alone in the oppressed role. Many women find themselves in the position of Bert's or Charles's father. Forced by tradition and socioeconomic forces into subservient roles, they often find that they must be aggressive rather than assertive simply to be heard at all. Many a wife feels the need to "use a two-by-four" just to get her husband's attention.

Oppression and acquiescence will inevitably build to a disquieting confrontation. What is significant here is that the son (or daughter) who internalizes a weak father may have some difficulty learning about setting firm, fair limits as an adult. He may live a life of acquiescence, hoping for the elusive acceptance, punctuated by occasional dramatic rebellious outbursts.

The Secretly Vulnerable Father

Some men present a strong front. They do not appear to be weak or vulnerable. They appear to accept the mantle as the male head of the family. However, their bravado may conceal a fearful, hurt, ineffectual reality. The father who seems like a hero outside but cannot stand up to his wife or set limits for his children at home

may have a son who sees women as dangerous and as hero break-
ers. That son may grow up to become a despot in his marital home.

When the division of responsibility in a home is characterized
by the father being in charge of the outside world and the mother
being the emotional caretaker, she is in a position of great power
in the family. She serves as a translator between the father and his
children. In that role she may control the nature and amount of
information that is transmitted. Often a man's connection with his
children is mediated by his wife's perception and emotional needs.

In many American families the mother serves as an affective
switchboard. All emotional communication between children and
their fathers are directed through her. Not only does this put the
mother in a very powerful and uncomfortable position, but it colors
every emotional message with her perceptions. It also underscores
the notion that when it comes to interpersonal communication,
fathers are just like children. They must be protected from feelings.

In such a home children and mothers unconsciously promote
the illusion of Dad as the titular head of the household, all the
while maintaining a secret alliance in which he is exiled. If a father's power in the home represents form without substance,
what's a little boy to learn about being a man? The young boy who
remains dependent on his mother to understand his father may
develop images of Father that are colored by her anger, frustration,
and needs. He may then grow up with an inadequate sense of
male modes of feeling and parenting, likely to become a distant,
translated father to his own children.

In post-feminist-movement America, sons often are far better
trained to be Mother's companion than are fathers. Growing up in
an era in which sensitivity and verbal skills have been more rewarded than traditional male skills, the son is better able to talk
with and understand his mother and other females. When a son is
drawn into this drama, he may well win Mother, but he will lose a
chance of having a male model of the world, and of the male mode
of feeling. One thing is clear to the son: Adult males are vulnerable
and flawed, at least in the home environment. If a son can defeat

a father and win his mother's affection and confidence, it means that fathers, with their secret vulnerability, are inferior to mothers. The son's male legacy is that when he is a father, he will also be inferior to a woman.

Of course a son who has this experience may also lose out on a sense of his mother as a life-giving source. Instead, lacking a personal sense of male potency, he will perceive her ability to destroy a man. The son may well internalize a sense of women as castrating and dangerous. His more tender sides must then be hidden from her. As an adult he may relate to women only by avoidance or domination. He will disarm her before she can destroy him. This will cause him to put her down or play caretaker to her weakness. Thus the cycle reoccurs in another generation.

An interesting parallel of secret vulnerability may also be observed in some traditionally male-oriented cultures. When I was in Japan, I was struck by what I saw as an interesting counterbalance to the male-dominated Japanese culture. Japanese men were accorded all the rights of the powerful. They decided about all worldly and political matters, they often spent much of their free time with other men or mistresses; they came and went as they pleased. Yet there were three areas in which they typically had little control: The wife was in charge of the home, their money, and the rights to the children. By keeping control of the purse strings, she exercised far more influence than her husband in many personal areas of their lives. Indeed, in traditional families her father had the right to claim his grandchildren as his own children, despite any feelings her husband might have. From my "outsider's" perspective she held a great deal of power, as long as it was not acknowledged.

Masculine Denial. Another way in which fathers are secretly vulnerable results from the unfortunate male trait of avoiding acknowledgment of losses or admitting pain. When fathers fail to come to grips with their aging, loss of physical power, and potency, their sons may learn that male vulnerability must be kept hidden. The message to younger males is that men are not strong enough to recognize or admit failings. It is then natural for sons also to learn to hide frailties and weaknesses, thus promoting a sense that they will also need protection from their feelings.

The Internally Wounded Father

Similar to the secretly vulnerable father is the wounded father. Many men have an internal sense of masculinity that is judgmental, angry, needy, vulnerable, and fearful. A man who cannot love his children enough because he wasn't loved enough is often reacting to his internal wounded father. The feeling of woundedness is a reflection of a deep sense of loss and disconnection and of holding in the pain without access to healing.

According to Dr. Sam Osherson,[7] an internalized wounded father is characterized by three aspects:

1. The son may remember his father as wounded, with father's deep sadness, incompetence, or anger dominating his image of the man.
2. He may also remember the father as wounding. This can evoke the loss and needy feelings the son experienced when he was rejected by, or disappointed, his father.
3. He may internalize distorted and idealized images and memories of his father as he struggles to synthesize his identity as a man.

For sons who saw their fathers as emasculated and weak, a shame of being male often emerges. The son absorbs his father's pain as his own birthright. His role is to be responsible, to serve women, and to be at work.

Will a son with a wounded father feel the guilt or pressure to show his father how to be a man, how to stand up to a woman?

The Angry Father

A recent survey of men indicated that they were most disappointed at how often they expressed anger toward their children compared with how infrequently they expressed love. A corresponding survey of elementary school children indicated that children also wish that their dads were less angry. For many men the anger is directly related to their own internal father.

Men who grew up in homes with distant, judgmental fathers are quite likely to internalize a combination of a low self-image, a sense of failure, and a disparaging outlook toward others. Criticized constantly as boys, they grew up feeling that they would never satisfy their father's expectations. As they grew, they internalized their father's angry, judgmental qualities. What they incorporated into their own psyches, as adults, was a constant personal commentator and critic.

Constantly aware of their fathers' disappointment and disapproval of them and with life in general, they feel insecure and inadequate. They project the opposite. Emulating their critical fathers, these men become critics in their own right. For such men male authorities provide constant reminders of the anger and violence that lurks just below the surface. The authorities are reacted to as surrogate fathers. Instead of their boyish experience of fear they felt around their own fathers, however, the emotion experienced is instantaneously transformed into anger—a safer, more protected emotion.

Woody was perceived as brooding, moody, and easily provoked to wrath with his children. When asked about his own childhood, he initially responded that it was "fine, you know average." After some thinking, he added, "I guess it was a pretty angry place. My dad would bristle at my mom and us kids. He was like a powder keg, and anything—mostly my oldest brother—could set him off. It wasn't that he criticized us so much . . . it was just that he took it all in and then exploded. . . . Mom used to excuse him because 'his work was so hard,' but I never got to know his softer side. Even now he's weak and frail. He still makes like he can do everything himself and gets frustrated when he can't. . . . You know, he sounds a lot like me."

Internalized Anger. A father's anger may also be turned inward against himself. When a man takes out his anger on himself instead of directing it toward others, he becomes depressed. Many men, such as Bryce, had fathers who were withdrawn and unhappy. "Even as a young child, I knew how angry my father was inside. I guess it was intuition, because he never expressed an angry word. Mostly he just sat around and seemed depressed. He hated the marriage situation with my mother, especially with his mother-in-law, who moved in shortly after they were married. When he talked to me, which was rare, he would talk like an indentured servant, tied to a job and a life that sucked the juice from his body. All he did was work . . . two jobs. . . . He was unwelcome at home. My mother and grandmother were inseparable. I know that my mother suffered also. She was kept in line by her guilt."

When a son intuits his father's hidden anger at exile and a life of work with few rewards, he learns early to be angry, too, and to develop a hard, protective shell. As a father himself he fears dropping the shield for two reasons: (1) he may be injured and become depressed like his father; (2) the rage that has collected from his father's life and his own will spew forth and be harmful to his loved ones.

This is one of the reasons that Robert Bly gives for his powerful proposition that the way to male feeling is through grief—grief for his father's exile and grief for his own.

Whatever the nature of a father's life (and grief), a son honors his father by emulating him. What better way than to carry my father's emotional life inside me? If my father is hurt and angry at being exiled from the home, I will unconsciously carry some of that hurt, anger, and fear of my own exile. Unfortunately, as much as it protects me from hurt, it also predisposes me to take it on as my own and to become just like him.

Consider the poetic example provided by Harry Chapin in his song "Cat's in the Cradle":

My son turned ten just the other day.
He said thanks for the ball, Dad
Come on, let's play.
Can you teach me to throw?

I said, "Not today.
I got a lot to do."
He said, "That's okay."
He walked away, but his smile never dimmed, he said,
"I'm gonna be like him, yeah. You know I'm gonna be like
    him."

MEN'S STRUGGLE TO SEPARATE FROM FATHER

As indicated earlier, a boy's task is to separate from his mother and identify with his father. Identification with his father or other male figures is necessary, but insufficient for him to take his place as an adult male in our culture. If he is to take his own place in the world as a man and father himself, he also needs to separate from his father and family of origin in order to form a new family of procreation. He must become independent enough from his parents to have his own adult life. This separation from one's real parents is normally progressive over years of effort by both parties.

Leaving home is difficult for both parents and children. Separating from the internalized images of our parents is far more complex for a number of reasons: We cannot get help from our parents; we carry the dilemma around inside, rendering geographical distance fruitless; we are unaware of the depth and breadth of the influence of the unconscious internal images. Yet to become fully functioning man and father, a son must separate both from his real father and from the internal father he carries with him. Only after a man gains some understanding of, and independence from, his internalized father may he reconcile with his real father.

Fathers and Sons: Separate and Together

A host of factors makes the father-son relationship particularly problematic. The struggle by which they connect and separate tends to push them apart.

At the time of each major separation-individuation stage, the relationship between father and son is likely to change for social, cultural, and emotional reasons. Each transition provides an opportunity for the rift between them to grow.

Early Separation-Individuation. At the earliest stages of a boy's life, at least until he is verbal and mobile, he is most connected to the primary caretaker, normally a woman. As the son begins to individuate from her (at eighteen to thirty-six months) he becomes more involved and connected to his father or substitute attachment figures. During the preschool years this attachment develops a competitive quality. The son tries to challenge the father as well as to continue developing a nurturing relationship. This stage (named the Oedipal stage by Freud) frequently becomes a prototype for later competitive peer-group relationships during a boy's school years. It provides a mild indication of the difficult father-son interaction during the boy's adolescence, the tension created as the son individuates from the father and prepares to leave home to go out on his own.

Adolescence. Adolescence is difficult under the best of circumstances. Powerful changes occur in the family structure. Sons need to reject parental values in order to establish their own. Issues of independence and sexuality often challenge parental standards.

For fathers and sons adolescence is often especially problematic. Sam Osherson describes the tension between father and son in modern culture as "impossible." Symbolically the struggle often takes on mythic proportions. When the son is old enough to leave the father's care, he assumes the responsibilities and rights of a man. Being younger, less concerned with traditional values, and motivated to make his own mark on the world, the son stands as a major challenge to the father in at least three ways: (1) he is the rejector of what the father has accomplished; (2) he will replace the father in the world of men; and (3) his emergence as an independent man is a powerful symbolic reminder of the father's mortality.

Having to face and grieve rejection and exile throughout their lives, it is no surprise that fathers might not welcome the challenge from their adolescent sons. Often they will actively resist the occasion of their replacement, seeking to eliminate the threat, delay the inevitable, and avoid the conflict. A father may do this by criticism, creation of roadblocks, withdrawal, or by using his experience and guile to defeat the challenge for as long as he can.

Separation and Reconciliation

Robert Bly reminds us that this conflict has always been so. However, he notes that modern societies have been able to rely less adequately on rituals to ease the processs. In less-industrialized societies there were institutions and initiations that supported the transition of adolescent males coming of age. In tribal cultures, male elders, other than the father, directed the adolescent's initiation. It was presumed that the paternal relationship was so complex that the father was not generally involved. Rather a reconciliation was encouraged following the initiation process. The reconciliation was imperative because it was assumed that a son needed to keep his father's love.

Modern institutions such as schools, sports teams, the military, and entry-level jobs prescribe certain initiations today. The adolescent survives the ordeal of basic training in order to become a man. Unfortunately these modern initiation rights do not include a reconnection with the father. Instead as the young man begins to take his place in the adult world, he becomes increasingly distant from the source of that love.

Today a son makes his mark in the world of work by his own deeds. Independence, achievement, and competitiveness are all honored traits for young men in our culture. None of these coincides with reuniting with one's father. Indeed it is just the opposite. The role of the young man is to replace the old, "to put them out to pasture." These traits also encourage an avoidance of a man's inner life, where his feelings of loss, sadness, and need for his father's love reside.

Thus a young man may carry around a competitive or aggressive feeling toward his father and men of his father's generation for many years. His business success usually entails replacing these older men, defeating them to achieve the rewards society gives to successful males. They may also compete for females. With the increasing frequency of divorce, more older men are remarrying younger women, in a sense competing, with their wealth, experience, and acumen, against the younger males.

When a young man is in the throes of such a rivalry, there is little room for him to experience his own or his father's inner pain during the conflict. To feel the older man's hurt and fear of rejection makes the young more compassionate and less of a soldier. To show concern for your enemy in combat is to be personally vulnerable. Thus in modern society there are many forces pulling for a detachment and objectification between generations of men. The internal needs for love, understanding, and mentorship are suppressed in the service of winning the competition. Thus the desire for reunification with Father is undermined by more common social values. Of course both fathers and sons suffer psychological losses at these times. Male socialization to ignore or suppress such feelings is quite strong. It usually takes other events or internal pain to overcome the pattern.

Separation from Father, Separation from Self

In the struggle and aftermath of separating from Father, men become distanced from the texture of their own inner life. To do otherwise would force them to face their own sense of loss, isolation, aloneness, and emotional pain. Many men compensate by repressing most of their vulnerable feelings. Knowing little of their actual father's inner life and suppressing their own, their internal image of what it means to be a father is to be distant and judgmental, detached from their fathers and disconnected from their own selves.

It seems logical that a man with a remote, mysterious, puzzling, foreboding internal representation of Father will unknowingly replicate with his children the lessons from his own fathering, the opposite of what he desires.

To avoid this legacy, a man must gain some insight into his internal father, understand the unconscious tendencies that emanate from this internalization, and face how he wants to be different. He needs to discover what his internal father is like and to make peace with him. Before turning to the issue of reconciliation, here are some hints for finding your internalized father.

ADVICE FOR FINDING THE INNER FATHER

To find my inner father, I must explore three interconnected path-ways: my actual father's experience of his life; how I internalized him as a child; and how he is represented in me as an adult. This is no easy task. We have to ask hard questions that don't have ready answers. My motivations as an adult may be quite elusive when I try to pin down their origins. Consider how the problems we experienced as children unconsciously emerge in our relationships and in the way we parent our children.

Did you grow up in a home with an alcoholic father who was prone to rages and violence when he was drunk? What images of your terror as a child remain with you as an adult? How does it impact on how you relate to your wife and children? Do you avoid anger at all cost to avoid being like your father? Do you find the same anger coming out of you when you are frustrated by your own children?

Because each of us is different, the following ten hints are dominated by questions rather than suggested answers. You will need to look within and find the answers that are true for you. There may be clues from your "natural tendencies" or from your automatic reactions to certain situations. Sometimes your dreams or yearnings provide clues to your hidden past. Sometimes your father's values or clichés will provide valuable information. Whatever forms it will take, discovery will involve taking a personal inventory and taking the time to recall your past.

1. Begin with your own father and grandfathers. Try to get to know what their lives were like both with and without you. What are your earliest memories of your father and grandfather? What emotions accompany your early memories? When you recall your childhood with your father, do you feel sad? Scared? Loving? Are there gaps in your memories? Perhaps you could get help from others to fill in the gaps. Many men find a complex array of emotions when they remember their fathers: frustration, sadness, love, hurt, and so forth.

2. Think about how your father expressed his masculinity. Where didn't he? Was he primarily concerned with safety and security? Was his life dominated by a search for freedom? Did he consider himself a workhorse? Did he always have to put on a strong face? Did he think of himself as special in some ways? Do you agree with his assessment? Was his maleness expressed sexually? How do you express your masculinity? How similar or different is it than his?

3. Consider his relationship with women. How similar or different is it to your own? What do you remember about how he and your mother interacted? What feelings did you have when (if) they were close and loving? When they were arguing? In what ways are your current relationships similar to your parents' relationship? In what ways do your romantic relationships replicate your relationship with your father when you were young? Where are the areas of your adult intimacy in which you feel blocked? How might these relate to your fathering?

4. If you see him as a caricature of omnipotence, infallibility, weakness, woundedness, and so on, consider what impact it has on you to view him that way. How might

that vision of him serve you psychologically? How might it restrict you? Consider completing the sentence "If I didn't view him the way I do, I'd have to face _____."

5. What grieving do you need to do for his life and for your own childlike sense of loss for not having had the father you wanted? If your father suffered a sense of exile from the home and from you, what was his pain at those losses? What suffering did he have because of distance from his own father? What was it like for him to be incapable of changing his interactions with you? Robert Bly believes that grieving our fathers' lives is a prerequisite to confronting our own grief as men.

6. If he is alive, try to make a meaningful contact with him, alone, away from others. *It is imperative that you, as the son, recognize that any change must come from you. After all, it is the son who has the internalized image of his father.* Reconnection and reconciliation with father is the topic of Chapter 9.

7. Persevere at point 6. Your early attempts will probably not be very fruitful.

8. Consider what kind of father you want to be. How is that different from how you are? Subconscious identification with, and internal images of, your own father may represent much of the difference. As a therapist I can say with assurance that men who try to do everything exactly opposite to their father have a frightening tendency to be similar. For example, when you find yourself holding in frustration to avoid expressing anger the way he did, you may well end up being very short or distant with your children, and they may feel as frightened of you as you did of him.

9. Consider what kind of husband and friend you desire to be. How is that different from how you are? The unconscious identification with your father may represent much of that difference as well. How do your childhood fears unconsciously dominate your present friendships?

Do you keep more distant than you would like? Are you
overly dependent?

10. Whether or not clear answers emerge from these considerations, the questioning itself and self-exploration may
well promote positive personal growth.

*Above all, do this self-exploration alone or with an older expe-
rienced professional male therapist.*[8] Trying to explore yourself
with your spouse or other loved ones will be less effective. Their
own unconscious needs for you to be a certain way will interrupt
your process. Your loved ones are accustomed to you the way you
have been. They may resist or complicate your efforts.

Once you are becoming more aware of your personal inner
journey, it is important to share the new perceptions and desired
new behaviors with your loved ones. Your personal exploration portends changes in the way you live. Changes you make in yourself
affect those around you. They will have to adapt to your metamor-
phosis. It may require a lot of time to discuss these personal
changes.

Remember that self-generated changes are naturally more ap-
pealing than reacting to change that begins in another person.

9

REUNION AND RECONCILIATION

"All I ever wanted was a father like you [Peter Pan]."

—from the death scene in
Steven Spielberg's film *Hook*

Whatever the nature of my real and internal father, I need to separate from each to become a mature man and effective father myself. In the course of that separation I will feel the loss of my daddy, my connection to some forms of maleness and to some of my heritage and personal grounding.

For some time between my adolescence and my finding a life partner, during which I may be embarking on my career or laying the groundwork for my future, I may not notice or be deterred by these deficits. I may truly overlook my father, his values, and his influence. I may define myself by being not him. It is possible that I will experience considerable worldly success without paying much heed to my actual or internal father.

However, for me to be successful in a long-term intimate relationship, and to be a good father myself, I will need to reconnect with my father and what he represents for me. It is through him, and my internal image of him, that I may pick up the missing threads of my heritage, my masculinity, and my emotional birthright. With a fuller awareness of my history and my fathering, I will be more aware of what it is I offer my future partner or children. To be the kind of man, partner, and father I want to be, I need to better understand who I am inside, and the path to that awareness runs right through my father's house.

REUNION

It is never easy to reconnect with parents. When adult children return home, they often find themselves feeling like children again. The normal tendency in families is to reestablish the former interactions and forms of communication. As James wrote in his journal, "Whenever I go home, it's okay for about two or three days. Then things begin to change. My parents start to pick the same fights we had when I was a teenager, and I fall right into the rebelling, obnoxious adolescent role. It's almost like we don't know how to be with each other as adults, so we revert to parent and child. It's like a trap that's automatically sprung, one I fall for every time."

The older methods of communication may be irritating, but they are predictable. Most families opt for the familiar pain rather than face the fear of the unknown. It is within this context that a man will have to find his way to his father. It may take some perseverance and creativity. Even when our fathers are still alive, they may not be easily accessible.

In modern society, family members often live in distant locales. Conversations are limited to visits that are characterized by short periods of intense proximity, or phone calls over the distances, neither one an optimal situation for sensitive communication. Even with proximity many men, such as Ron, describe their fathers as "nontalkers." Steve says his mother "won't let Dad get a word in edgewise." Many of us can identify with the following phone conversation:

FATHER: [*answering telephone*] Hello?
SON: Hi, Dad. How are you?

FATHER: Fine, wait I'll get your mother.

SON: No, wait. I want to talk to you.

FATHER: She's on her way. Hang on.

SON: Dad, I want to talk with *you*.

FATHER: You need money?

SON: No. Things are good. I've been thinking about you and wanted to talk.

FATHER: You been drinking? Oh, here's Mother.

As his mother got on the phone and began chatting comfortably, the son wondered why he even tried to get through to his father.

Lee's father told him, "I don't want to talk long. Your mother's asleep and she'll be real mad if she knows she missed your call."

After years of being in the verbal background, feeling unsure of their ability to communicate, or fearful of reopening a wound, our fathers are not always ready for serious conversation. Even when the situation is face-to-face, it can be difficult. Whit waited months for his father to visit. He arranged for them to spend a whole day alone. Nonetheless the experience was tense. "I was alone with my father yesterday. The whole time I wanted to talk to him, make connection, hear about how he felt about me, talk about all that's happened between us but . . . we just drove in silence for hours. The first time I started to broach the subject in a restaurant, he got up and went to the john. I think I said about 5 percent of what I needed to say. Disappointing . . . but . . . a start."

When Does a Man Seek Reconnection?

There is no specific time line for going back to your roots. For most men other family events instigate the need. My intensified desire to reconnect may be precipitated by my father's illness or death, or his sudden reappearance in my life after many years of absence. Often the need arises from inside: when I suffer personal losses, when I become a father myself, or during the mid-life years.

Relationship Failures. Rob is like a legion of men who "never made a real decision in my life until I got divorced from Sandra. Before that it was which job, which college, which major—choices between two or more attractive options. Divorce was yes or no. . . . I was devastated by the sense of rejection I felt when it was over. I felt like a little kid who had made some huge blunder and I was waiting for the inevitable exile."

After being in the postdivorce dating world for about a year he realized, "I keep being in the same relationship, over and over. I keep getting to the point where I know there should be something more, but I don't know what it is."

At times like these some men find their way to their fathers, father substitutes, or therapists. Seeking a mentor, they begin an internal journey of discovery. Often what they discover is incomplete is their relationship with their father. Sometimes each failed relationship mimics the lost relationship with Dad.

Becoming a Father. When a man becomes a father for the first time, he is naturally prone to consider what it was like for his own father and to be drawn closer to him by their shared experience of fatherhood. Reflecting on the imminent birth of his daughter, Louis thought out loud: "I wonder how it was for Dad when I came into the world. Was he as proud? As scared? Did he feel so responsible? He never told me what it was like for him. Maybe it was just another thing he took in stride, and just handed out the cigars. I want to ask him all those questions, but I just don't know if I'll embarrass him or he won't answer, or whether he'll just have the same reactions as Ma."

When his own child is born, the new father is replaced as the youngest generation; he shares with his father the experience of being pushed back a generation; he feels his own mortality. He also feels the intense love and pride of a father and wants to share it with the man, who, he hopes, felt that way when he was born.

The Mid-life Crisis. During the mid-life years men must face the limits of their careers, their relationships, and their mortality. As they begin to accept their losses and the ceiling on their potential accomplishments, they are naturally thrust into an examination of their inner lives as well. As Tyrone speculated,

> I always figured that I just didn't have many feelings. I was just like my father and all the other men I knew, except for sissies and [gays]. My wife kept telling me I was a rock. I never knew what all the fuss was about caring for the aged, etc. . . . Then about thirty-nine or forty it began to change. I saw how my advancement cost Reggie his, and I felt something for him and his family. Then, when my sister got sick back East, I just had to go see her and prayed (hadn't done that since I was a kid) for her . . . she's okay. Anyhow, on that plane back from Philly I was thinking that I would die, too, and what have I really accomplished in my life. Sports, good money, a couple of friends, two kids I don't really know. So I get off the plane, and my son is at the airport and runs up and hugs me and I start bawling right there. I guess I don't know what it's all about, and for some reason . . . now that matters. I want to be different for my boy.

When men reach this stage, and allow themselves to feel the lost connection with their own fathers, the subject often brings tears to their eyes. When Teddy began talking about his father in a group of men, he had to leave the room to compose himself before he could continue. Lee said that the most crucial moment in his personal psychotherapy was when he could mourn the loss of his grandfather twenty years previously. Howard described his fifty-year hope that his aging father would ever tell him "I love you." He confessed that he had not said those words to his father either.

Connection and Introspection

No matter when I become aware of the need to reconnect to my feelings and my past, the primary goal is learning about myself. As I become increasingly aware of my own needs and automatic (unconscious based) predilections, it becomes increasingly important to better understand my relationship with my father. Ultimately as I get to know him better, I will also have to face the images of fathering I internalized as a child. I must gain a fuller conscious comprehension of how the vision I carry of my own father often impacts on my relationships with significant others, with my self-esteem, and with my real father. Only when it becomes conscious may I face the internalized images, square them with objective realities, and alter the antiquated programming to suit me better as an adult.

Father and Child Reunion

The single largest step a man can take to confront and heal from the dysfunctional aspects of his relationship with his father is to initiate one-to-one contact. There may be some preliminary psychological steps for a man to build up to that one. For example, he may well have to face his own fears, anger, and confusion about his father. He may also need to carefully prioritize his goals and plan his method of approach.

Many men have lost touch with their fathers over the years, and even though they feel the hunger for their lost father, they are reticent to make the move. Many men feel that their father should be the one who makes the move rather than themselves. In a fair world that might be so. Unfortunately waiting for our fathers to fix the rift is fruitless. All the evidence points in a single direction: *It is the son's job to initiate the process of reconciliation. It is especially salient for sons as they become fathers.* Most of the time long silences are not easily broken. The son (or daughter) who wishes to reconnect with a father may need perseverance as well as courage.

Your father, fearing upset in his life or a larger rift, may dodge your attempts to be closer. He may be uncomfortable feeling that close to a child or to another man. He might not have the skills for a closer connection. Perhaps he is unconsciously angry at your desertion of him when you left home. Perhaps he fears renewed closeness that will be followed by another rejection. Perhaps an adult-to-adult connection will burst his own illusions of how he was as a father when you were a child, forcing him to take a personal psychological inventory. Finally, he might fear completion of the relationship with you as the symbolic equivalent to finishing his work on earth. At an unconscious level reunion may bring forth the specter of his own demise.

On the other hand, your father has much to gain from a reunion. He may regain his feelings of closeness with his child. He may be able to see himself in you and take pride in the person you've become. He might get closer to your children. He may feel loved and respected as he did when, as a youngster, you would race toward him calling "Daddy" with delight.

RECONCILIATION

In the previous two chapters recommendations were provided to get to know both your actual father and your internal father. That knowledge is necessary for self-awareness, but insufficient to grow fully as an independent father yourself. To do that, you also need to reconcile with your father. If you are to grow fully into your role as a father, you need to make peace with both your natural father and your unconscious, internal father images. How do you reconcile with your own father?

How do you learn to face feelings about your own father, recognize what you love about him, accept those things you don't like, and forgive him for being who he was?

Reconciling with Your Natural Father

My father's name was John Kinsella. It's an Irish name. He was born in North Dakota in 1896 and never saw a big city until he came back from France in 1918.

He settled in Chicago, where he quickly learned to live and die with the White Sox: died a little when they lost the 1919 World Series; died a lot the following summer when eight members of the team were accused of throwing that series.

He played in the minors for a year or two, but nothing came of it. Moved to Brooklyn in '35, met Mom in '38, and was already an old man working at the naval yards when I was born in '42.

My name's Ray Kinsella. Mom died when I was three and I suppose Dad did the best he could. Instead of Mother Goose, I was put to bed with stories of Babe Ruth, Lou Gehrig, and the great Shoeless Joe Jackson. Dad was a Yankee fan, so of course I rooted for Brooklyn. But in '58 the Dodgers moved away, so we had to find other things to fight about. We did, and when it came time to go to college, I picked the farthest one from home I could find. This, of course, drove him right up the wall which, I suppose, was the point.[1]

In *Field of Dreams,* a remarkable film that explores many facets of the father-son relationship, Ray and his father reconcile when Ray reaches out to his father after the latter's death. He is able to honor those things that his father valued, recognize his limitations, and in so doing meet him as a person rather than an image.

Bryan, a sixty-two-year-old man, recalled with pain, "My father never told me he loved me. Toward the end of his life I wanted to tell him how important it was to hear it from him, but the closest I ever got was to tell him I loved him, hoping he would respond in kind, but he died first."

Kenneth was still angry at his father thirty years after his death. "He wasn't there when I needed him. He never protected me from her. He just left the house every day and I was the one who had to live with her tyranny. She was his wife. I was only a kid. I couldn't control my mother. He really let me down. . . . When he died, I was surprised at how sad I felt."

Each of these men was limited to an internal psychological reconciliation. Their actual fathers died before they could try to work it out. Dick had a quite different experience. After his mother passed away, his father made a cross-country train trip to visit him in California. Dick's hope was that they would finally have the opportunity to work out the rift that began in his adolescence. His initial verbal efforts seemed to fall on deaf ears. Then one day he took his father to his workplace with him.

He kept saying that he didn't want to get in the way, but I just told him to do what he wanted. When we got there, there was chaos. A major report was due, the copier was down, and the copy shop across the street couldn't get the project done in time. Somehow I resisted my usual M.O. (which is to take over), and I asked my dad what he would do. He started out by protesting, then he seemed to brighten and asked if he could take the copier apart. Well, he had it up and running enough for the critical job in less than an hour. You should have seen him . . . black toner on his shirt cuff and cheek, and a smile like a kid in a candy factory. At lunch I told him how much he helped me out, and he spontaneously started to tell me stories about how I was as a kid, his joys at helping me out, his pain when I left home. . . . I told him how I needed to be out on my own so I could live up to my image of him, not so I would reject him. . . . We both cried when he got back on the train to go home. I call more often now, and he calls me too. Last week he called and asked for my help . . . made me feel like a million bucks.

It isn't often easy to square long-term disputes and silences.

Richard had always felt close to his father, but he still found it difficult to tell him some things. He discussed what he wanted to say for six months in therapy prior to a visit back to his parents' house in Indiana. He always knew his father loved him, but had never actually told his father how he felt as an adult. He was in Indiana for a week. On the sixth day he and his father went for a walk on their small family farm. Richard reported, "We walked and talked. I wanted to say 'Dad, I love you.' He knew it I'm sure."

THERAPIST: So you never actually said it.

RICHARD: No, but he knew.

THERAPIST: What stopped you from saying those words?

RICHARD: I don't know exactly. I was anxious, afraid that I was wrong all these years.

THERAPIST: Afraid he wouldn't reciprocate.

RICHARD: More or less. I will tell him. It's important.

THERAPIST: How old is your father?

RICHARD: Eighty-six.

THERAPIST: So how old will he be when you tell him?

RICHARD: [*grinning*] Okay. You made your point. I'll do it this weekend.

The next session he came in and reported, "Well, I did it. I told him. . . . He got choked up like I thought he would. . . . He said it's the most important thing he ever heard . . . that he feels that his life was worth something . . . then he told me that I was the best thing that ever happened to him. We both cried on the phone a bit, and then he told me about the crops. I'm glad I did it. Mandy, my wife, said she was proud of me. She really loves him too. He's been much more of a father to her than her own father."

As Richard described, not only is it difficult to talk intimately with a person of few words, but there is also a fear for the son of discovering what his father feels about him.

Personally my reconciliation with my father has come gradually over the years. I was not an easy son to father. I have always pushed against conventions and "rules." I chose a profession that is impossible to describe effectively. I have lived six thousand miles away for most of my adult life. I married twice. My female partners were not of the faith or background that he would have preferred. In my thirties my connection with my father became particularly salient as I began to know myself better and as I struggled with personal losses.

As I took each step, he has responded. Among the steps was a letter of thanks in which I enumerated the positive things I got. Even though he projected some criticism into it, he replied. We then talked about some of the negatives. I followed this with new physical closeness—hugs and a kiss on the cheek when we met. He was uncomfortable at first, but didn't shy away. I asked him to be the best man at my wedding. He accepted. I initiated talks about becoming a father and my concerns. He shared a few of his memories. I shared my children with him; he loved them as a grandfather.

My father has been ill for a long time. In addition to numerous heart problems, he recently had a stroke. While he was recuperating at a nursing home, only one question was important to him. He wanted to know if he had been a good father to my sister and myself. Thankful that I had worked through so much of the childhood fears, angers, and disappointments, I could honestly and enthusiastically answer affirmatively. In return he was able to tell me that he loved me and was proud of me; the message for which I had yearned since boyhood.

I feel lucky. My father responded fairly readily to my efforts. Not everyone is so fortunate. Like most sons, I was harboring some anger and fear along with my love. I may have felt that my father didn't understand me, that he questioned my judgment, that he had different values, or that he insufficiently stood up for me the way I wished, but I never questioned that he loved me. I truly didn't expect him to reject my efforts at reunion or reconciliation.

If your relationship with your father is more problematic, you will have to overcome more fear, anger, and resentment of your father and of his treatment of you. You will need to carefully detail for yourself what your anger, fears, and resentments are. You will have to determine which are the most important to share with him and how you might relate these. Most of all you will have to develop a sense of what he could do at this point to make it right. What do you want from him? Finally, you will have to be able to accept him for who he is and forgive him for his failures and inabilities. What will be enough? Is it understanding of his life? Is it an apology? Is it a promise of something better in the future? Or is it an agreement to stay apart recognizing irreconcilable differences?

No matter what the outcome of your attempt at reconciliation, for your personal psychological good you will want to be able to know in your own heart that you made the best effort you could.

Reconciling with the Internal Father

Making peace with my actual father may be the beginning or the culmination of internal psychological work. To begin the process I need to accept that there are big parts of my father in me. I need to acknowledge that these parts play no small role in who I am.

I will become increasingly aware of my unconscious needs that I expect my partner to fulfill and my resentment of her when she unknowingly fails to do so.

As I become more aware of what parts of him I own, I must face the pain of what I wanted as a child and never got, at least in sufficient quantities. I must also face the pain of recognizing what I get and give to my own children. I will progressively feel more vulnerable to, and responsible for, everyday events in my important relationships.

Most of all I will have to face my fears of abandonment and rejection as a child and my susceptibility to these feelings as an adult. Often I will have built an extensive system of protection against potential rejection. To gain freedom and connection, I will have to face the loss of security. Dismantling that psychological fortress will make me more subject to pain and hurt, and much more alive and free in my relationships with my partner, my children, and my friends.

For most of us help from a guide, mentor, or psychotherapist makes this internal journey go faster and more effectively. To choose the struggle and face the fear of the unknown is an arduous journey. The alternative is to unknowingly replicate our own hurts upon our children—an unfair, unreasonable, and ungrowthful enterprise.

How do we gain the courage to approach and reconcile? How

a son unravel his lifelong male training that requires an immutably strong front? How do we reverse the automatic unconscious internal shift that instantaneously makes anger out of fear? It isn't easy. I wish I had some facile, "one size fits all" advice. Having been a psychotherapist for a quarter of a century makes me believe that each person must find his own path.

There are some commonalities. I know that it involves facing the fears of the unknown. I know it involves accepting ourselves for who we are instead of who we think we should be. I know it involves recognizing our personal loneliness and feeling the sadness that brings. I believe it also means accepting our mortality, and once we do, endeavoring to spend what time we have in the best way we can.

For my understanding, the only antidote to mortality is intimacy: with myself, with my partner and family, and with humankind. Intimacy requires that I understand my personal boundaries and limitations and be willing to stretch myself and face the fears of being close with others, particularly my partner and family.

This isn't easy. One way of knowing that we are on the right track is that it feels scary. One of my clients once said of his personal attempts to forgive his father, "I was so anxious, I knew I must be doing something right."

There is one final point. Although the heart of reconciliation requires forgiving my father, it does not mean forgetting. Quite the contrary. I need to remember. I also need to understand that he probably did the best fathering he could under the circumstances. When I forgive, I must face a frightening reality. The only person I can blame for my own future difficulties is me. Blaming others inhibits the ability to face ourselves. When I forgive my father, I must forgive myself for my past behaviors and take charge of my own present and future; a daunting endeavor. After all, I am the only one I will ever be able to change.

In a sense it is a choice to live fully, growing through challenges as long as we're alive. We'll be dead for a long time, there's no sense acting that way during the short time that we're alive.

GUIDELINES FOR RECONCILIATION
WITH YOUR FATHER

If your father is still alive and available:

1. Make the effort to talk with him. It won't be easy. There may be a tradition of noncommunication or communication through a third party, such as Mother. He will be reticent to just be open—as will you. As unfair as it seems, it is the son who must make the first (and probably second, third, and fourth) attempts.
2. Carefully choose the setting to maximize your likelihood of success. For many men it is often best to get him to do something with you. Randy, for example, asked his dad to help him refinish the basement. Sandy asked his dad for advice on installing a new computer system at home. Russ spent a week helping his father repair fences at the family farm. While you are working on a mutual task with your gaze on some object, talking can begin.
3. Prior to any conversation, think through carefully and prioritize what you most want to know about his life, feelings, and thoughts.
4. Know in advance what you want to say to him. Do you want to express anger, hurt, sadness, love? How can you say it so that you maximize your opportunity of being heard? Keep it simple!
5. Be certain of your own motives and needs. Take the time to discover and vent any anger prior to confrontation with your father. Before you are ready to work directly at altering your relationship with your father, you need to be clear on your goals. These can be muddied by a reservoir of stored-up hurt and anger. One method of gaining perspective on these is individual or family psychotherapy that focuses on recalling and resolving long-buried con-

flicts that remain indirect influences on current living. The unique advantage of therapy is that it provides a safe environment for men to become more comfortable with their feelings and prepares them for a constructive approach with their actual father.

6. Try to diminish any requirement you have for a particular (or any) response from him. If you have your hopes pinned on your father's immediately "seeing the light" and asking for forgiveness, you may well be disappointed. Similarly if you are certain that he will dismiss you, criticize you, or put you down as he has in the past, you may be surprised. Be clear on what you want to do and say and be prepared to have the chips fall where they do. One particular danger is to expect him to be your daddy and take care of you during this time. If you are approaching him man to man, you must not expect that he will help you out as a father might help out a son. Not only is that unlikely, but in fact the reverse may be closer to reality.

7. Recognize his limitations. Try to understand that he was also a man with limited resources struggling with these roles himself. Rather than being all-knowing and omnipotent, he probably used his emotional and intellectual resources as well as he could. His way of parenting was only his way, not the best way to be a father, nor the way he would have done it if he had another chance.

8. Don't delay.

If your father is already gone:

Reconciling a relationship when the other person is unavailable is somewhat more problematic than when he is alive and present. However, in either situation most of the work primarily requires internal psychological changes. If your father is dead or otherwise unreachable, you may still benefit from the process of searching and reconciling.

1. Find out as much about his life and motivations as possible. Your relatives, old neighbors, or former co-workers of your father may all be excellent sources of information. Old photos, family stories, or the family Bible might also be rich sources of information.
2. Imagine that he is alive and present. What would you like to say to him? What would you like to learn from him?
3. Tell your image of your father what hurts you have, what angers, and what sadnesses about him. Tell him of the losses you suffered for lack of sufficient fathering.
4. Write down a list of traits you have that reflect his positive and negative traits. What was your inheritance in skills, appearance, habits, and relationships?
5. Make a list of what you would like from him now if he could or would give them to you.
6. Think of some ways that you could give those things to yourself or get them from others who are available.
7. Consider getting help from a professional. An experienced older male therapist might be particularly helpful in evoking, and helping you work with, those important feelings and perceptions.
8. Make forgiveness your long-term goal. It is not appropriate or possible intentionally to forget what has occurred in the past. It is important for your ability to rise above the hurts of your past that ultimately you let go of a need to change your father. If possible, try to forgive him for his inadequacies and fully examine your own life without passing the negatives on to your children.

The task may seem formidable. Many men have succeeded before you. The chapter closes with a few examples.

SUCCESSFUL RECONCILIATIONS

A successful reconciliation with your father will result in a shift in your personal feelings. It may also alter the way he relates to you, but that is far less important. You should feel more complete with him, more understanding of his life, more accepting of your own, and less resentful, fearful, or angry. The other results that normally accompany a successful reconciliation are a greater ability to be close with your partner and children, a better understanding of, and love of, being male and of other men, and a sense of having more balance in your life. Some men also report a greater comfort with their own frailties and losses, and more confidence in their personal ability to "make a difference."

When Ralph felt freed enough from his anger at past actions of his father, he was eager to test the possibilities of an adult relationship with him. As an initial step he chose a safe vehicle for time together, asking for help to remodel his basement. In the course of this "productive" time, his father slipped out with a term of endearment, calling him Dolly, a name he had not used since Ralph was a toddler. That one word of affection initiated a transformation in their relationship, because it altered Ralph's basic assumption about how his father felt about him. Over the next several months their relationship changed for the better.

Of course establishing or reestablishing contact on an intimate basis with your father may not be possible or this easy. Moreover, such contact is not usually magically healing. Normally when it's successful, it initiates a slow process that may have only limited potential for change in the real relationship, yet great potential for change in the internalized relationship.

Neil tried to reconcile with the father who virtually abandoned the family after he and Neil's mother were divorced. It took several months for Neil to work up the courage to ask his father to play golf with him. Golfing with his father had been one of the few positive memories he'd retained. The event took place with symbolic perfection on Father's Day and went without a hitch, except for the fact that it was utterly boring. They had little in common, and the man's father was just as narrow-minded in later life as he had been before. The tangible outcome was a decision to maintain occasional contact to keep the relationship alive, but the more important result was a feeling of being unburdened from the years of anger, guilt, disappointment, and feeling cheated that came as baggage with the abandonment by his father. Having the opportunity to discover and express the painful feelings connected with his father was more important than changing the relationship in this case, because it was essentially all that was possible.

Clint was only eleven when his father was killed. The family was left with debts, no immediate source of income, and only a small farm to live on and survive from. Despite knowing that his father was not at fault for dying, Clint harbored resentment and anger toward his father and most older men. When he became engaged to his college sweetheart, his mother insisted that he return to Iowa for a visit. While he was there, she took out all of his father's belongings and told him stories about each one. Later he visited his uncle to ask about his father's boyhood. When he understood better how hard a life his father had endured, his feelings mellowed. He said, "Much to my surprise, I actually felt proud when the store lady told me I was the spittin' image of my dad. I never before had thought of what his life was like. . . . How we were alike, and how strong he was. Until then, I only thought of Mother's strength of character."

Randall's mother divorced his father when he was just a little boy. He visited his father occasionally while he was growing, but "never liked him much. He seemed so aloof and distant, not like my stepdad." When he returned as an adult to find his "roots," he discovered that his biological father "was always threatened by my successes. He withdrew from me because he was in competition with me. It really made me angry all over again, but then my therapist asked me what it must be like for a man to fear his own son. My heart just melted. I wept for about a week for all his pain and fear . . . some of which I've spent my own adult life fighting. It was really pathetic when I thought about his life. His wife kicked him out; his kids rarely visited. He just sent the support checks every month, but couldn't enjoy me or himself. . . . It was an important insight. Now I'm committed to not letting my own fear stifle me, and to being with my own kid. . . . I guess in some ways inadvertently he is giving me what I need from a father."

10

THE MAKING OF A FATHER:
LIFELONG LEARNING

Considering the significance of changing social contexts, one's biological and internalized progenitors, and one's own psychology, this business of becoming a good-enough father seems quite intricate. There seems so much to learn. Surely the whole training process cannot occur during the nine months of a first pregnancy. How do men learn the desired and requisite skills? Where do they hold the classes?

I have arbitrarily divided the lifelong learning into eight stages. They are presented as an overview of the germinating and maturing learning process. What is clearly evident is that fathering is learned from elders, children, and peers. It is interactive. Sometimes a man is primarily the teacher, sometimes the student. Throughout a man's life the core of the process involves learning from mistakes. You don't have to be perfect. None of us can be. We do need to be consistently learning, involved in a dynamic process, more focused on the moment than on any ultimate goal.

The eight stages of fatherhood development include:

1. Preparation
2. Beginning
3. Fathering babies and preschoolers
4. Fathering school-age children
5. Fathering adolescents
6. Letting go (launching the children)
7. Mentoring
8. Grandfathering

PREPARATION: EARLY IMAGES

Watching and Listening

I remember mornings, as a young boy, sitting in the bathroom watching that intricate male ritual called shaving, watching my dad mix and apply the lather, sharpen his razor, pick it up and deftly remove the twenty-four-hour growth of facial hair. It was a fascinating ceremony that had a clear, almost religious protocol. It felt good, as a boy, to know that someday I would also take the sharp (dangerous) implement in hand and similarly prepare for my day. I remember the smells of the soap, shaving cream, after-shave lotion, the slapping sound of hand on face and the slight wince as it was being applied, the sight of the cigarette-smoke-blended bathroom air and occasional frightening blood. It all had a sense of importance. This was part of Basic Training for men and fathering. Someday my son would be in the bathroom watching me as the big man.

There were other male ways to learn in the bathroom: how to hold my penis and aim the urine stream; how to achieve mastery over urinary and bowel functions as bigger men do; how to gain my father's praise for my male skills.

Being in the bathroom with Dad was being in the world of men. The other places where men gathered alone were the barbershop, the card games (which I wasn't allowed to watch much, because of my bedtime and giveaway joy at the sight of a good hand),

and of course the baseball diamond. Here were men doing male things, enjoying themselves, being close. I imitated my dad's batting stance, learned how to warm up my arm as if it were the arm of a thirty-five-year-old, learned when and how to take risks, how to strategize, be part of a team. These were the male things that were to serve me when I became a grown-up.

I would learn how to be a man by hanging around with my father and other men. I would grow into my role just as I would grow into progressively larger shoes, clothes, and baseball gloves. I would go to work with my dad, and he would teach me the jobs of men.

Somewhere along the way, for most boys, this expectation begins to die. Our dads don't really understand what it's like to be in school or to be an adolescent. They are gone so much, away at work, busy with chores or projects on the weekend, helping mom. They have little time for their friends or for us. We can join them while they work around the house, in the garage or workshop, but there's precious little time for them to join us—if they live with us at all.

When Daddy's Away

Can I learn the skills of men without growing up in the presence of the look and feel of those skills? The skills themselves may not be as important as my father's presence and my emotional connection with him at both conscious and unconscious levels.

I can learn how to shave without the masculine ritual and never know anything more than clean-shavedness. I could learn how to avoid nicks and how to take care to get the tough places from my mom. She shaves too. But it isn't the same.[1]

I don't have to model my batting stance after my dad—in my youth there was Ted Williams, Stan Musial, Bobby Thompson, Duke Snider, and a host of other batting "heroes." Today's sons can emulate Joe Montana, Kirby Puckett, Wayne Gretzky, or Michael Jordan. Yet Dad's way has some extra appeal—he represents our personal destiny. Few fathers will ever threaten DiMaggio's hitting streak, but to a son Dad's way far outweighs social recognition. Even in a little boy's dreams, there's some sense that he won't grow up to be Willie Mays, but he may well grow up to be his father.

If the individual male skills are secondary to the connection and feel of fathering, what if my father is unable to trigger my genetic and psychological program, "How to Become a Man"? How will I learn those masculine and fathering skills? Without a proper masculine initiation will I ever fully identify with all the male traits that will serve me and my community? As previously indicated, several studies do indicate that males with absent fathers or father substitutes never quite grow into their own manhood. Psychologically they remain adolescents, have difficulty with commitments, tend to reject masculine values, and have an incomplete sense of exploration or self-affirmation. In his absence a son may be more inclined toward hero worship and media images of men. Inappropriate images of heroic men in popular media may mislead a boy into excessive aggressiveness, exclusive orientation to winning, or a superficial sense of manhood. To begin to learn balance, a boy must emulate sources closer to home.

More importantly, what lessons do I get from my absent dad? Do I learn that being a father means being absent, disconnected, or unavailable? Do I learn about how to be a father from a woman's perspective?

For a young boy, imitating a father and practicing male gestures, skills, and interests, and internalizing a sense of a male heritage are the most powerful sources of learning. Whomever he emulates, he will be practicing to be a man and father himself. There is no difficulty observing this. Children identify so fully with parents that they frequently say and do exactly the things we say and do—often at the most embarrassing moments.

PREPARATION: PRACTICING MASCULINITY AS AN ADOLESCENT

Adolescence is a time of passage from the dependence of childhood to the independence and responsibility of adult life. During this time a boy makes the transition to manhood by testing limits and by practicing traditional adult male skills.

The two predominant areas of adolescent learning are work and relationship.

Work/School

As an adolescent a boy learns work skills by schooling or training programs and by experimentation with the world of work. This is commonly a time for the first part-time after-school job, the summer or school-vacation job, or even some entrepreneurial endeavors.

Ned began working early as a paper boy at age eleven. By the time he was thirteen, he held a regular after-school job with a local merchant. At sixteen he was behind the counter at a fast-food restaurant. He reflects, "My folks were supportive of my work, because they couldn't give me any money for extras. Dad made enough for food and rent and precious little else. When I worked, I didn't put any added strain with my expensive tastes."

By the time he was thirty, Ned owned a chain of car washes and was "on the way to my second million."

Luke also followed a fairly common pattern. At age sixteen he got an after-school and weekend job at the local soda fountain. During summers he drove a delivery truck for another merchant. He kept those jobs until he went to college. During his four years as a scholarship student at his college he worked in the lunchroom.

Many adult men simply do not remember any time when they were not required to work and earn income. Like Luke and Ned, most of us began our psychological training program to develop a work orientation by the time we were in our early adolescence. We got the cultural message. Men work for the money that provides access to the prizes of our culture, especially females. We are still expected to cover the costs of dates.

Adolescent work wasn't bad practice. Many of the important social lessons were well learned. My personal initiation into the world of work occurred when I was thirteen years old. My father broke an ankle that spring. Because his work required legwork, I was pressed into service. Although I was not pleased with the rigors of work versus a summer of baseball and bodysurfing, I was pleased to be able to be with my dad and to be doing what men in this culture do.

School is the other dominant scene for teenagers. High school, college, and training programs are the crucible where culture, trades, and lessons about life are forged. Reminiscing, Cliff indicated, "High school was disillusioning. It was there that I figured out that life wasn't fair. Good kids didn't get the girls or the grades. Honesty was rarely rewarded, and if I was going to go out with a girl on a Saturday night, I was sure to get zits by Thursday."

Dating and Mating: Trial-and-Error Relationship Learning

Few events in life are more potentially emotionally hazardous than early dating. Before men can be good-enough fathers to their own children, they have to master enough relationship skills to find and develop a relationship with a partner. Having separated from girls during the later grammar school years and associated primarily with the other boys, males have a lot to learn. Especially since everything has been transformed by their body chemistry (i.e., puberty).

The numbers of questions about male-female relationships that are clearly answered for teenagers are few to none. We all learn in a painful trial-and-error way. We can't learn from our parents; to us as adolescents they seem very out-of-step with "reality" as we know it.

There is also a shift in social patterns. During the elementary school years girls tended to be more isolated and boys were involved in larger groups. During early adolescence, at least with regard to opposite-sex relationships, this trend reverses. Girls often learn the dating games and flirtation by interactions with other girls. Boys typically do not talk about their fears with other boys, who represent the competition; they have to learn about relating to girls all on their own.

Dating is commonly considered a process with a purpose: finding a proper mate. The period has become prolonged by the complexity of modern society, including extensive years of necessary education, earlier puberty, and social custom to marry later in life. Dating also provides an experimental environment for learning how to be intimate with that certain someone. Few of us have an easy time of it. Prior to having any opportunity for training and practice, we are judged, and judge ourselves, by standards appropriate for experienced adults. Furthermore the onus of making the first move is still left to the male. He takes the emotional risk of rejection. What makes this risk especially threatening is that rejection from same-age females may replicate the sense of being rejected as a little boy by Mom during earlier phases of development.

How do I ask a girl out? When is the right time?

Jimmy is an attractive seventeen-year-old high school junior. He gets better-than-average grades and is college bound. He has lots of male and a few female friends at school. His only high school date so far was his junior prom. "To tell you the truth, I went with a girl who I knew would say yes. She wasn't the one I really like. I couldn't ask her—Carmen—because I think she likes me, too, but if I ask and she says no, then I won't be able to go back into that school—no way."

Among the major dilemmas for young males is the problem of being the initiator of the first kiss. As Cal recalls, "I don't know. Maybe I was naive or something. Maybe I did mature late, but I was terrified. I even remember her name—Mary Ellen. I was okay at the movie, but by the time we went out for Coke and fries, I could feel the nerves growing. Then at her door I just didn't know what to do—made a real ass of myself. I was sure she was angry with me for not being good at it. I liked her, but I was afraid to call her back until her friend told me she wanted me to. I still get retroactively embarrassed about my naiveté, and I was all of fifteen."

Lawrence said he "was shocked when my wife told me how prepared she was for that first teenage kiss. She knew to close her eyes. She and her girlfriends had talked about it for months. I just blundered in and kissed her while she was trying to talk—my reaction to the worry that she might say no when I tried. . . . At least we didn't get our damned braces locked like a couple of dogs in oral heat."

Ron solved the problem by avoiding the issue completely. "I knew I'd be a screwup at dating. So I just didn't go out in high school. I turned to academics and science. . . . I just decided by the time I was eighteen that if any woman really wanted me, she'd have to come and get me. I wasn't about to get shot down. . . . So my wife was in my college Organic lab, and she decided that I was the one for her. . . . We've been together for nine years, so I guess she was right."

Our social customs have made the "dating and mating" game somewhat more hazardous because of the lack of clear guidelines and rules, and of course the essential pressure on males that they must be the initiator.

It is not a short learning project. Most of us take years to "get it right." During this time, our self-esteem is in jeopardy and our learning involves doing what we think will be acceptable rather than learning how to be ourselves. This insecurity may generalize to our relationships with everyone and everything. We always feel that our very being is on the line, a state of mind that is anathema to intimacy.

Lacking models, a viable instruction booklet, or the necessary emotional maturity, many men do not completely master the ability to relate immediately during their dating years. Instead the early years of marriage and parenting become a continuation of the training for fatherhood.

Most of the skills of parenting that adolescent boys do acquire will have to be seriously modified when they become fathers. This is one of the reasons that adolescent fathers might have such a difficult time providing adequately for their children's emotional or financial needs. Still partially children themselves, they find it hard to be self-sacrificing or wise enough to provide something for their own children that they have yet to experience personally.

BEGINNING

Expectant Fathering

While the actual biological event that makes a man a father is almost instantaneous, the psychological development of fatherhood is quite a bit slower. Men lack the biological verification of parenthood that women experience. For an expectant father (and for many men long thereafter), access to the baby is controlled by the pregnant mother. She may encourage his connection to the baby growing in her womb or discourage it. Because his physical attachment to the fetus is secondhand, and because of a variety of other social factors, fatherhood may develop more slowly than motherhood. Of course there are expectant fathers who are more involved than the mom, but they are the minority. Many expectant fathers don't develop a deep sense of their fatherhood until there is felt movement in the womb. Others don't begin to experience feelings of fatherhood until the birth itself. There is also a smaller group of fathers who begin their deeper emotional attachment when their children are walking and talking. Most men, however, describe with awe, and what Martin Greenberg calls "engrossment," the first experience of holding their child.

In the past five decades, fathers' involvement has been profoundly affected by the revolutionary shift in childbirth practices in the developed world. Beginning in the 1940s the natural-childbirth movement, spurred by the pioneering work of Fernand Lamaze in France, Grantly Dick-Read in South Africa, and Robert Bradley in the United States, there has been a progressive interest in father involvement and participation in pregnancy and birth. As recently as 1965 only 15 percent of all fathers expected to be present when their children were born. For the most part these men were health-care professionals or lived in rural areas. By 1985, 85 percent of all men expected to be present.

Most professionals and the vast majority of parents believe that father involvement in childbirth-education classes has the short-term benefit of increasing the man's connection with his wife and newborn. With a few celebrated exceptions, such as Kimberley Hefner, wife of *Playboy*'s Hugh Hefner, most women strongly prefer their partner to be present. Most men want to be present as well. In a 1986 survey 74 percent of the expectant fathers interviewed chose to be present, 15 percent had "mixed feelings, but would probably be present," and 9 percent were uninterested or unwilling to be at the birth. The remainder who responded left the decision for their participation in the birth entirely up to their wives.[2]

Martin Greenberg, author of *Birth of a Father*, believes that the effects of father attendance at birth on paternal-infant bonding are extremely significant and long lasting. Few authors dispute the short-term positive impact of father presence at birth on men and on the family. As Horace so clearly indicates, his presence at the birth truly enhanced his feelings of well-being and affection for his family, at least at the time surrounding the birth: "We be havin' lots of problems during the pregnancy. Not sure if marriage was the right thing. Not sure if we could make it go. But when Nicola was born, I just felt like a million. Good for me, proud of the woman—she bear so much pain with courage. I just figured maybe we could make it. It got hard later, and I don't know if it will last but I got my little girl, and even when Wilma gets to raggin', I remember when the baby came. It was the three of us against the world."

During the period of pregnancy, the man makes adjustments that help to prepare him for birth and parenthood, yet they may also be stressful, because they often compound other—usually work-related—demands. Katharyn May, a pioneer researcher in this area, makes the point that men who have difficulty adjusting to the pregnancy must be considered personally at risk for emotional disruption.[3]

Whatever the impact, expectant fathers go through a great deal during that first pregnancy. They experience new fears and anxieties, begin "nesting," and sometimes develop physical symptoms themselves.[4]

Among the most powerful learning that takes place is an almost-universal protective feeling among new fathers. I must provide a safe environment for mother and infant. Financial responsibility also changes. Men who were uninterested in conserving resources or saving for the future find themselves doing things "that older guys do."

Irv, a father of four, recalled, "When Tammy was pregnant with the first, we weren't even married or nothin'. I worked when I needed the bread, but mostly I was what you'd probably call a bum or a biker. I used to hang glide, ride a chopper, anything for kicks—the bigger the risk, the better. Then, when she started to get big, I don't know why, I just started to clean up my act. So now with four of them and Tammy being my wife, instead of a Harley we got a station wagon. . . . It's not bad. My life is probably better for it. I wonder what will happen when the kids get old enough to figure out the birth dates before the wedding, or see some of my old pictures. I looked like 'Easy Rider,' man."

In addition expectant fathers report becoming much more attuned to the human life cycle and to their own and loved ones' mortality. Many desire reconnection with their own parents, particularly their fathers.

All the sensitizing that occurs during this time provides valuable fathering skills of caretaking, empathy, and sacrifice and builds the feeling of love for a child and for children in general.

FATHERING BABIES AND PRESCHOOLERS

The next stage of fatherhood is parenting infants. In our culture men have traditionally not had a significant role in these early stages of their baby's life. Newborns need a great deal of nurturance and physical comfort. Fathers have typically assumed these roles only when mothers are unavailable. Gender-related sex-role expectations are very powerful for new parents. Many fathers spending time with their newborns are frequently queried whether they are "baby-sitting." The inference is that Mom is the parent and Dad the "hired help" or second-string relief.

Fathers with newborns often describe being supplanted by their wife and other women when they engage in child care. This is well depicted in the recent film *Modern Love,* in which Robby Benson, playing the role of a new father, is excitedly preparing to give his new daughter her first bath. He is emotionally devastated to find that his wife had acceded to her mother's request to bathe the infant in his stead. Mother and grandmother did not arrange for this switch in plans out of malevolence. They had no idea that this "maternal activity" would matter to him. It represents a powerful social perception. We have yet fully to accept active, equal father participation with babies.

When my own daughter was a newborn, my mother-in-law came to visit and help my wife during the first two postpartum weeks. For the first few days each time I held my daughter, she was spirited away from me and into the arms of Mom or Grandma. The clear message: Fathers are not supposed to be home holding newborns if a woman is available. It's her job and her prerogative. In addition another question arises. If Dad is a copartner with newborn care, what is Grandma's role? Didn't she come to be with the mom and her grandchild? If she doesn't help with infant care, what does she do when the new parents' place is cleaner than it has ever been and there are enough cooked meals for a week? If she feels left out, she may return home prematurely or she may subconsciously create other things for Dad to do by changing the organization and placement of his belongings.

Bill recalls his early battles with his mother-in-law: "I swear, she made my rocking Lissa to sleep a very expensive proposition. In the ten days that she was visiting to 'help,' she damaged my car, pulled out wires to the stereo, and rearranged my drawers. I still haven't found some of my clothes, and it's been five years since the last baby. She was fine as long as she was busy with the baby or cooking, but the moment I started to spend time with the baby, she disappeared and in no time at all something of mine was being 'accidentally' damaged. I like Annie, so don't get me wrong here. She just didn't know what to do with herself. . . . So she got into trouble. I guess she was unconsciously resenting my participation and she kind of got even by giving me other things to do so she could get back to Lissa."

It is appropriate for most fathers to establish their early right to hold and nurture their baby. This must be done without getting into a "baby as rope" tug-of-war. The women in the baby's life need to learn that Dad also feels protective and desires the close bonding with an infant.

Why Fathers Are Important in a Baby's Life

Oftentimes fathers naturally provide additional and alternative resources. We hold infants differently, we play with them differently, and we respond differently to their needs. Some of these differences were detailed in Chapter 3.

Where mothers naturally offer warmth and security, fathers encourage freedom and exploration. They are both very important. The natural male way is complementary to the natural female way.

Similarly, when women play with babies, they tend to be very visual and auditory in their play, promoting attachment. Jane, a childbirth educator, described the "proper method of interfacing with infants" in her baby-and-mother's class. Holding the infant close to her chest and speaking in a loud, high-pitched, almost squeaking voice, she continued, "Hello there, you sweet little beauty. How's my favorite little perfect baby?"

Michael Lamb,[5] Ross Parke,[6] and Frederick Bozett[7] all point out that when fathers play with children, they typically assume the role of social interactor, particularly in the mother's presence. More of a father's time is spent in interactive-play activity. Father's play is generally more tactile and "rough and tumble," especially with boys. Fathers serve their babies not only as attachment figures but also as a primary source of affiliating; the good father is both a playmate and a caretaker. Shirley Hanson and Frederick Bozett[8] state, "It is of the utmost significance that infants attach to fathers as well as to mothers."

Considerable research observing infants and parents strongly suggests that infants soon learn to use their parents for different purposes at different times. Infants normally turn to their fathers to meet their comfort and security needs when mothers are not present. When they are available, fathers provide more for their social needs.

In his role as promoter of social interaction, the father helps the eighteen-month-to-three-year-old child to begin to separate from the mother. During these crucial months the child has to begin to develop a sense of a personal self, distinct from the mother-baby bond. The father, as a secure person who is not part of that symbiotic relationship, is able to promote the toddler's early separation from Mother. The baby can separate from Mom to explore and can still have the safety of a loving parent by affiliating with Dad.

As a part of the family system who is outside the umbilical mother-child connection, a father also offers the young child an opportunity to learn cultural mores. For example as a species we are instinctually aggressive. Young children express this aggression without regard to social etiquette. Because the mother is commonly so much more a part of the same emotional unit as the baby, she may be more likely to accept the natural impulses than the father. He is in a better position to model, channel, or guide the children's innate aggressive urges into socially acceptable pathways.

Fathers and Attachment

Until recently fathers have been considered as primary attachment figures for infants only when mothers have been unavailable or inadequate. In fact many writers seem to believe that infants attach *only* to mothers or other female figures. My colleague, Martin Greenberg, beautifully describes the connection between men and their babies. Using the term *engrossment,* he states that fathers have

1. A visual awareness of the newborn in which it was seen as beautiful or attractive

2. A tactile awareness with a desire to hold and touch the newborn
3. An awareness of the newborn's distinct features
4. Perception of the infant as perfect
5. A strong attraction to and focus on the newborn
6. An extreme elation described as a high and
7. An increased sense of self-esteem[9]

Fathers are seen smiling at, verbalizing to, vocalizing to, touching, rocking, and holding their babies. Infants also *affiliate* with their fathers by cooing and smiling and *attach* by crying or seeking to be held. Michael Lamb points out that infants employ the friendly affiliating behaviors with individuals regardless of relationship, whereas "attachment behaviors are focused more narrowly only on attachment figures."

Caretaking by Fathers

A father who wishes to have a positive impact on his young children needs to be involved in their physical caretaking: feeding them, changing diapers, reading to them, and playing with them.

Although "involved fathering" is a developing trend, the actual amount of time that a father spends interacting with his infants or children may be minimal. Actual statistical estimates vary widely. In general, studies that rely entirely on maternal reports show the lowest estimates, whereas research that has both mothers and fathers fill out time charts show the highest amounts of father-infant time. The range is quite broad, running from a few minutes per day to over three hours.

The differences between these studies lead to some tentative conclusions:

- Fathers, almost to a man, feel that they don't have enough time with their infants.
- There is a positive correlation between a father's presence

at birth and his comfort providing primary care for his infant and young child.

- It is somehow acceptable for mothers to minimize the actual amount of time that fathers spend with infants.
- When both parents are present, fathers will defer to the mother. It is therefore important that fathers caretake their infants alone.

So what does the father learn about fathering from infants and preschoolers? He learns patience. He learns to go at the other person's level of competence. He learns about his own innate nurturance. He learns to focus on the relationship. He learns not to try to accomplish anything else at the same time he is caring for a preschooler. He relives and reevaluates parts of his own childhood. He discovers that some apparently logical solutions are less effective than emotional relationship skills.

FATHERING SCHOOL-AGE CHILDREN

During the preschool and elementary school years (ages three through twelve), fathers have several important tasks to accomplish. At a behavioral level fathers may support the child's growing competence and independence. Particularly with sons, fathers serve as role models in "male activities." During these years, children learn how to act in culturally appropriate, gender-specific ways. Traditionally, girls practice becoming mothers through nurturing play with dolls and developing home-based skills, whereas boys learn about teams and outdoor skills.

As sex-role models, fathers provide the opportunity for their daughters to learn about male modes of feeling, the community, teamwork, and the limits of nurturing and early sexual behavior. Boys can model their fathers' community participation, competition, ambition, and dedication to work. As parental models fathers offer all of these skills to children of both sexes.

Individuation and Separation

During the elementary school years gender learning is particularly powerful. The male and female roles that are modeled and adopted during these years are often played out later to extremes during the adolescent years. In this period, children begin to become increasingly influenced by peers and other out-of-home social forces. It may be quite important for Father to confirm, expand, or dispute specific information that his children attain at school, on television, or through the media. For example in 1991, when my daughter came home from school with stories of "the heroism, glory, and righteousness" of the "Desert Storm" Gulf War, it seemed important for me to provide some understanding of the losses of war as well.

Because fathers are identified with the out-of-home environment, they exercise the greatest influence on their children's realization of social demands. A father does this by accepting and containing the child's anger at increasing separation from Mother during early school years. He helps the child channel the anger into appropriate competitiveness, competency, and motivation. Similarly he may help the child learn how to deal with a need for connectedness by encouraging the developing of group relationships with peers. Teamwork and group identification may be supported and modeled.

Male Modes of Social Interaction

Male play and interaction have often been characterized as more goal oriented than women's, more aggressive, less concerned with the socializing than the product, and so on. When a father teaches male forms of play to his children, he encourages healthy competition and competency.

As an acculturational agent he can teach both sons and daughters tenderness (through physical contact) and toughness (through separation). He can support gender-role development, teach morality and fair play, and convey the masculine approach to social interaction, as a balance to the feminine.

Time and Young Children

During these years in their children's lives many fathers express frustration over the conflicting demands of work and home life. Many men report feeling inadequate as fathers because of the limited time they are able to spend with their school-age children. They describe being out of touch with the children's school lives, daily ups and downs with playmates, and developing goals. All too often men are called in primarily as summary disciplinarians.

Some fathers report that their relationships with daughters during this age period are often less close. This is presumably because as their daughters become more immersed in gender-role practice, there is less understanding by fathers of young females' special needs. Of course other fathers find their growing daughters to be better companions and encourage the relationship growing closer. They share greater interest in similar activities. This is greatly influenced by the number and ages of other children at home. When Mom is involved with younger siblings, older daughters will often seek out extra time with Father. Most fathers report increasing connection with their sons during this time.

A recent survey of ten- and eleven-year-old children at a local elementary school highlights this limited-time dilemma. Asked what they would like their fathers to do more or better, approximately half of the girls listed "more time" as their number-one priority. The other half listed "make more money" as a top priority.

FATHERING ADOLESCENTS

Adolescents have a most important task to accomplish. They must find a way to separate from their families of origin and move into the adult world on their own. As our culture becomes increasingly complex, the adolescent stage of development has expanded to meet the escalating demands. Compared with that of the past three generations, adolescence today begins at a younger age and extends to an older one.

It begins earlier for a number of reasons. Biologically the onset of puberty occurs sooner. In addition mass media romanticizes this stage of development, encouraging preteens to experiment with adolescent behavior. Increased social incursions into the home and school by outside influences also tend to extend the adolescent period downward into the elementary school years. Finally, familial financial and career needs have left many preteens with lots of extra, unsupervised time for experimentation.

It also extends later in life. The journeyman's level of schooling has expanded commensurately. The college degree, a generally accepted "ticket," at least in middle-class homes, has extended most adolescents' financial dependency at least into their twenties. With the increasing expectations of advanced degrees, this may well be prolonged. Economic trends also perpetuate young people's increasing financial dependence on parents.

Father as Sustainer of Adolescent Individuation

In order for adolescents to move into the world of adulthood, they must begin to deal with a significant psychological question as well. They need to discover who they are, what their values are, and whom they want to be as adults. This issue of identity can play havoc with their relationship with parents. Often adolescents attempt to answer the question of who they are by defining who, or what, they are not.

As the parent who most represents the outside social work world, the father becomes the authority figure with whom adolescents test and work out their own fears and difficulties. Dad becomes a representative of society and is asked to support his adolescents as they battle against him—no mean task. To be effective, a father must provide firm and fair limits, often while being provoked.

Adolescents form their identity by battles or comparisons with "safe" authority figures. This usually means parents and teachers. Despite what teenagers might request or demand, they are experimenting to learn adult roles. If they must rebel to make their mark, they need something reasonably solid to rebel against. Without limits their behavior will have to go to excess. William Golding, in his *Lord of the Flies*, depicts this in frightening detail. The boys' extreme behavior is only curtailed with the arrival of the adult male sailors (father figures).

Parents with Lax or Rigid Limits. From my twenty-five-year perspective as a clinical psychologist, I believe that the most effective way for parents to promote promiscuity and drug abuse in their adolescents is to set inappropriate limits. Adolescents need to learn about themselves by testing what they know and by asserting their knowledge and desires. Parents who are excessively restrictive force delayed and often explosive rebellion. Similarly when there are no firm limits, teenagers are pressed to find a way to rebel, and they will inevitably be drawn to extremes. Two brief case examples illustrate this point.

Cathlyn grew up in a very restrictive home. She was denied the chance to listen to music, dance, or socialize in her family of origin. Punishment for errors was swift and extreme. She recalled being locked in a closet for a whole night for "cussing at the dinner table." At fifteen she decided that punishment was inevitable, "so I might as well be punished for something big." She regularly sneaked out of the home at night, became involved with petty theft, and was sexually promiscuous. By the time she was seventeen, she had been pregnant four times, ending each with an abortion. She left her parents' home permanently before graduating from high school.

Dave's family was the opposite of Cathlyn's. His parents were invested in being their children's best friends. They joined their teenagers at rock concerts, invited them to adult parties, and made alcohol and marijuana available at home. Finding a way to rebel against such parents was not easy, according to Dave. "They were more like my friends than I was. But I also wasn't about to become some kind of ultraconservative. Those guys were really weird. So I just turned to 'coke.' I was shocked that they freaked when I did smack."

Dave finally found the necessary form for his rebellion. Because his parents had lax standards, he was pushed to try more dangerous ways of establishing his independence.

Additional Conflicts for Fathers of Adolescents

The timing of adolescence frequently coincides with other emerging concerns for men.

Role Conflict. It is hard enough for a father to withstand the provocation of adolescent testing and respond with appropriate limits and consequences without any complications. Because an adolescent is both rebelling and learning how to take his place in the adult world, there is a concordant conflict for a father. While being an authority figure with clear limits, he must also be the advocate of his children's transition to adulthood (college, apprenticeship years). Being supportive and steadfast at the same time is difficult for most adults. Only a father who has some self-knowledge and comfort with himself can truly serve both of these demanding masters. *These two are the vital keys to success.* When we are unaware, we are most likely to respond unconsciously with those internalized messages from our own adolescence. Furthermore teenagers will instinctively root out and exploit parents where they are psychologically weakest. To be the father I want to become, I must develop awareness of my own personal tendencies for rigidity or cowardice and resolve them.

Parallel Conflicts. An unfortunate coincidence occurs in many families. Just as adolescents are struggling with issues of their emerging identity, their fathers are struggling with the troublesome questions of mid-life. In significant ways the adolescent and mid-life transitions are quite similar. Men in the throes of a mid-life crisis are asking lots of questions themselves. As their teenage children are questioning who they are, these fathers are rethinking their own personal issues of identity and meaning. It is hard for a man in this stage to have the kind of firm limits and boundaries that are most efficacious for the adolescent. He has less time and emotional energy available for the teenagers. When a man is going through his own mid-life crisis, an adolescent's challenging of authority can be more than a petty annoyance; it can be explosive. It doesn't need to be. If I can lay a groundwork of a reciprocal give-and-take between my offspring and myself during the infant, child, and teen years, we may be able to comfort and encourage each other during these difficult times. Of course I must maintain my mature parental role, giving far more than I ask of my child.

Time may also become a factor. Fathers, worrying about their own retirement or college tuition, may expand their workday, coming home late and tired. Adolescents also lead busy lives with school and homework, social lives with peers, extracurricular groups, lessons, and so forth. They have less time for father-child activities than they had during the preadolescent years. When fathers and teens are together, they are often tired and irritable. Much of the time spent in the same room may be parallel, such as watching television, rather than interactive. However, shared activities, though rare, acquire special psychological importance for fathers and adolescents when they do occur. College students in particular seem quite influenced by the "special time with Dad" that was spent during their high school years. That relationship and their perception of it, when solid, seems to be particularly sustaining during the emotional ups and downs common to college-age students.

Sam was in his mid-forties when he seriously began to question his career, his life goals, and his relationships. His wife was returning to school for her degree. She was physically unavailable, emotionally distracted, and beginning menopause. Their three children were eighteen, sixteen, and fifteen. Sam came into therapy two days after their youngest son was suspended from high school for cutting classes. He described his sixteen-year-old daughter as "completely out of control." It took several months of therapy for Sam to get a handle on what was happening in his own life. Subsequent family-therapy sessions were successful at having the parents regain control, set limits, and give the adolescents a firmer ground on which they could experiment more sanely and safely.

Who Will Be Graduating Next? Stay-at-home moms often feel a need to pursue outside interests during the children's later school years. Many women return to jobs or pursue previous careers at this time. Others return to school to complete degrees or train for new fields. These changes are usually accompanied by a healthy dose of anxiety. Many women become less available to their families as they pursue their own long-delayed interests. Fathers in these homes often find themselves with many more of the home duties. The father becomes the parent who is available for demands from his adolescents. He may also feel the loss of support and encouragement from his now more inaccessible partner. As Kyle put it, "When LuAnn went to graduate school, I was the parent in demand. She was out three evenings a week, and when she was in, she'd fall asleep studying. So the kids needed me, the house needed work, and whenever there were exams and papers, I'd be doing the shopping and errands. . . . I think I liked the time with the kids the best; the thing I disliked the most was that she never gave me any credit for all the additional work I was picking up . . . and the lack of a sex life."

Fathers learn a great deal from adolescents. They fully discover the importance of setting limits. They come face-to-face with their own rebelliousness and questions about authority. They must face their aging and recognize their biological replacements as procreators. Some may also find that their teenagers ask questions that they wish to ask themselves. Many a teenager today has parents who persuaded grandparents to protest the war in Vietnam or otherwise question authority.

LETTING GO (LAUNCHING THE CHILDREN)

Beyond Adolescence

It would seem that the bulk of fathering would be done by the time the children leave home late in adolescence, but as Craig

Roberts and Kay Zuengler point out, "The longest phase of fathering begins with the children's departure from the home and ends with death of the father or the child."[10]

Clearly, fathering at this stage of life is less active, less "hands-on," and more reciprocal. Many events can affect the father-child relationship after the children are grown. Illnesses, divorces, remarriages, birth of grandchildren, one's own retirement, loss of the mother, financial setbacks, and in-law problems can all test even the strongest parent-child bond.

Unlike earlier stages, these events do not unfold in a genetically determined order. They occur for different families at different ages and sequences. There is less of a uniform game plan. Fathers have to cope with these issues as they occur, uncertain of the terrain ahead.

Launching

After adolescence, children continue to mature and eventually leave home to begin their lives as independent adults. During this launching stage a father gradually develops more collegiality and mutuality with his children. He needs to become less authoritarian and directive as his children become more receptive to his input and suggestions. The father-child relationship is characterized more by sharing and negotiating as the children successfully leave home and become more independent. The eventual goal is for children to develop permanent companionship, marry, and have children of their own, creating for their father the role of grandfather.

Difficulties with Launching. This transition is not necessarily turmoil-free or natural. A new conflict, possibly born during the teenage years, may emerge. It reflects the mixed feelings parents have about their children leaving the nest. As long as the adolescents remain financially and emotionally dependent, their parents may be able to avoid potential psychological conflicts of their own.

These conflicts may involve fears of changes in lifestyle, or of alterations in intimacy.

It is interesting that studies of children leaving home have almost exclusively focused on the mother's reactions and intrapsychic conflicts. Many mothers do have a difficult time with the "loss" of the children at home.

Faith is a fifty-six-year-old married mother of two grown children. She has been married for thirty-three years and has a part-time job, which she enjoys. She and her husband travel and socialize frequently. She is in relatively good health after a long recovery from a skiing accident. "Bert is a good husband, but I'm glad I work a few days a week, so I don't feel like he's always underfoot now that he's retired. He's a little finicky and needs to clean constantly, but after thirty years you don't notice that anymore. Besides, I always come home to a clean house and cooked meal. The thing that bothers me is that he doesn't care about his children the way he should. He goes out even if they might call or come over. He wouldn't pick up our son at the airport. He just said, 'Why can't he catch a cab?' For me, Martin's still my baby. If he wants his mother to be at the airport, I'll be there. So Bert gets angry with me because we were supposed to go to a lecture that night. But to me there are other lectures, other nights."

Faith is still very tied to her children. She will literally stay home and wait for a phone call after her twenty-five-year-old daughter goes out on a date—a call that rarely comes. Although both of her children have been out of the home for over four years, she retains the emotional commitments to them that she had when they were babies. It is clear to everyone in this family that Faith and the children need to separate further. It is also likely that she and Bert will have to renegotiate their own relationship as partners without the children.

Mothers are not alone in the separation difficulty. Some fathers become just as unwilling to let go. Bob is a fifty-year-old college professor, father of three children. Although he was "not close or connected to" the children until they could "walk and talk," he has been deeply involved in all of their school and extracurricular activities. Because he had the more flexible schedule, he frequently went on school field trips; he was the car-pool parent and he coached all the children's soccer teams. When the last of their children graduated from college and decided to pursue graduate studies fifteen hundred miles away from home, Bob and Diane were alone in the home for the first time in twenty-eight years. It didn't last long.

After three months Bob went on a trip to visit and "help" their oldest son. When he returned home, he reported, "I felt so lost when I was leaving Curtis, he really didn't need me anymore, and the girls are doing fine also. Diane can just enjoy their success and take pleasure in the fact that they are off and she's done her job. I just have this empty feeling inside. I spend my time thinking about a sabbatical in England so I can be close to Louise, but I know it's not good for her."

Within three months of this conversation he was becoming involved with a single mother of three school-age children. Despite Diane's and a marriage counselor's efforts to help him understand that he was unconsciously trying to avoid his sense of loss by "adopting" other children, Bob continued down that path. Today he has divorced his wife, married the other woman, and reports that he is happy again, although "the truth is that Marilyn and I don't have that much in common except a good sex life and interest in the kids. She'll never be the friend that Diane was all those years. The good part is that I can really be close to those three kids and make up for their own father's disinterest."

Bob's inability to be a husband as much as a father precipitated this particular run of events. According to Diane, "It was hard at first, but I'm strong and have good friends and a loving family. I'll recover. There were obviously some marital disagreements, particularly around sex. I just don't think they were enough to break up a thirty-year relationship. . . . The biggest tragedy in the whole scenario is that he has created a rift with his own children. They're still angry at him and they feel displaced now by these other children . . . sad . . . very sad."

Bob and Diane are not alone. Marriages are often tested during the "empty nest" period. The launching stage is dangerous for marriages because of the sense of loss of the lifestyle and because of the need for partners to face each other (perhaps be intimate for the first time). In the face of this frightening challenge some, like Bob, opt out. Others leave, ostensibly for different reasons.

Margaret left her husband to seek "peace and solitude," claiming her work was done.

Mary left to find her "true love" after "doing my duty for twenty-five years."

Fred instigated a separation from his wife of thirty years "to find himself."

Launching is a particularly difficult phase of family development if the parents have an insufficiently developed relationship as a couple. In many marriages the parents and children form an emotional triangle. Conflicts are indirectly confronted by use of a third party. This may take several forms.

Sometimes the children are the recipients of the emotion, as in families where the anger one adult feels toward another is displaced onto the children. Some families blame the children for whatever ills may occur. Other families do not allow for direct affection between mates; instead the children receive all the love from one or both parents.

When the children leave the nest, the couple is often faced with the prospect of encountering each other without the buffer of the emotional triangle. They have to find new ways to work out their conflicts. This can be a period of great growth and intimacy for a couple. Unfortunately many couples resort to finding new triangles: work, friends, pets, grandchildren, and so on. Many of these couples simply seduce the children back into the middle of their relationship, asking for their adult children's help with a host of problems.

Bill and Jean took the opposite tack. When their children moved out, they reified their separateness by taking over their children's bedrooms and creating a symbolic "Maginot Line" down the center of the hallway of their apartment. Accustomed to living more as roommates than as marrieds, they altered their home to reflect this choice.

What can a man learn about fathering during the launching stage? Who he is alone. Who he is with his wife. How to be a man without being a father. How to be with kids when they are not as physically present. How to let go and move on, facing this loss as a precursor of other losses in life, facing his own mortality, and determining how he wants to spend the remainder of his time. What contribution he will make to his community.

MENTORING

There is a stage in a man's life where his fathering is extended beyond his own family and children. During this time men focus on their contribution to their career field, to the next generation, and to the world in general. They become fathers to the younger generation of males (and sometimes females). As a mentor a man provides support and instruction to younger people, who may safely apprentice themselves to him to learn his skills and his style.

Walter said, "For the first time in my life I felt like I was just going to be myself. No longer would I be what I was supposed to be; no longer would I do things because someone else decided that I should. I figure that it's time I just let the chips fall where they may. If I'm not socially acceptable by now, I probably won't ever get to be . . . You know, I feel twenty years younger than I did when I was in my forties."

For some men mentoring others is far easier than fathering their own children. There is little of the tension common to the father-son relationship. There is less of a psychological threat of being replaced in the family. For his part the younger disciple challenges less and receives the mentor's experience with less defensiveness.

This is a stage more typified by generativity than specific creative discoveries. A mentor is called upon for his wisdom and lifelong experience. He doesn't compete with those younger so much as he challenges them to excel. He encourages their contributions and offers advice for improvements.

Precursors to Mentorship

Mentoring rarely occurs until a man has struggled with his serious mid-life questions. Until he has begun a series of "inventory takings" concerning himself and his offspring, he will be too ego-centered not to be competitive with younger people. In therapy during this time men often have to acknowledge their personal lack of in-depth fathering as boys. They explore their longing for that experience, which, to a great extent, molded their own patterns of parenting. They reconcile with their internal and material father so that they are free to father others more fully. To some extent a therapist can provide some of that deficient parenting. More significantly, the therapist can provide an environment for the father to find ways of parenting himself, to accept himself for who he is, and to mature psychologically. By virtue of his role, the therapist offers a model of mentoring.

As for all other forms of fathering, the mentor encourages individuation and separation. He promotes adult-adult interactions.

Latter Stages of a Father's Career

Mentoring comes most frequently when men are in the latter stages of their career path. They are beyond their peak creativity, past the need to compete with others for advancement or rewards. Cary is a sales manager at a large department store. Pointing to a younger salesman, he reflected, "You know, years ago I would have crushed him. I would have risen to the threat he posed and found a way to beat him to every sale, to every promotion. I would use guile, trickery, and politics—anything at all to win. Now I look at him and I don't feel threatened, although I know he is trying to replace me in this job. In some ways I appreciate his aggressiveness. It actually looks good on my stats. . . . But more than that, I can see myself years ago. . . . I know I'm not moving up any higher in this organization. I'd like to leave it better than when I came in, and I would even be open to seeing Norman climb above me to the vice presidency of sales and marketing. I might just help him, so long as he isn't climbing on my bones."

At this point in his work he can clearly see the limitations, come to accept them, and move on to other pursuits. Some men take this opportunity to launch a new career. Jake retired from a thirty-five-year career as an engineer and began actively to pursue his college dream of writing poetry and short stories. Malcolm began making high-quality, hand-carved children's toys after retirement from his machinist's job. B.J. and his wife followed a long-time dream of being in business together, starting as real estate novices in their sixties. My own father, retired from running his own business, did some part-time tax work for a large national firm. He really enjoyed "working with the numbers" and "helping people." He also enjoyed being able to leave the office behind when he went home.

Other men pursue hobbies or other interests. Carlos left his position with a large automaker in Detroit and moved to "a golf community."

There are also men who remain with their organizations, taking on new roles as ambassadors of the company or the whole industry. The famous Napa Valley wine maker Robert Mondavi has become an international traveling spokesman for California wines since turning business operations over to his sons. Several men have played an increasing role in their community's affairs.

Finally, there are men who simply cannot let go of their work routine. Many of these men literally "work till they drop." They do not envision any life for themselves other than the daily rigors of their job. These men enter psychotherapy rarely. When they do (usually after some physical disability), they describe feeling purposeless, disconnected, lonely, and often depressed. These fathers, so locked in to the role of provider and worker, are unlikely to evolve as their children grow and leave the home. They will not adopt the mentor role.

dication to Family

ccurred in Robin's fifty-fifth year of life: He became
r and he became an environmentalist. Speculating that
the two events were related, he said, "I looked at her in that crib
and I knew it was my job to do whatever I could to make the world
she would live in safe for her whole generation. I never much
thought of the future beyond me and my sons before, but with a
granddaughter, I know that I can do a lot for the future of my
granddaughter's granddaughter."

It is common for mentors to become increasingly interested
in their families. Their wives, adult children, grandchildren, and
community become a primary focus. My wife's grandfather, William Sullivan, who was always involved in community to some extent, used his retirement time to become involved in a Meals on
Wheels program in his community. He also gave pony rides to
handicapped children on his One Horse Ranch.

I first met Bill when he was in his seventies. I know about his
"toughness and temper" only through reports of my in-laws. Since
I've known him, he has been exceedingly generous, kind, and free
with his recollections, enjoying his numerous grandchildren and
great-grandchildren.

As in the case of Robin and Bill, many men's interest in their
family expands to the community. They provide valuable support
for others and use their time and resources to better their environs.
In many nuclear-family communities the absence of mentors is
particularly felt. Older people and retirees live far from their families, making it difficult for their children and grandchildren to receive it.

When a man shows acceptance and encouragement for the
contributions of the younger generation, he expands his fathering
role dramatically. No longer competing with those who would challenge him, he is in a position to truly enjoy the advancement and
accomplishments of others. To some extent, this is the most powerful form of direct fathering. Sam Keen speaks of this role as "hus-

banding" the earth.[11] It shows an acceptance of one's own life, with its inherent limitations, and a desire to make a contribution. From mid-life on, "leaving the earth a little better than when I arrived" is a primary goal of fatherhood.

Mentoring is a stage of fatherhood that is often mixed with other stages. Quite often it occurs simultaneously with grand-fathering.

GRANDFATHERING

Having a child is the only necessary precondition to becoming a grandparent. Yet, unlike each of the prior stages of fatherhood de-velopment, becoming a grandfather is completely dependent on others. If my children remain childless, I do not become a grand-father. To a large extent my children, as parents, will determine the frequency and possibly even the quality of grandparent-grandchild contact. In addition to proximity and transportation concerns, the parents' relationships with their own parents may dominate the children's experience of their grandparents.

Being a grandfather offers a man special opportunities. He can be a model, a mentor, a wise elder. He can be playful. He also has the chance of being the kind of dad he wished he could have been with his children.

It is clearly easier for many men to hug and kiss their grand-children, to play with them, to listen to and understand them, more than their own children. The generational buffer, aging process, and reduced responsibility all appear to make the grandfather-grandchild relationship far less anxiety provoking and easier than the father-child connection.

What does grandfather status afford? It gives us a second chance to "get this parenting thing right." It provides us with an opportunity to teach and pass on the learning of a lifetime to future generations. A grandfather can teach his son or son-in-law how to father in a way that was personally impossible. A grandfather can serve as a surrogate father for a child whose father is unavailable.

In a family in which positive intergenerational relationships exist, grandfathers are encouraged to develop a close, special relationship with their grandchildren.

In the Dimuro family, for example, "Gampa Dan" was a constant visitor to the family home. He frequently "baby-sat the kids" and took them out to the park or special events. On family events and holidays it was customary to find Dan; his son, Tim; and the children away from the adults, engaged in long hours of play. When Michael, Tim's middle son, began to have trouble with other children in intermediate school, it was Grandpa to whom he confided and from whom he sought (and received) help and support, much to the satisfaction of his parents.

By contrast Ken was the only son in a family of five children. When he was growing up, he experienced his father as cold, distant, and critical. As a child he felt that he could never live up to his father's standards. When he had children of his own, it was common dinner conversation to criticize and express anger toward his father. Is it any wonder that his daughters infrequently saw their grandfather? Is it a surprise that they never wanted to go to the restaurant that he owned and found his stories and company "boring"?

Tim and Ken were best friends who grew up in the same neighborhood. Both of them considered Tim's father to be Grandpa.

Many adult men who feel negative toward their father may discourage the grandfather-grandchild relationship. If I despise or feel distant from my father, I will not likely let him get at my children. I may punish him for all the hurts I felt by depriving him of my children. It may also be painful for me if my father gives my children the love that I was denied as a child. I could actually become competitive with my own children for the emotional goodies. In the presence of affection shown by my father to my children, and a memory of being deprived as a child, I may once again begin to believe that it was my fault that he didn't relate to me that way, a severe blow to my self-esteem.

Grandfathers and Grandchildren

Dr. Stanley Cath states, "The advent of a grandchild is a developmental milestone that can revitalize the older man and assure him of a future connected with his biological and psychological self. It is this opportunity that accounts in part for the grandfather's idealization of his grandchild, the two of them are also linked by other transgenerational dynamics: by their common resentment of the father they both have reason to envy, and by the corrective possibilities offered by grandfatherhood to compensate for guilt felt about inadequacies as a parent."[12]

Grandfathers also provide a different model of masculinity for grandchildren. They may be softer, less competitive, more yielding, and patient. They may be more comfortable with their grandchildren's play with opposite-sex-linked games. Often this may assist grandsons to express more positive feelings toward other males.

Of course not all grandfathers offer such psychologically healthy messages. After a thirty-year career with government intelligence and his own security business, Gus exemplified the traditional masculine role model. He regularly lectured his young grandchildren on the importance of being tough: "You need to be prepared at all times. You never know when someone will try to catch you off guard. . . . You got to be real careful around softies and intellectuals—they're the most deceptive. . . . A man who needs friends is either a weakling or a queer."

Gus, who was abused by his father, used corporal punishment liberally with his sons and grandsons. He is seventy-one years old and remains unable to accept his own softer side. Any healthy, passive yearnings for a man's love and approval remain repressed. He is neither favored nor sought out by his children or grandchildren.

The Modern Grandfather

Most men find grandfathering pleasurable and important. They enjoy the luxury of indulging their grandchildren without guilt, since they are not responsible for teaching that generation to be socially acceptable adults.

In the past century many more men have had the opportunity to grandfather. Increased life expectancy has made it possible for more men to become grandfathers for longer periods of time. In addition, as the average number of children has decreased, the number of years between the first and last child has also decreased. Thus most men experience grandfathering as a separate phase of life from fathering.

By contrast, men who are marrying and having families later in life may have no expectation of becoming grandfathers. In addition, with fewer children men can expect fewer grandchildren. However, population statistics indicate that men who live to be in their mid to late sixties have a high likelihood of becoming grandfathers.

Many grandfathers experience a sense of biological renewal and continuity in their grandchildren. This is often enhanced by the lack of responsibility, threat, or competitiveness that characterizes adjacent generations. In line with that, many men also experience greater emotional fulfillment as grandfathers than they did as fathers.

In many families, grandfathers also achieve a special role as a resource person, expert, or mentor without the challenges to which they were accustomed. Oftentimes grandpas can also provide financial assistance to their children. Many men were like Kirk, a grandfather of four: "You know, when my father came to this country, he had nothing but the clothes on his back. There was no chance for me to finish high school. When Bradley and Roberta came along, my biggest desire was that they could go to the state college. I can't tell you how much it means to be helping the young ones go off to private colleges. We're quite a success story. When Marcia showed me her report card, I think I was prouder of it than she was."

In return for helping his grandchildren with finances and encouragement, Kirk gets to experience vicariously adventures that were denied him as a child and adolescent. He also gets to fulfill his family's dream of increasing success for each generation.

Two additional advantages of grandfathering were addressed by Fujio: "It is a joy to reminisce about the old days and remember the good times with my parents and the children. I remember the one time I saw my mother's father. 'Ojiji' was a very stern, old Japanese man, but I knew he liked me. When nobody else was looking, he'd slip me a treat and almost smile. I probably tell too-long stories, but I enjoy the look in the grandchildren's eyes when I tell them of old Hawaii or their ancestors growing up in Japan. . . . Sometimes I get to spoil the grandchildren too. Treats, games, surprises. Last week I took the little one out to the merry-go-round and just kept buying tickets."

Most men seem to feel satisfied and comfortable with their grandfathering. Where do they learn how to be a grandfather? There are few set norms or cultural rules. Grandfatherhood and status in the role is achieved through contact and behavior rather than any automatic eventuality.

Like Fujio most men seem to replicate their own positive feelings toward their grandfathers with their grandchildren. Fujio's grandfather's indulgence with small treats translated two generations later into unlimited merry-go-round rides. Many men disclosed that their relationships with a favorite grandfather had a lifelong effect on their subsequent familial relationships. For reasons described in depth earlier, this seems more important for boys than for girls. As Roland remembers, "My 'pa' was the only older man who ever took any interest in me. He was close and nurturant, and when things got bad in the house, I could always go through the back fence and spend safe time with him—no questions asked. He just always seemed glad to see me. I've always thought that I'd like to be a grandpa like 'Pa.' "

There is no set way to be a good grandfather. Each man needs to find a balance that suits his values and personality. Some grandfathers are more formal than parents, prescribing proper behavior for their grandchildren. Others are more lenient than a child's parents; unconcerned about formality at this late stage of their own

lives, they try to bring a sense of joy and freedom to their relationship. Many grandfathers specialize in that role, always being playful
with the grandkids.

A fairly large group of grandfathers stay fairly distant from
their grandchildren. They have intermittent personal contact.
These grandfathers rarely get involved with any parenting. They
occasionally play "Santa Claus" or provide financially more than
emotionally. At times these men also play the "family expert" role
with their grandchildren. They are the clear authority, the patri-
arch.

Knute is a good example. He claims that he genuinely loves
his grandchildren "at a reasonable distance. I really enjoy their
visits, but I have my own life also. Mostly I try to tell them the
importance of their family history. I want them to be proud and to
honor the family in school and work. . . . I probably spoil them too
much when they get good grades, but what the heck."

Finally, a new form of grandfathering is emerging: surrogate
parent. With the breakdown of families through divorce, desertion
of children, the high rate of unmarried pregnancies, and other economic and social problems, many children are being raised by
grandparents. Historically this role fell to the maternal grandmother, but increasingly grandfathers are being pressed into service. This is particularly true of younger men who are already
accustomed to being an active father and still have enough stamina
to keep up with young children.

Tom's son and daughter-in-law were both incarcerated, leaving him with their three children. He became the primary caretaker for three years until the parents were "straightened out." "It
was hard. I had to do things I never did before. Those three kids
were an armful. But after a while I got into a routine. . . . I'm a lot
closer to them than I ever was to my own kids."

Some Difficulties for Grandfathers

Grandfathers and grandchildren generally connect the best when
the grandfather is in his fifties and sixties, the children are younger,

and there is no great difference in values. For younger and older grandfathers, adolescents and value conflicts can become quite problematic.

Grandfathers and Divorce. When a man's children divorce, he may be in jeopardy of losing contact with his grandchildren. This is especially true for paternal grandfathers, because the mother retains custody in 90 percent of divorces. When a grandfather's child does not have custody, he may find his contact with grandchildren restricted or denied, especially if the divorce was messy or the result of his son's misconduct. Many grandfathers expressed great pain at the loss of contact. They felt that continuing contact with their son's ex-wife was disloyal, but still wanted to be close with their grandchildren. With 50 percent of marriages ending in divorce, this is no small problem. Many former daughters-in-law also felt conflict about continuing contact with their former fathers-in-law.

Karen described her conflict well: "I want Billy to have contact with Grampa Wes, but I don't know how to do it without constantly running afoul of Martin. Each time I see him, I end up a wreck for a few days at least. Then, too, I worry that his parents are criticizing me for leaving him. I never know what to tell Billy when he wants to see his grandpa. I also have to deal with Greg's jealousy when I have any contact with Martin's family."

It's easy to understand her reluctance to encourage contact between her son and former father-in-law.

As described earlier, a grandfather-grandson relationship may be particularly influential in a boy's development. Loss of his paternal grandfather may subsequently adversely influence a man's relationship with his own grandchildren when he becomes a grandfather.

Maternal grandfathers tended to do better, but family breakup and their feelings about their divorced in-laws can create conflicts. In addition, remarriage creates step-grandparents, and as the number of relationships increases, intensity and time lessens.

If his daughter has custody of her children, Grandpa may be

called upon to provide increased financial support for the grand-children. There is also a higher likelihood that he and his wife will be asked to serve as surrogate parents at least until his daughter gets her life together again.

Grandfathers, Family, and the Culture

Grandfathers may play a special role in transmission of family values across generations. There is a true need for the wise old man, with his stories of days gone by, to provide continuity between generations. There is a place for grandfathers to give to their grandsons and granddaughters whatever their parents cannot provide. Where grandmothers symbolize wisdom in nurturance, and connection to the earth, grandfathers are the surviving warriors who know of the world and the hunt. They can teach survival with a love that is often obfuscated by tension between fathers and sons.

Grandfathering and Gender Roles. One of the primary forms of grandfather-grandchild communication is about sex roles. In our culture men are often the carriers of the distinctions between male and female behaviors. Grandfathers' topics of conversation with children are usually more men-centered. They make clear distinctions between men's and women's roles, and they focus most often on the paternal line. Historically the strongest bond with grandchildren is likely to be with the sons of a son. By contrast, it is not uncommon for fathers to have the most special relationship with "Daddy's little girl."

Because of their significance in passing along gender-role expectations, grandfathers who violate sexual boundaries with grandchildren may be especially devastating to these children, creating severe emotional and psychological dysfunction.

"The Best Darn Granddad"

It is important for men to know as much as possible about their grandfathers' lives in order to understand their own father better.

It is equally imperative that grandfathers develop the skills to communicate their feelings, hopes, dreams, and demons to their children as a way of helping the next generation grow.

The unique joys of grandfathering may have been best summed up by a taxicab driver in New Orleans, who treated my wife and me to the following spontaneous description of his feelings about being a grandfather for the fourth time: "I gets to come and go as I please, feeds 'em what they like, spoil 'em, play with 'em till they's all riled up, then leave and gives 'em back to the parents."

He laughed heartily and then proudly pointed out the snapshots of the grandchildren on the dashboard of his cab.

A LIFETIME TO GET IT RIGHT

Becoming the father you wish you had requires lifelong learning. As we progress through the stages from infant to elder, there is something to give to others and something to receive. The progression is never easy or smooth. Most of the learning involves on-the-job training and lots of anxiety.

Men who attempt to avoid facing the fear of these successive stages risk truncating the process, becoming stuck in an early stage of development. As they age, these men will continue to use their "tried and true" methods to solve problems that they face. Unfortunately solutions that worked at one age of father and child development are anachronisms in the next. They apparently will be doing everything right and still fail to reach their desired goals.

To go from the hopes and dreams of a young boy to the wisdom of an experienced grandfather requires regularly facing the fears of change and the unknown. It is easy in the face of such fears for any man to back off and to try to stay with the status quo. Yet only the man who will take the less-traveled path, who will strive for greater intimacy with his children and with his community, will find the fullest rewards of fathering. He may also discover an antidote to the despair of mortality. At each stage a man would do well to be as fully present and aware as possible.

III

HARD
FATHERING

SINGLE FATHERING

Happy Father's Day to all the dads:
Those with custody
Those who see their children all the time or rarely
and especially those the system chewed up
Who are denied this priceless right

This Father's Day message on a national computer bulletin board continued with a plaintive plea from a noncustodial father seeking help from anyone in the electronic expanse. He was desperate to find some way to be closer to his children and to deal with his loss of them. Many men and women responded with empathy, support, and advice. He responded later that the outpouring of caring was helpful, if not reparative.

Few issues bring as much pain to men as the loss of their children. Yet many men must face this loss. For a variety of reasons, modern divorce often translates into a separation of fathers and their children. Over the past three decades, as the number of divorces has swelled to approximately 50 percent of all marriages in America, there has been a corresponding trend of disengagement between fathers and children.

"The System"

Since the late 1960s the general position of the courts and social agencies has been that women are better parents by virtue of their gender. This general prejudice in favor of mothers has created a situation where mothers are almost automatically granted custody of the minor children in a divorce.

It has not always been so. At a time not too distant in our past, children were the "property" of the father. Indeed, so was the wife. This was clearly an inappropriate and indefensible position, and we have seen these practices eliminated in Western developed nations. Unfortunately while the legal system has ceased treating women as less than fully functioning persons, it has compensated by considering men as inadequate parents, quite a swing of the same scythelike pendulum.

When it comes to divorce and custody, social scientists, judges, legal practitioners, and elected lawmakers all shy away from politically incorrect public acknowledgment that women might not be superior to men, particularly as parents.

In the past few years small groups of men have begun to call such characterizations into question especially when it comes to the relationships with, and safety of, their children. These men argue that the near-automatic assumption that mothers are superior and the legal reification of that conjecture leaves fathers in very difficult positions. Many divorced men feel little freedom about how they can be with their children. They have a perception of diminishing input on matters of discipline, a need to provide support for two households, anger and resentment toward their former spouses, and a sense of failure. Combined, these feelings place a father in a precarious emotional situation. Either he will muster the courage to persevere in the face of frustration or he will succumb to the temptation to drift away from the family and the battle.

How is the single father to cope? We begin with fathers who have custody, then focus on those who do not.

SINGLE CUSTODIAL FATHERS

In those rare circumstances where a father is granted custody, he must face a myriad of dilemmas. The task for any single parent is immense, replete with time conflicts, dual responsibilities to make a living and maintain a household, no relief, and special emotional needs of children who have lost their family of origin. Because of the extremely low probability of spousal support, single fathers may have an additional financial burden. According to family-court attorneys in California, Illinois, Massachusetts, and Texas, it is not uncommon in many jurisdictions for a father to have physical custody a majority of the time and still be required to pay "child support" to his ex-wife.

Men become single custodial fathers as a result of separation, divorce, adoption, or widowhood. Of these, separation and divorce are the most common reasons for fathers gaining custody. Only 10 to 15 percent of children in single-parent families live with their fathers. The most recent estimate is that approximately a million American fathers now have sole custody.

Dual Standards for Custody

Custodial fathers are generally better educated, higher wage earners, have higher-status positions than the average, and have the wherewithal to seek custody. This is in sharp contrast to single custodial mothers, who all too often live in poverty. This represents a curious dichotomy. In many jurisdictions fathers are restricted from receiving custody of their children *unless* they have exceptional financial resources, whereas mothers will automatically receive custody, even if they are financially distressed. Most custodial fathers choose to be so. Many single mothers, deserted by a husband, have no such choice. Mothers end up with sole custody by default. Fathers can only achieve sole custody if they show special circumstances.

A national survey of (primarily Caucasian) single fathers who were members of Parents Without Partners indicated that the three most frequently cited reasons why the father had custody were the ex-wife's emotional problems, the children's expression of a choice to live with the father, and the father's superior financial status. A group of fathers who do not fit these criteria includes those who become single custodial fathers because of the death or desertion of the mother. It is notable that none of these reasons address the quality of parenting.

Rick is like many men who sought and received custody after his wife of twelve years requested a divorce.

> I love my children. . . . I couldn't imagine not coming home to them after work, but the truth is that I didn't really know what I was doing. . . . My dad was very loving when I was growing up, but Mom was really the parent we learned from. I don't think my dad ever changed any of our diapers. I had no training at all, [a point] that was driven home to me [repeatedly] after my wife left. One thing worries me. I wonder if it's normal—I think I used to be more of a father to my kids before the split. Now I sometimes feel like I'm taking care of the house more than the kids. There's so much to do, and I just don't get it so well organized.
>
> There sure wasn't any training for this. My dad always played with us and came to my Little League games, but he wouldn't have been ready to do what I'm doing now.

During the interview Rick was emotionally and physically affectionate with his two sons as they dropped by to check out what was happening. In response to a question he replied, "Yeah, I've always hugged the boys and was affectionate. My parents are like that, too, with all of us kids and the grandchildren."

Most of the men who had custody of their children reported that they were consciously making efforts to show their children affection in the absence of a maternal parent.

Lack of Support

One interesting finding is that fathers neither use nor seek much community support. When possible, they kept the home and community constant following divorce. This is consistent with the

Western male value of "doing it all by myself"—a prescription for long-term burnout and depletion.

Jeff is a good example of this. When his wife left suddenly for her "new life," he was left in sole charge of the three children under ten years of age. His reaction was to redouble his efforts to be a wage earner, involved dad, and homemaker. He succeeded for fourteen years, until the youngest graduated from high school. At that time he came into therapy suffering from a number of stress-related disorders and appearing fifteen years older than his chronological age. Is Jeff's experience normal? What is the lot of single fathers?

Kyle Pruett, in his book *The Nurturing Father*, writes, "The single father, not unlike the single mother . . . can expect . . . exhaustion, boredom, worry, confusion and disappointment, [along with] exhilaration, emotional rewards and pleasures unique to this experience never before felt or thought possible. Career advancement is often put in cold storage."[1]

Pruett, and others such as James Levine,[2] have frequently noted that this is particularly difficult for men in the corporate world, because, unlike mothers, fathers are not expected to put their children first.

Brian was thirty-three and progressively advancing in management in an Ohio automobile company when his wife of seven years left him and their two children. His "first surprise" came from his boss: "He pretty much indicated that I must have been a sexual failure. Then when I asked for extra time off to take the kids to doctors' appointments, lessons, or games, there was that disapproving look. My work didn't suffer, because I made up the time, but after I had the kids, there was a different atmosphere, and I was real aware that promotions would not be coming as quickly for me, because the company didn't come first. If I were a woman, I know that my family would not have been held against me the same way."

Geoffrey Greif, in *Single Fathers*, reported that the biggest problem faced was of juggling the multiple demands of career and fatherhood.[3]

Elroy described the following problems in his life: "When she took off, at first I think I was relieved . . . the fighting was over but then reality, like, set in. Whew, man, I got to figure out how hard my mamma worked when we was kids. I was up at five every morning just to get the house together and work out before the kids got up, then it was breakfast, drop 'em off at school, over to my job by eight. Lunch break was errands, then after work at five I'd get 'em, feed 'em, help them with homework, get 'em to bed by nine-thirty and then have to study for my own night school. Usually I just read three pages and passed out."

Cam, a twenty-six-year-old salesman, became overwhelmed by the conflicting requirements of his job and his two young sons. "I just lost it. The job required me to be on the road overnight, and with the boys, that was impossible. So I asked my boss for local routes and he tells me that if I pursued that, I'd be out of a job. . . . The day-care place was unstable, and I couldn't afford a live-in person. So I had to quit that job. Then, when I was out of work, the lawyer told me that I could lose the kids. . . . That was the blackest time. I couldn't let them go back with their mother . . . she was still on drugs and runnin' around, but I just couldn't handle them either twenty-four hours a day and no money comin' in. After about five months I just packed up the boys and came back to my folks' place in Arizona. My mom helps out now when I have to go to Tucson overnight."

The Importance of the Predivorce Relationship

Researchers have consistently shown that the predivorce relationship between father and child(ren) is the most significant factor in postdivorce adjustment to custody. Fathers who have been very close to their children and most involved with them tend to be most likely to seek, gain, and maintain custody. These men usually have been very involved in child care since the pregnancy, feel more comfortable with their children, and react better to single parenting.

Changes in Custody Arrangements

Despite the small numbers of single fathers vis-à-vis single mothers, single fatherhood and equal physical custody are definitely increasing. As more women enter the work force, as their salaries achieve equity with males in similar jobs, as our culture becomes more comfortable with involved male parenting, and as more men fight antiquated gender-based court decisions assigning custody, men will be granted sole and joint custody more often. More fathers will have the opportunity to participate in childrearing after divorce. California, which sometimes reflects, and sometimes creates, national trends, has had a policy of joint custody wherever viable.

Many women have already begun to relinquish custody in favor of career aspirations. In addition, men's activist groups are proliferating, upholding men's rights to custody of the children following divorce. In Texas the term *custody* is being seriously questioned, and many people prefer alternatives such as *residence* or *possession*.

Researchers have distinguished between single fathers who seek custody versus those who merely receive custody. The seeker aggressively goes after custody with the belief that he is the better parent. The assentor is either passive or resistive to custody and custody occurs in instances where mothers could not or would not assume primary custodianship. Men who seek custody report being involved in child care since early infancy.

NONCUSTODIAL SINGLE FATHERS

Most divorced, separated, or unwed fathers do not have primary physical custody of their children. Reliable figures on numbers of such men vary, but there is no question that they are in the millions.

Custodial Rights?

Often fathers have no say at all in the matter of custody. An unwed father only has rights and responsibilities to the extent that the mother allows or demands.

Author Thom McFarland wrote in *Mothering* magazine, "I hadn't planned on becoming a father that New Year's Eve in 1979. In the heat of passion, when I asked Marie point blank, 'Are you using any birth control?' she replied, 'It's all right. Everything's okay.' She didn't tell me she had decided against using her diaphragm. Months later, I learned from a friend that I had become a disposable dad."[4]

Thom was one of the increasing number of men who were with a woman who wanted children without marriage. Following the dictates of popular women's magazines and talk shows, and believing that a mother was all a child needed, Marie had no expectation that he would contribute to child support nor that she would demand his involvement with the child after that New Year's Eve.[5] She simply made a unilateral decision that had serious implications for Thom and their baby, Shawn. His feelings about being part of the conception, about being a father, or about being tricked were just not considered.

Deciding that he wanted to be involved in Shawn's life, Thom McFarland was able to discuss the matter with a sympathetic Marie, began paying child support, and visited frequently.

Other men are not so fortunate.

Chuck was twenty-three years old when his brief relationship with Patricia ended. He was unaware at the time that she was pregnant. The next contact he had with her came two years later, when he was subpoenaed into family court and ordered to pay child support. He was not invited, nor allowed, to develop a relationship with his daughter.

Similarly Gene was married to Stephanie for seven years. Their prenuptial agreement included a strongly worded agreement that they would not have children. In the sixth year of their marriage Stephanie had a change of heart and approached Gene about having a child. When he confirmed his desire to remain childless, she stopped taking birth control pills without his knowledge. When he discovered that she was pregnant and that she had deceived him, he filed for divorce. The court, acting on behalf of the child, ordered him to pay child support and denied him visitation "because he had not wanted the child." A year later Stephanie remarried and quit her job. On the basis of her new incomeless status, Gene was ordered to double his child-support payments. Her new husband's income was not considered because of another prenuptial agreement.

Legal Rights, Actual Rights. Gene and Chuck got the "worst of all possible worlds": financial responsibility for a child they would never be able to know or parent. Such apparent injustice is not altogether unusual.[6] A father who wants equal custodial rights definitely has an uphill struggle in most of America's divorce courts. Mothers are awarded custody of minor children in approximately 90 percent of divorces. Parenting by most noncustodial fathers is thus largely determined by the visitation arrangements set forth in the divorce settlement. A common form of such visitation is the father having the child on alternate weekends and holidays and one weekday evening per week. To an involved father this means that he will regularly not see his children for seven consecutive days every other week. Such a separation punctuated by a single evening together can be very painful. These men feel that much of their time together with their children is spent on greetings and leavings.

That is not the worst of it, however. Legally visitation rights may not be denied or terminated unless a parent is deemed unfit. However, many unhappy noncustodial fathers report that their visits with their children are often shortened or eliminated for a host of reasons. In a petition to family court Mark indicated that his ex-wife was late in transferring the children for forty consecutive weeks. "Whatever the time that I was to pick them up, it wouldn't happen. Easter vacation was the worst. I was supposed to get them Sunday night and have them until the next Saturday night. I went to pick them up at five o'clock as agreed, and got to wait outside in my car for four hours. At nine or so she pulls up and says they went to a movie instead of coming home. Then it takes another two hours to get them packed up. So we leave at eleven-fifteen and don't get home till after one in the morning. Then she shows up two days early to bring them back, and when I say no, she tells the kids that I refused to let them go to the rodeo with her."

It would be facile simply to consider ex-wives like Mark's as "passive aggressive," resistant, withholding, or manipulative. That could be unfair, perhaps hypocritical. These women who have the burden of most of the child care are losing out on some of the best (play) times with their children on weekends and holidays. They are also likely juggling very complex lives. Indeed many women report that their ex-husband is unreliable in picking up or dropping off the children on time. There may be many reasons for the lack of compliance.

However, from the male perspective Mark is being cheated out of some of the precious few moments he does have with his children. Furthermore divorce is, by definition, a condition sought by people who do not get along well and who probably lack the communication skills to resolve such conflicts with each other. Normal compromise and negotiation are frequently unavailable.

In such a relationship lingering animosity can well generate an environment in which limits are placed on visitation as a way of punishing a former spouse. This battle, like the withholding of or noncompliance with child-support payments, uses the children as munitions to hurt or retaliate for old injuries inflicted by an ex-spouse.

Fathers Who Don't Exercise Rights. There are many men who do not seek or desire much contact with their children, nor do they make their appropriate child-support payments. They have been well described as deserters, deadbeats, or avoiders. Other fathers become parental dilettantes. These "Disneyland Dads" are available infrequently and make every visit with their children a whirlwind of exciting events. There are also cases of "forced visitation," an unfortunate concept based on research that concludes that post-divorce adjustment of children is best when there is regular contact with both parents. This practice is destined to create more harm than good.

Visitation Patterns and Problems

It is common knowledge that the noncustodial parent (90 percent of the time fathers) has diminishing contact with his children over time. The longer the time since the divorce, the farther apart the visits seem to occur. Fathers who do not pay or are behind on child support are unlikely to visit often. Distance is another factor. As geographical distance increases, the less frequent the contact.

Why the abysmal visitation for fathers who claim to suffer deep longings for their children? Many fathers are quite verbal on the subject. They feel that their ex-wife's anger, vindictiveness, tendency to tie visitation to the child-support check, job-related moves, and their own pain of repeated and regular losses were crucial.

Many fathers cited the continuing conflict as a reason for diminishing contact. D.B. wrote of his difficult circumstances:

My ex and I have supposedly agreed through our lawyers on an increase to child support of about 150 percent and on standard Texas visitation rights for me. We officially have joint custody. Now she has given me a letter that flies in the face of the court's visitation order. I'm supposed to have visitation with the kids from June 15, when they get out of school, to July 28. She has signed them up for camps and activities until July 27 and wants me to have them from then until August 20, after my vacation from work. Also she has told the kids that they have a choice of being with me or going to cheer-leading and basketball camp. It's the same during the week. She has them signed up for so many activities with sports and church that either I don't get to see them or they get cheated out of fun activities. So I get to be the heavy. I got the revised court order spelling out exact visitation so that I could schedule their time with me to involve activities and family time. This weekend I really feel like the heavy. It is my weekend, but she has the kids scheduled from Friday at six (the exact time my time begins) until Sunday at four P.M. (an hour before I have to return them to her). So even with the revised court order I'm the "bad guy," and my time with the kids will be with them being angry and resentful at me. I am going to enforce the order even though the kids will be mad, because they have to understand that this is my time with them and that means sacrifice for all of us in terms of the other things we want to do. The damnedest part of it is that this is one of the reasons why I divorced her—keeping me from being with my kids.

D.B. gets to see his kids under poor circumstances. Scott, who claims that his ex-wife is physically abusive with their three school-age children, feels frustrated by the roadblocks he faces in seeing his children at all.

Easter vacation is coming, so now I have to look forward to whatever hoops the ex has planned for me to jump through in order that I realize my court-ordered visit.

She has lived in three states, moving to keep the girls from me. I now live in Virginia and she in Arkansas. She moved there under false pretenses and has recently changed residence and refuses to give me the new address or phone. I talk to my oldest daughter at her aunt's house from time to time.

Last summer I had to drive to Kansas where she was living because she refused to put the kids on a plane, because she has to pay 40 percent of travel. I had to have the Kansas authorities arrest her before she would reveal where she had the kids hidden (at the house of a friend from church). Only then did she let them go with me, without her 40 percent contribution. I was very lucky the police officer who accompanied me to make the request for visitation was sympathetic to the cause. His little girl, he explained to me, is somewhere in Europe with his ex.

I now have a great wife, and our sons love their stepsisters. I have always paid child support—even send the check to her parents in Maryland when I don't have her address, and I've never done anything to hurt my girls. She reported me to Child Protective Services in Arkansas anonymously a few years back and lied that I was hitting them and not sending support checks. I was denied visits for three months while they investigated. Then, when they found out that she had lied and made the call, they just laughed it off. It was okay for her to say those things, and I was considered guilty until the CPS saw my canceled checks and asked the kids. So I lost out for three months. The worst part is that she has threatened to do it again, and she tells the kids I refused to see them. Nobody seems to care that she's the one who illegally took them out of Virginia.

Another reason men give for dwindling contact is personal pain. There is an inherent conflict in the postdivorce family. First of all the couple has resorted to divorce because they have conflictual communication and values. For most recently divorced adults divorce brings with it feelings of failure, anger, and guilt. Each contact with the ex-wife reactivates those feelings and may feel like a setback in the healing process.

In addition, if a man's true personal demon is the fear of abandonment and rejection, he must face that demon twofold at each visit: once by contact with the ex-wife, their failed marriage, and a host of related feelings, and the second by the feelings of loss of his children brought about by the intense time together followed by another lonely separation.

Many men try to avoid those feelings and conflicts by avoiding the situation altogether and refraining from visiting with their children. A common destructive social cycle may then be set in motion. Having little contact with children, he is likely to become less willing to pay for their support. Mothers then retaliate by further restricting visitation until payment is made, which makes fathers angrier and less willing to pay, and so on.

The Predivorce Relationship. A primary factor in visitation patterns and problems is the historical relationship between the father and the children. Men who have had distant relationships with their children are naturally less likely to be involved fathers after a divorce.

Marshall was a very uninvolved father when his children were growing up. He was away from home on sales trips two or three weeks a month. When he was home, he "felt like a visitor." He and his wife were divorced in 1985 when the children were thirteen and sixteen. Because he was accustomed to little contact, he did not seek custody or regular visitation. He describes his current relationship with his children as "pretty much the same."

Kenny, by contrast, was, according to him, "the more involved parent. . . . When the children were young, I was the Indian guide, scoutmaster, Little League and soccer coach, car-pooler, suburban dad." He describes himself as continually working with his children on homework and projects. At the time of the divorce his two sons asked to be with him, as did one of his two daughters. Kenny speculated that the oldest daughter only chose to be with her mom because she felt that her mom needed someone. Despite the children's desire, and the agreement of his ex-wife, the court ordered equal custody and visitation for both parents. The court also ordered him to pay child support even though three children were living with him most of the time. After the divorce, according to Kenny, he spent "more quality time with the children because there were no fights. So it was better in that regard, but then whenever they spent the night with their mom, I just ached with missing them. So that was the bad part."

For both Kenny and Marshall, divorce essentially continued a pattern of contact with the children. This is generally true. Most men who were involved with their children before the divorce remain so. Those who were distant remain distant.

Occasionally men change their contact patterns. Manuel and Carol had what she described as a

> traditional marriage. He would go to work and bring home the bacon, and I'd stay home with the kids and cook it. . . . He was never that involved in the kids when they were little. He'd just discipline them and let me do most of the child care, you know. . . . The marriage came apart when we had four kids and I went back to school to get a career to help pay for college. . . . The truth is that the house kind of came apart. Nobody did the housework. . . . I expected him to do it, and he expected me to continue. . . . I just got fed up and decided to move out, closer to the campus. It came as a real surprise to me that he wanted to have the kids stay with him. . . . I didn't know he even noticed them. . . . Anyhow, to make a long story short, as soon as I was out of the house, he was completely transformed. He was with the kids all the time, and the house was almost as neat as when I was there.

To Manuel the role of traditional father did not include much time with the children. That was the mother's job. Once he became the sole parent, he naturally assumed the duties of that role as well. Role fulfillment and duty are well ingrained in modern men. They do what they perceive is the appropriate thing rather than what their partners desire.

Competence. Manuel was a competent father and homemaker. His skills were not evident until he determined they were necessary. Not all fathers are that way. In his book *Creative Divorce* Mel Krantzler describes the great difficulties for some men in learning how to cook, clean, or do the wash.[7] Oftentimes wives think of their husbands as incompetent little boys who will fall apart if they spent a twenty-four-hour period alone with the children.

As strange as it may seem, there are fathers who do feel this way. Roger "panicked whenever Lois would leave me alone with the baby for more than three hours." After his divorce Charlie "always found excuses to have my mother or mother-in-law around when it was my day with Megan." He loved his daughter but felt inept as her caretaker, something his ex-wife predicted and complained about while they were married.

Ed wasn't concerned with his fathering "outside the apartment," but was very uncomfortable with the household tasks that would make his "apartment a place for my son."

A particular form of competence involves communication with children. Many men are ill trained at verbal relating, particularly with children. They are not accustomed to the emotional or nonlinear logic that is normal for children. Untrained in many verbal parenting skills and lacking access to a built-in support network within which these are easily learned, some men avoid the uncomfortable situation by avoiding their children or restricting contact to clear-cut activities where talking is less likely.

Gerald was quite revealing in his comments:

When we were first divorced, I didn't know what to do with David. His mother spoiled him, I thought, and I wanted him to be much more responsible and grown up. I think I expected that when he was four. Well, we had a lot of uncomfortable adjustments until I finally figured out that he was doing the best he could and I was the screwup, not him. Over the months and years we've worked it out. Now I welcome his visits instead of dreading them. We don't always have to do something. We can just hang out together. He likes that a lot. I also know now that he isn't spoiled, my ex was just responding to him at his level. . . . [*laughing*] Now I bribe him with dessert too. The last three years have been a time when we both grew up. It sure wasn't easy. Lots of times I just wanted to miss our visits. I'm glad now that she pushed the issue and didn't let me take the easy way out.

The Influence of New Relationships on Visitation

When people divorce, they often feel loneliness and fear that they will never again have a viable relationship. New relationships will occur for most divorcés; some earlier, some later.

Bringing a new romantic relationship into a family remains problematic. Fathers will likely face the task of introducing a new sexual partner to their children, an introduction that is rarely met with acclaim. Frequently children of divorced parents hold the hope, belief, and unconscious desire to have their parents reunited. The newcomer is a threat to the realization of that yearning and is likely to be treated with distance, disrespect, or disapproval. The attempt to have his children like his new lover is described by Peter:

I was so worried the first night they were to meet, I almost felt like it was my own first date. What if they hated each other? What if there was a scene? Well, my picture was wrong, but the worry was right. You could cut the tension with a knife. Nobody talked except me, and I sounded like an idiot. Marlene was being too careful with them and they were having none of her. It took a long time before they finally accepted the fact that I would be with someone else . . . after their mother was living with a guy. It wasn't Marlene either. Sandy was the third one they met. She had an edge. She was a kindergarten teacher and knew how to talk to them at least . . . probably she knew how to talk to me the best. I am not fond of those memories. Monday-morning quarterbacking tells me that none of us was ready for that first meeting.

New relationships often lead to new marriages. The vast majority of divorced persons remarry.[8] Remarriage of the custodial parent usually results in less closeness and time spent with children from previous marriages. This becomes more pronounced when there are children from the new marriage. The new spouse's feelings about the children also have an impact.

Melissa was so threatened by her husband's children that she would make herself scarce during their visits and subsequently resent them for interfering with her time with her new husband. Rick was so worried about losing Melissa that he failed to confront the issue of her jealousy of his daughters. Instead he allowed his time with his daughters to diminish. To avoid conflict, he began to call them only from his office. "I finally came to my senses one night when she accused me of talking to Julie behind her back. When I heard myself lying and making excuses for talking to my own daughter, I knew things were crazy. I let her intimidate me by her fear and I just went along. That's exactly how I got into hot water in my first marriage. She'd pressure me, I'd make promises I couldn't keep, and then instead of standing up to her, I'd sneak around."

In therapy, Rick and Melissa had to work through her mistrust and jealousy and his intimidation. They also had to come to grips with the presence of Julie in their lives. What made this particularly difficult was Melissa's personal history. She was still angry at her own stepmother for "kicking me out of my father's house."

Personal Emotional Issues

Going through a divorce is rarely easy on anyone. Few people enter a marriage with less than a lifelong plan. Divorce means failure of a commitment and of the life plan. Divorce also means trauma for children and reduced contact for fathers. A man's grief at losing his family and the fantasy of growing old together is palpable, even if he precipitates the divorce.

Divorce requires a reassessment of one's beliefs, behaviors, and self. It is typically a time of greater emotionality. Feelings of insecurity and fears of loneliness are described by most men during the divorce process. This disequilibrium can be most troublesome as a father also tries to parent effectively and help his children go through their own fears and the disruption in their lives.

Facing Prejudice. Because uninvolved and underinvolved fathers have been so evident and their behavior so well chronicled, there is a general tendency to think of all divorced fathers in this light. Frequently "experts" cite these examples, along with "data" indicating that the majority of divorced fathers have diminishing contact with their children, as evidence that all divorced fathers are irresponsible and disinterested in their children. Clinical practice with men, and interviews with over one hundred single fathers, belie these "facts." However, involved fathers often experience themselves unfairly treated as "deadbeats" or described as "different." Either definition is unfair and distancing.

The Pain of Loss of Contact with Noncustodial Children. Many men suffer a great deal from the loss of daily contact with their sons and daughters. They consistently seek extra time with their children. Wayne, a divorced father of three, with joint custody, reported, "When the kids are at their mother's house, I sometimes just get overcome with the sadness. It even begins when they're with me and I know they'll be leaving the next day. I feel so bad that I withdraw. Especially if it'll be a long stretch—like the one week a month I don't have them at all." Wayne's sadness about the weekly separation from his children precipitated his emotional withdrawal even while they were still present. He began missing them before they had actually left.

Ken, a busy professional, went so far as to ask that his ex-wife call him every time she would normally use a baby-sitter. He has arranged his schedule around her schooling, job, and social events for four years. From a psychological perspective he has to face his own jealousy and discomfort each time she has an overnight social engagement, but he feels the reward of having the extra time with his children is worth that price. It is also commendable that she is willing to place her children's and ex-husband's best interests above her own convenience.

Noncustodial fathers who lose contact may also feel a deep, persistent longing that defies easy description, even when the lack of contact is their own fault.

Normally those fathers who have the most regular contact with their children have not remarried, live close to their children, and are more highly educated. Similarly the more highly educated the mother, the more likely it is that Dad and children will spend more time together, especially if the mother has remained single.

Facing Personal Decisions. If you go through a divorce, your personal emotional upheaval and need to be distant from the person who is becoming your ex-wife may obscure the children's needs to keep you active in their lives. It is important to consider what your life will be like as a noncustodial father. What role do you want to take in your children's future? What role do you want them to play in yours? Knowing what you want, how can you work out a parenting agreement with the woman you are divorcing? What impact will your children have on your new relationships? Would you be happy with a woman who rejects your children?

Fighting the System

Many men, recognizing the difficulties, missing their children, and despairing of any help from courts and agencies, have begun taking matters into their own hands. First, children are being kidnapped by their own fathers and taken across state lines where legal authorities have difficulty apprehending them.[9] Second, fathers'-rights advocacy groups have burgeoned. As a result of these two phenomena, combined with the personal loss of contact with their own children, lawmakers have begun to clarify the nature of visitation and to strengthen the enforcement of visitation orders.

Child Support. Child support is another major problem for noncustodial fathers. Although sex roles have shifted, fathers are more often ordered to pay child support than mothers who are in similar circumstances. It is still "newsworthy" when wives are ordered to pay alimony, as the 1992 front-page press coverage about Joan Lundin and Jane Seymour indicates.

According to a variety of population surveys, only one half of all noncustodial fathers meet their support obligations. The problem has become so serious for homeless and other children who live in poverty that federal legislation has been passed enabling states to enforce mandatory child-support payments. In addition "deadbeat" fathers' tax refunds can now be withheld for overdue support payments.

Just as with visitation, the more highly educated the parents, the higher the socioeconomic status, and the mother remaining single are highly correlated with regular support payments.

Men's Problems with Support. The two biggest complaints that noncustodial fathers have about child support are the *intertwining of visitation and support* and the *unfairness of the payment amounts.*

The problem of creating a vicious cycle between visitation and support has been previously addressed. When there is any connection between access to children and payment of support, there are serious grounds for trouble. Both are prime ways to hurt the person from whom one is divorced and who presumably is not among one's favorite intimates.

Many men feel cheated and treated unfairly by the amount of support that is court ordered or negotiated by divorce attorneys. Under most circumstances the only people who are fiscally better off after a divorce are the attorneys and therapists. When couples divorce, they normally require two households, double expenditures for common items, disruption of routines, changes in childcare arrangements, and possibly adjustments in work hours. Each of these is likely to cut into family financial resources.

Generally both parents have less to live on after a divorce. Commonly cited statistics (e.g., Tom Brokaw's *American Family in Crisis*) indicate that after divorce a woman with custody is likely to have her income reduced by 25 percent *and her ex-husband's increased by 35 percent,* an unfair and outrageous outcome. Like most statistics, however, this one bears more careful scrutiny. In fact those statistics hold primarily in blue-collar and lower-medium-income families where the mother has full custody of the children and when she does not remarry. There is some indication that the reverse is likely to be true in white-collar and higher-medium-income families, that a woman's standard of living will increase while her ex-husband's wages stay roughly the same or deteriorate.

This is particularly common when both parties remarry. One

reason for this is that with remarriage there is a general tendency in our culture for women to marry up the socioeconomic ladder. Thus she is more likely to remarry someone who has a higher income, and he someone who has less. Many a second wife, such as Linda, bitterly decries her family's standard of living, which is lower than her husband's ex-wife's:

I am the second wife (now married for fourteen years) and I have never been able to shake his first from my life. She is vindictive toward him even seventeen years after their divorce. He is paying $400 per month for each child plus expenses of $100 plus $120 for health insurance. So altogether he pays $1,120 per month for the two boys. That's out of his take-home pay of $1,985. Here's the problem . . . the children are with us more than half the time, which we both like, but why do we have to pay so much when she only supports them three days a week. . . . Then she insisted that we get a separate insurance policy, not put them on mine (which would have been no extra charge) . . . plus she has a teaching credential, but won't work because then the support would change. Do you think it's fair that she can just ride free after seventeen years while I end up having to work (plus his job) to support us? She lives in a big house; we rent. She eats out and buys expensive clothes; we can't. She goes on fancy vacations and we can't. She also has lived with a guy for nine years, but since they aren't officially married, she doesn't report his income. I know their marriage was horrible for both of them, but I don't think it's fair that we should have to pay for so long. Also, we have promised both children that we would pay for their college expenses (at the state school) and she won't pitch in a dime.

Even without inequities generated by remarriage men may get the worse deal. Debbie and Tom are a good example. Married for fourteen years with three children, they both had careers as helping professionals. As a hardworking, overly generous, and underpaid social worker, Tom was much too accepting of Debbie's long and intimate relationship with a supposedly homosexual male colleague. She constantly compared Tom unfavorably to her friend and ultimately became involved with him romantically. At that time she ordered Tom out of their home and moved her friend in. Characteristically avoiding conflict, Tom left as requested.

In the subsequent "no-fault" divorce action filed by Debbie, the financial settlement favored her. She received the family home, one half of his retirement savings (and all of her own), one third of his income (and all of her own). Tom was left with no equity until the family home was sold at her discretion and had to live on $2,000 per month (a small sum in Silicon Valley). By contrast she had $4,500 per month (her salary of $3,500 plus $1,000 from him). The three children spent three days a week and the whole summer at his apartment. In addition she is still living with her friend, who makes a decent salary and pays half of the rent and expenses for their living space. His income is not counted by the court.

By comparison Sean (an engineer) and Mica (a stock broker) were divorced after ten years of marriage. They have two children. The divorce was a direct result of his affair with his secretary. He moved out of the home and into an apartment to facilitate this affair in 1988. The divorce settlement in this case was roughly identical to the one that involved Tom and Debbie. Even though their incomes were roughly equivalent, Mica received child support of one third of his income, one half of his retirement funds, and spousal support of $800 a month for three years. She also got to keep the family home and had primary custody of the children. After the divorce her income for herself and the children was roughly three times his.

It is easy to conclude from this situation that Sean "made his bed and now he can sleep in it." Unfortunately this conclusion can hardly be applied to Tom. It was his wife, after all, who had the affair and he who was the loser. One conclusion that might be drawn from this is that, at least in some circumstances, the husband may be the financial loser no matter who creates the grounds for the divorce.

These examples are not isolated. Among white-collar, upper-middle-class professionals the man rather than the woman may be victimized in a divorce. This flies in the face of conventional wisdom and the financial devastation wreaked on lower-middle-class and poverty-level women who are divorced. It goes without saying that the primary victims of divorce are of course the children. At this point the man's feeling that he is being cheated is the focus of our attention.[10]

Tom and Sean have both sought relief from the court on appeal. At this time Tom has received a reduction in the payments based on his increasing time with the children. Sean had the spousal support reduced by one year. However, the legal costs make these victories more emotional than financial.

Two Pots: Hers and Ours. Another man's experience exemplifies this unfairness. Jose was a devoted father and husband for twenty-five years. After a successful career his position was eliminated at a California engineering firm. Semiretired, he began consulting out of his home. His wife, Laura, who had returned to work when the children were grown, found her own career blossoming at roughly the same time. Despite the fact that she was earning the lion's share of their joint income, they had a curious, yet common agreement: The total income in their home was divided into *their* money (all that he made) and *her* money (her income). When she left him for a man she met at work, she insisted on keeping that arrangement. She wanted half of his income and all of her own, arguing that his income was payment for the years she stayed home with the children. What is shocking is that the divorce-settlement agreement coincided with her belief.

Jose was informed that unless Laura remarried, she had the right to half of his income, even though his was less than hers. His lawyer, arguing that he also deserved half of her income, was unsuccessful. Both Jose and Laura believed in this double standard. However, the result was that she will live out her life in luxury (a result of her higher income combined with that of her lover and half of Jose's), whereas he will live just above subsistence levels.

Two supposed facts make this possibility difficult to confront: the previously cited belief in the "fact" that women's income decreases by comparison with men's, and the "fact" that women receive only a fraction of the pay for equivalent work. The data on which these supposed facts are based have been shown to be seriously flawed, more political than scientific conclusions. However, these erroneous beliefs are so strong in our culture that many men rightly feel that the correction for inapplicable social ills is being extracted from them personally.

The social injustices that many women do suffer must be corrected. However, a broad-based assumption that any particular man is gaining from such unfairness is erroneous. Dispensing justice for social ills based on group identification instead of individual cases is prejudice. In today's divorce court some women are treated as if they belong to a protected group, and their husbands as if they were perpetrators of an injustice, without any evidence to support that assumption. Too often it is precisely the wrong people who get the special benefits; truly needy women and men are sometimes treated less kindly.

In Brief

The sum of these psychological, financial, and social problems faced by noncustodial single fathers no doubt contributes greatly to these fathers' gradual withdrawal from the lives of their children. Fathering relationships do not seem to weather such obstacles readily and therefore tend to attenuate over time.

Because it is unlikely that the number of divorces will decrease soon, the goal for fathers, children, and therapists is to help support men through this process while encouraging continuing or increasing contact with their children. If men do not actively resist the natural tendency to withdraw, all levels of our culture will be affected. The fathers will long for their lost children, the children will grow up without fathers—and thereby replicate in the next generation the impact of father absence—and mothers will again have the burdens, and the power, of solo parenting.

There is no question that both fathers and children suffer from withdrawal after a divorce. How do you face all the difficulties and remain a constant and important force in your children's lives? Most men who have "lost" their children through divorce carry a deep pain for many years. They suffer the personal loss. They also feel guilt at leaving their children with a person they personally dislike. They lose their connection of biological continuity with the next generation. Most important of all, fathers who leave expose their children to emotional, psychological, and economic harm. It is rare to find any man who would not be bothered by that.

WIDOWERS AS SINGLE FATHERS

There have always been single fathers. Two generations ago the most common cause of death in twenty- to forty-year-old women was childbirth. Thankfully, high maternal mortality rates, which created instant single fathers, have dramatically diminished, although the United States trails other Western nations significantly in this regard. Recent research indicates that over 200,000 American children live with widowed fathers.

Right after the death of their spouse widowers may have difficulty dealing with the emotional problems of their children. This is because they are grieving the loss of their partner while expanding their role to replace what she gave the children. The initial adjustment will be affected by the preexisting relationship between the father and children, how much division of labor characterized the household, and the father's ability to deal with his own feelings of loss. Over time most widowers do quite well, as well, or better than custodial fathers.

The death of a mother often draws the children closer to the surviving father. Most widowers describe their former marriage as happy, and this prior good feeling and communication are transmitted to the children. Some idealization of the deceased is normal and healthy, although carried to excess, it can delay working through the grief process. Often fathers and children, having shared a mutual loss, are therapeutic for one another in the grieving period following death. This is more true when the children are not at preschool or younger ages. By the time they are in grammar school, children have more ability to care for themselves and to help competently around the house.

Many widowers report that they felt closer to their children than before their wife's death.

Sudden Adjustment

One of the biggest problems that faces most widowers who are fathers of young children is the suddenness of the loss and the shock of being instantly the sole parent of their children.

Bernard's wife was killed in an automobile accident. At the time of her death the children were eleven and seven. As a stay-at-home mother Margo was very active in the children's lives. She was always available to them, was active in their schools and lessons, and supported their social lives by providing a center for their friends as well. According to Bernard, she also took very good care of him.

Following her sudden loss, he had to assume many family duties that were new for him. He suddenly inherited the roles of cook, launderer, driver, and social director for the two children. Initially, community and family support helped him get through some of the particulars, but that soon faded. "You know, when she first died, someone brought over a casserole or drove the kids every day. They also supported me emotionally as best as they could, but in three months we were on our own. I guess I'm proud of how much the kids and I have done. We really have most of it under control. We all miss her terribly, and I still cry myself to sleep some nights—or end up sharing my bed with both the kids when they feel sad or scared. . . . But you know, we are doing okay. We eat takeout more than I'd like, I'm not as on top of my work as before, but there are clean clothes and the house is clean (not neat). All in all I'm amazed at how well we've done."

Bernard's adjustment, eighteen months after his wife's death, wasn't atypical or unique. Most fathers, forced to pick up their late partner's roles and responsibilities, adjust fairly well over time. These men do not report any insurmountable problems other than what they previously had. Their younger children become more independent and supportive. The family unit often becomes more tightly bonded.

Bernard's children were both school-age. Gregory faced an additional challenge when his wife died suddenly: His daughter was only two years old. He was accustomed to caring for her at home, but it was no easy task finding proper child care at an afford-able cost while he was at work. The long hours and a lack of sick-child care plagued him for years. He reported on the day of his daughter's graduation from college, "I was lucky so many times. I am also glad that I gave her priority over my work. I never did get to be manager of my own store, but just look at her. She's worth every minute, every compromise . . . even during those awful years when she was an early teen. . . . I guess that's when Beth [his wife of ten years] really helped out. . . . You know when I married Alysha, I thought I had met the best woman in the world. Her death, in a funny way, makes me believe that I have been triply blessed" (*pointing to his current wife and his daughter*).

Although some fathers initially experience difficulty with the demands of child care, they eventually discover they can deal with their children's emotional and daily needs. Often the children be-come a positive force in their facing of their grief and in their lives.

This is not to suggest that their lives are easy. The sudden loss of a family member is traumatic and painful for everyone.[11] The grieving process is frequently prolonged. Many adults who lost par-ents as children feel that they have never fully recovered.[12]

Widowers and Divorcés

Are widowed fathers different from divorced fathers? To some ex-tent they are. Normally speaking, they feel more positive about their former marriages and describe the relationships as having been highly satisfactory. In addition ongoing conflict continues in divorced families, whereas generally it does not in widowed families.

Another difference is related to the behavior and coping capabilities of the men. Widowers and divorced men experience similar loss reactions: feelings of shock, denial, helplessness, panic, self-pity, confusion, and depression. However, divorced men often feel a heightened sense of guilt in addition. Most widowers do not believe in retrospect that they could personally have prevented the loss.

The community will also support widowed fathers more. Friends and family will not be prone to blaming or avoidance, which may accompany a divorce.

For the children the reality of their mother's death eliminates hope for a reunion between their parents. Because they have only one living parent, it also promotes greater closeness between fathers and children.

A Single Exception: Suicide

When a wife's death is self-inflicted, all survivors and community may be far more prone to feelings of responsibility or blame.

After Nelson's wife committed suicide, leaving him with three children, he found community support to be absent or minimal. "Those first weeks were terrible. My brother flew in and actually dealt with cleaning up the mess and arranging help for the kids, but he couldn't deal with everything. The church wouldn't bury her in the church cemetery. . . . I kept wondering if I had done anything or could have done anything. I feel so guilty. . . . I mean, I knew she was depressed and wouldn't take her pills, but nobody thought it would come to this. . . . You know, her aunt committed suicide, and maybe her grandmother also, so I worry about the kids. . . . Most of my neighbors were polite, but when the story got out, they just treated us like lepers. . . . I am really angry at the church. I always went there for support. . . . They just didn't make room for us. Why do they make me feel so ashamed?"

For many in our culture, death by suicide invalidates the support anyone who has suffered such a loss will need. In many ways these mourners need extra caring because of feelings of guilt, shame, and the sense that the death could have been prevented. Widowers who have suffered this type of loss normally need extra assistance. Psychotherapy is strongly recommended.

WHY SINGLE PARENTING MAY BE MORE DIFFICULT FOR MEN

Most men do not initially choose to be single parents. We gain that status through a loss, by divorce or death of our spouse. This is similar to the vast majority of women who are single parents, although there is an increasing number of single women who opt for single parenthood.

There are some differences among men and women in this regard. Even as our cultural revolution in gender roles progresses, few boys receive much training in parenting. They are not encouraged to place much attention on the care of younger siblings or to plan to be a father, as much as they prepare for a career.

There are fewer support systems in place for us as single parents. We are also less prone to seek such support when it is available. Men usually do not get as much time with their children as women.

In addition, there is considerable evidence that we fare less well after divorce than females. Married men even live longer. Psychologically, males seem to handle divorce worse than their female counterparts. Divorce from a wife may well reflect an unconscious replication of the pain of earlier separations from our mothers. Divorce may well reactivate the pain of separation and loss we experienced from an emotional exile, as young boys, in our families of origin. Working through the emotional pain of divorce for men may involve dealing with a lifelong fear of abandonment and loss. Men who fail to address these psychological connections may be prone to remarrying quickly, only to find themselves replicating their old relationship with a psychological clone.

ADVICE FOR SINGLE FATHERS

1. Try everything you can to resolve your conflicts and avoid the divorce altogether. Marital counseling is a good first step. If divorce is inevitable, seek mediation rather than litigation. Explore divorce therapy and individual therapy to avoid working the conflicts out through the children.

2. You may divorce a wife, but fatherhood will remain. Find a way to **stay connected** to your children and to actively provide what fathering you can. The greater the adversity with your ex-wife, the more the kids need you to be a positive model for them.

3. Try your best to put the hurts and anger with your ex-wife behind you. Although you will probably never become good friends, it is important that you learn to parent cooperatively. The more you can put aside your desires for revenge or attempts to change her, the better it will be for your children.

4. Whatever your personal feelings, as much as possible keep your negative feelings about your ex out of the relationship with the children. Don't compare your house with hers. Don't use the kids to send a message to your ex.

5. Introduce your new friends to your children carefully. It is usually appropriate to introduce your children and lover only when the relationship appears to have a serious future potential. When you consider new partners, keep your children in mind. For example, if your prospective new partner has children of her own, or dislikes children, figure out what the impact will be on your children. Make the necessary adjustments.

6. Be prepared to fight for custody rights if you want them. You won't get them automatically.

For the Custodial Parent:

1. **Seek help.** Often men tend to try to do it alone. Other single custodial fathers can be of help. Fathers in intact

families and noncustodial situations may also provide input. Single female parents may be most helpful in articulating resources and providing emotional support.

2. Recognize that you have two full-time jobs. **Don't try to be Superman.** It will not be possible to do everything perfectly. You need to examine and prioritize your values and do what you can. Try to make peace with the parts of your life you will have to downplay. Perhaps fathering will have a higher priority than some work endeavors. From my interviews with many others who share your difficulties I can conclude confidently that career delays are not as debilitating to most men as putting one's family on hold. You will probably have your career long after the children have left your home for good.

3. Community resources are normally geared toward female single parents. You will need to **get connected** to these "female" networks. As forbidding as that might seem, you will probably be welcomed as a parent, not rebuffed because of your gender.

4. **Find other single fathers.** This is frequently not such an easy task. Like you they may also be isolated and remote. In addition to churches, community centers, classes, and school organizations, computer bulletin boards and electronic mail provide opportunities to connect with others.

For the Noncustodial Parent:

1. It is easier to abdicate responsibility for children if you see them infrequently and your ex-wife does things differently than you do. However, a child does much better with two parents. Try to maximize the time you are available and **find ways to stay involved with your child.**

2. **Attend the major events in your child's life:** school; athletics, dramatic performances, and so on. In some ways

it is more important for you to go to these than it is for fathers who live with their children all the time.

3. **Keep the children aware of what is happening in your life.** They are usually much more interested than a parent expects.

4. **Find other single fathers.** This is frequently not such an easy task. Like you they may also be isolated and remote. In addition to churches, community centers, classes, and school organizations, computer bulletin boards and electronic mail provide opportunities to connect with others.

5. **Seek help.** Other noncustodial fathers can be of help. Fathers in intact families and custodial situations may also provide input. Women who are single parents may be most helpful in articulating resources and providing emotional support.

FATHERS WITH MULTIPLE FAMILIES: STEPFATHERS

My stepdaughter is visiting.
I love her as much as I love my biological kids.
Yesterday, on our eighth wedding anniversary, she said,
I love you, Mom, and you too, Dad.
I realized it was also my eighth anniversary with her.
It was the best present.

If being a good parent is a near-impossible task, consider the difficulties faced by a parent with children from different families. Stepfamilies are complicated legal, emotional, and social entities. They are also quite common. If we are to believe popularly quoted statistics, almost one half of American children will spend at least some time in a family arrangement that does not include two biological or adoptive parents. Over a third of all children will live in a stepfamily.

STEPFAMILIES

Stepfamilies have been in existence at least since biblical times. Men commonly married a widow and assumed responsibility for stepfathering her children, or a widower with children remarried, creating a stepmother. The prefix *step* is derived from an old English term that meant "bereaved" or "orphaned." In more modern terms a stepparent was seen as "stepping" in to replace a lost parent. In these families there were no living "outside" parents.[1]

Today most stepfamilies are created when children from a prior union are brought to another marriage by one of their biological parents following divorce. In a blended remarriage there may be "outside" parents, in-laws, and extended family on both sides. Such living "outsiders" often have a significant impact on the new "blended" family.

Stepparenting is no easy task. To all the problems of biological parenting are added a host of novel ones. For one thing all stepfamilies are built on the foundation of prior loss. For another there are no readily available models for new stepparents to emulate. The modern stepparent is an additional parent rather than a replacement. Finally a stepparent does not have a legal status with stepchildren; as a stepparent you may not have the right to obtain emergency medical treatment for stepchildren; you may not have the right to see the stepchildren's medical records; you will not be required to pay child support, nor will you have the right to visit the children if the marriage ends in death or divorce. Similarly it is extremely unlikely that custody would be awarded to a stepparent.

At least four areas of unique stress are commonly experienced in stepfamilies:

- Continuing emotional impact of divorce
- The difficulty of merging different family cultures and identities
- Incompatible family rules about distribution of resources
- Loyalty conflicts

Continuing Emotional Impact of Divorce

Divorce is the result of incompatibility, a legal correction to a social-relational failure. Frequently it is experienced as a failure by parents and children. Rarely is a divorce easy for the participants or their children. Normally divorce engenders pain, disillusionment, a sense of failure, and feelings of loss. Most people going through the breakup of a long-term intimate relationship suffer with these feelings for a lengthy period. Therapists generally estimate that it takes a minimum of one to three years to accommodate, and become adjusted to, a divorce when the marriage has produced children.

Divorces for families with children are particularly difficult. The parents are usually forced to be in contact with each other to make ongoing decisions about their children's schooling, finances, and activities. Custody and visitation rights often bring the divorced couple into frequent, uneasy face-to-face contact. This contact often reignites conflict and uneasy feelings for the adults. In-laws, who have a continuing love for and who fear a loss of contact with the children, often put additional emotional pressure on the couple.

Gus and Sally were married for ten years. They have two girls, aged nine and six. Although they have been divorced for four years, the emotional impact is ongoing. According to Sally,

> the nightmare continues. I try not to get hooked, but every Thursday morning when he comes to get the girls, there's real potential for a fight. Last week while he was waiting, he started to look at the mail on my kitchen table. He constantly pumps the girls for information about me and my life—as if I had one. . . . The money is constantly an issue too. He always brings the check on the eighth instead of the first. Last summer vacation he brought them back three days late so they could spend more time with his family. I don't object to his parents, I always liked them, but if they really wanted more time, they could have arranged it during the first part of his trip. I know it's just to provoke me, so I try not to get angry, but he still gets to me.
>
> Last week he was really nice when he came over, so we had a cup of coffee and talked a little. I should know better. He tells me that he still loves me and wants to get back to-

gether. Then, what's worse, he tells Kimmy [oldest daughter] that he wants to get back with me. Meanwhile he's the one who's living with another woman. It so bothers me that I'd even consider going back. My life was hell. . . . I have to really remember what it was like, and then I get miserable. I feel terrible saying this, but I sometimes think it'd be a lot easier if he just died.

Gus sees Sally as unreasonable and unfair: "Wanting all my money, making me fight to be with the kids, wanting everything her own way. What about my parents and sisters? They really love the girls. What's the harm if the kids spend some extra time with their grandparents and aunties?"

Although they have been living apart for five years, they are both still able to recreate much of the negative emotional intensity that existed during their marriage. This is partially true because of their constant contact over their children. The other reason has to do with their personal growth. Neither Sally nor Gus has taken the time to work through psychologically their personal sense of loss of the relationship nor the loss of their hopes and fantasies for their marriage. Both have avoided confronting their personal issues that led to their disillusionment and divorce. Instead of owning their personal part in the problems, they continue to use the partner as "the cause" of all their problems. Sally believes that she cannot have another relationship for fear it will turn out like her marriage. Although she has dated a few men, she hasn't gone out with anyone more than twice. Gus has lived with six different women in the five years since their separation. He stays with them until the time comes for a more permanent commitment, then he moves on. Until they can relinquish their ex-spouse emotionally, neither will be able to form a successful new relationship.

Sally and Gus are still single. Most people remarry within three years of a divorce. If there are children, these marriages create stepfamilies. When they establish their new home together, they may move in the emotional baggage from the prior relationship, along with the wedding gifts. This is especially true for men, because they tend to remarry much sooner than women.

Both parents and children must recover from the loss of a spouse, parent, and expectations. It is natural for everyone involved to go through a period of mourning, including anger, guilt, sadness, anxiety, and so on. When a new relationship forms before the original family is surrendered psychologically, the mourning will continue during the early stages of the new relationship, inevitably coloring it.

What is the impact of this carryover? On the positive side the new relationship can serve as a counterbalance and reality test. The new spouse can provide support for the emotionally turbulent times. On the negative side the old conflicts may invade the new marriage. Consider the position that Wendy describes:

> I knew when I married Quinn the kids were part of the package. I wasn't too surprised by how hard that has been . . . and it's been hard. What I was not ready for, and still resent, is how much Beverly [his ex-wife] has crossed the boundary. I mean, it's almost like she lives here. She gets him so mad and uptight that there's no talking to him for days on end. Or she calls me and tells me all these things about him that I don't want to know and that mostly turn out to be lies. I know you won't believe this, but one day I came home and she was in my bedroom with the kids. She asked them to give her a tour of their new house . . . in my bedroom! I put a stop to her commando visits, but I can't stop her from hurting Q and our relationship. He can just come unglued from one of her little "remarks."

A new marriage, and the desire to be released from the emotional bonds of a prior relationship, may not be enough to enable a divorcing man to feel free or to make peace with his past. Unfinished emotional separation is often problematic. It seems very important that new partners understand the continuing emotional impact of the prior marriage. After three years Mark is beginning to appreciate the power of his prior relationship in his unconscious mind. "I hate to admit it, but, truth be told, when I get upset with

Kate, I treat her with all the force of my anger at Maureen, my ex. I know they're different up here in my head, but I respond from my gut. I blast her with the full force of my rage at Maureen, and she doesn't deserve it. She doesn't even have a clue where it comes from. Three weeks ago she had a second glass of wine at a restaurant, and I had that fear clutch my heart that she was alcoholic like Maureen. I didn't say that. I just ragged on her all the way home about her 'drinking problem.' She doesn't have a drinking problem. It was all in my mind."

Children are a constant reminder of the prior bond. The former spouse lives in their appearance, gestures, habits, words, and actions. They are inadvertently the messengers that keep the old pains alive. Any concerns that an ex-spouse could harm the children will be provocative. Disagreements over discipline, activities, or styles that were present during a marriage may be exacerbated after a divorce. Sometimes new lifestyles of a parent after a divorce can also be problematic.

Len reports, "Since she got involved with this new guy, all the things that we agreed to are up for grabs again. I don't want the kids exposed to some of the things that they are. We used to restrict their television viewing. Now they each have their own TV and cable. Then, when they get to my house, they complain because I won't let them do lots of things they do at her house. One weekend they just didn't want to come over here at all, because 'the other house was more fun.' That really hurt."

The Difficulty of Merging Different Family Cultures and Identities

Within a larger social context each family develops its own culture and identity. In a remarriage the individualized culture must change as new people enter and previous members leave. Social rules evolve slowly as a family grows. However, with a remarriage conflicts may develop as fully grown cultures are forced to cohabit.

Merle remembered one of the first instances where the culture clashed:

. . . and crashed. We were one of those "Brady Bunch" family types. She had three kids and I had two when we got together. Never were two more different groups to be housed under the same roof. Her daughter was used to free use of the family car, gas and insurance all paid. My son, who was the same age, got it on the occasional Saturday night as a privilege or he got to drive it to work when he was on the late shift. But he paid for gas and insurance. Her youngest was used to a swimming pool and would turn on the sprinklers and run through whenever she wanted. My kids were used to water conservation and flushing toilets only when necessary. The first two years were tough. My kids suddenly thought of me as Simon Legree, and hers thought she didn't love them as much as I loved mine because she didn't set limits like I did.

Until a stepfamily develops a shared family history over time, members tend to have a tenuous sense of belonging. The blending of two cultures requires time and tolerance. To some extent a stepfamily will never have the unadulterated feeling of "the way it's supposed to be," because it is an amalgam. Pedro says he remembers the exact moment, and the emotional thrill, when his stepdaughter used the word *we* to describe the remarried family: "I can recall it like yesterday. We had been together about two years and we were at my company picnic. She just replied to a question from my co-worker, that 'we're the family from the valley.' Nobody else even noticed it, but I felt a joyous, electric charge of delight. I really felt accepted. My love for her had been growing, but with that incentive it just blossomed."

Another factor that complicates the new family identity is that many cultural values and roles are altered during the process of a divorce, single parenthood, and remarriage. Because these matters are in flux, less is clear and stable in the commencement of the new relationship. The only model we have is for the "happily ever after" marriage. When that fails, individuals have to find their own ways of re-creating expectations and reexamining personal values. As these evolve, the new relationship experiences a disequilibrium.

In addition a blended family is inherently less stable because of the remaining ("outside") parents, likely lack of a common surname, and an unreasonable anticipation that they should act like the model family of their expectations. In the words of nine-year-old Robby, "It's okay. We just make it up as we go along!"

Incompatible Family Rules About Distribution of Resources

Children who come from a single-parent family to a stepfamily normally are accustomed to certain allocations of time, energy, money, and affection. The children are not the only new family members who come with such expectations; adults forming the new couple also anticipate certain allotments.

It doesn't always work out according to plan. Often a stepfather finds himself in competition with his stepchildren for affection, attention, or time with his new wife. George, who was single until his marriage to Melanie, reports that he became a stepdad too suddenly: "When Mel and I were dating, it was just the two of us. I knew about her kids, but it wasn't so real. Then when we all moved in together, there were two little people that I had to deal with. Mostly I resented the time they took from me and Mel. They just acted like I didn't exist at all. It was about two years before I began really relating to the older girl. It happened because we were together at least one night every week. It was real slow. It's funny, because I always liked the kids as people, I just didn't know how to be their parent or stepfather."

Mary Ann was very resentful of the time her new husband's children took up in the evening:

> I just couldn't believe it. After dinner he'd help them with their homework, play with them, read them stories in bed. By the time he was done, he was exhausted and had nothing left for me. At first I thought it was the adjustment period, but after a while I got pretty vocal about it. It was a clear competition between me and his kids for time with him, and it didn't

matter how much time I spent with them. They always wanted special time with Daddy. In those early months I used to pray for their weekends with their mother. It was the only clear time we had.

When we went to counseling, I learned that he felt guilty about breaking up their family, so it made some sense to me, but he also figured out that he could do it again unless he paid some attention to my needs as well. The thing was that he didn't expect to get any time for himself either. He just did whatever anyone else wanted until he was exhausted and fell asleep.

The stepchildren may also feel very jealous when Mom lavishes attention on her new husband instead of them. Often they feel a great loss when she remarries. When she was single, they had her all to themselves.

Brett, who was a sophisticated sixteen-year-old when his mother remarried, "felt real lost and alone without her. It started when she was dating him, then she was gone more and more. I started to go out with an older girl from the neighborhood. I knew she was like a replacement for Mom, but I needed it. Jimmy was younger, so he got into trouble at school and with the cops. That way she had to pay attention to him too. When Dad first died, she was all for us. I think I also was bothered that she'd try to replace Dad. I know she needed somebody adult to hang out with, but I wasn't ready."

Changes in the way money is distributed may have a big impact. When Leslie, a single mother with three young children, married Cliff, she entered into a new world. Accustomed to careful budgeting and limited resources, she found herself in conflict with her new husband's wealth. She certainly enjoyed the end of her monthly stress when the bills came in. However, her children, who were accustomed to a conservative lifestyle, now could purchase anything they wanted. Leslie was deeply worried about their "losing their sense of values."

Nick's experience was almost the opposite. As a single man a good proportion of his income was discretionary. When he married Gwen and became a stepfather to her son, their joint income left them with less unallocated funds. He resented having to reduce his personal spending and reacted by running up charge-card expenditures for several months. The monetary adjustment became the major disagreement in their relationship.

Whatever the specifics, redistribution of family resources is often difficult for everyone in the new unit. Feelings of jealousy, anger, and rejection often emerge until the new allocations evolve and are accepted.

In blended families some children may in fact receive more of the resources. In one blended family there were two incomes; the wife's income from her late husband's insurance was solely for her and her children; the husband's income was for the whole family (minus alimony and support payments). In this household one sixteen-year-old girl had far more available resources and freedom than her sixteen-year-old stepsister, a situation ripe for bad feelings and competition.

Loyalty Conflicts

All members of a remarried family commonly experience loyalty conflicts. Children who develop affection and love for a stepfather may feel disloyal to their biological father. A biological mother may be torn between a desire to be with her new husband and her children's need for time and attention. Stepfathers who are also biological fathers regularly feel guilt over the inability to give as much time and affection to their natural children as they do to their stepchildren. In a blended family a parent may feel guilty about the relative amounts of time spent with step and biological children.

Kenny guiltily reported that he really was fond of his stepdad: "Mike is really a good guy. I called him Dad once and then felt weird. Like if I call him Dad, I don't care about my own dad. I do. I love him, but Mike is around and cares about me too. Do you think if I like Mike, it means I don't like my dad so much?"

His stepfather had similar conflicts: "I really am growing to love Kenny, but each time I feel myself getting close to him, I miss my own kids even more. I should love them all equally, I know, but you know, blood is blood. When the girls are over, I think I don't pay enough attention to Kenny, but when they're gone, I feel guilty when I'm affectionate with him. . . . I wish I could be more like Michelle or my mom. They just take in all kids and love 'em to pieces. They don't worry about who gets more. They just give a lot to all the kids."

Loyalty conflicts can be the most burdensome for family members. Often they are felt unconsciously. They may produce the deepest emotions without being rationally understood. Disloyalty to a biological parent may bring up a sense of failure. As Lee described it, "Being disloyal to my father, even if he is unavailable, is a violation of the Ten Commandments. I don't feel right doing that."

CAN STEPFAMILIES BE SUCCESSFUL?

Stepfamilies face additional challenges. Unless these challenges are acknowledged and met, adjustment may be elusive.

The picture is not all negative. Stepfamilies who struggle with and confront the adjustment problems actually show improvement in a host of areas. These include better psychological adjustment, a reduction of psychosomatic complaints, less delinquent behavior, and better sex-role development, particularly in boys.

The most encouraging information reported in the literature is that children raised in stepfather families are not different from children reared in biological families on measures of delinquency, stability, personality, school behavior, grades, drug use, psychosomatic complaints, self-concept, interpersonal relationships, and personal attitudes toward marriage and family.

Several of the conflictual areas are common and predictable. New stepfamilies can be prepared for some of the adjustments. For example, loyalty conflicts must be anticipated and respected.

Each person in a blended family will have to reestablish his personal territory and redefine his relationships with the new and old family members. Affectional bonds have to be nurtured as they slowly develop. New rules, duties, chores, and access to resources will have to be negotiated. Accommodation will have to be made for new extended family members.

The wise stepparent takes on parental responsibilities slowly. Integration and bonding require nurturing over time. Rushing them may paradoxically delay or eliminate the possibility of occurrence.

Most stepfamilies do somehow confront the common stresses and make the necessary adjustments. What stages might there be for stepfathers in working through this process?

STEPFATHERING

Considering the prevalence of stepfamilies in modern culture, there is a remarkably small literature providing understanding and advice.[2] Even within the small existing literature over 90 percent is addressed to step*mothering*. Stepfathers, who are the vast majority of stepparents, are almost ignored. This statistic mirrors the absence of a bountiful literature on fathers compared with that for mothers.

Because women receive custody of the minor children in 90 percent of divorces, there are a greater number of stepfathers than stepmothers. Whether you are a stepfather, bring a stepmom into your children's life, or remarry and have a second family, you are likely to encounter several obstacles unique to stepfamily life. The highest probability is that you will become a stepfather by marrying a woman who has custody of her children.

What do stepfathers experience when learning to parent stepchildren? For one thing stepfathers have a poorly defined role and are usually relegated to on-the-job training. They also tend to be overanxious to make the new family work quickly. Many new stepfathers feel discouraged or disillusioned at the lengthy process of adjustment.

Experienced stepfathers estimate that the integration of communication, authority, and discipline into family life takes at least one and a half to two years. Affection and loyalty concerns take longer. Rushing these can have a number of negative influences on the children, including poorer mental health and psychological adjustment, increasing dissatisfaction with the family, ongoing behavioral problems, and less-competent social behavior.

Predictable Crises

As a stepdad many of the crises you will encounter involve the discrepancy between what you expect and the realities of early stepfamily life. You may anticipate facing several of the six most common "myths":

1. Most new stepfathers expect that their new blended family will function just like a natural family. Because the stepfamily is founded on loss and is structurally different, **it will not function like a natural family.**

2. For some men adjustment is slow because they view the blended family as somehow abnormal. If your new family seems wrong by comparison with a nuclear family, you may be inclined to act as if the blended family were an embarrassment or an example of failure. This perspective may well inhibit realistic understanding or attempts to make changes.

3. Many men expect the adjustment to stepfamily life to occur suddenly or almost so. In fact **the adjustment will move at what seems like glacier speed.**

4. Many stepfathers expect that they will love their stepchildren the same as their natural children. Not only is the bond different, but **the lack of a long shared history makes this equal love very unlikely.**

5. Often stepfathers expect that they will get along better

with stepchildren who do not live in the home. In fact the **reduced time together** and the inconsistent nature of the relationship, dominated by hellos and good-byes, **makes the adjustment take much longer.**

6. Stepfathers will often be surprised that they feel disloyal to their noncustodial natural children when they are more loving to their stepchildren, an experience that is counterintuitive and disturbing. We expect that love given to any child will just feel good.

PERSONAL BOUNDARIES

Most of the special difficulties for stepfathers involve issues of personal boundaries. To what extent is a stepfather involved as a parent with the children? What is the relative prominence of the marital or parent-child relationship? What rights and influences will ex-spouses and in-laws have in the current marriage?

Because of a lack of evolved social rules for old and new family members, the new family boundaries have to be redrawn and recreated.

Stepfathering and Parenting

The stepfather walks an emotional tightrope. He is in the position of partially parenting children who cannot fully accept him without feeling some disloyalty to their original father, or to his memory. He must be a parental figure, yet stop short of trying to displace the natural parent. He must also shoulder the child's normal resentment toward him as being a block between their mother and natural father.

Stepfathers regularly report confusion over the degree of authority they may exercise in their parental role, especially about discipline and enforcement of rules. They are frequently unsure about how to demonstrate affection to their stepchildren and how much is appropriate. Finances may also impact on boundaries. In

addition to the very real financial strain of simultaneously supporting their original families and the new stepfamilies, many men feel
a real conflict about where the money is spent. To give more to
your own children is to make it more available to your ex-wife; to
give it to the stepfamily may make you feel that you are depriving
your own children while supporting others.

Emotional Baggage

For most men stepfathering is not only more complicated than
fathering, it is also potentially more emotionally laden.

While living with a stepfamily you may well feel considerable
guilt at your perceived "desertion" of your own children and your
sense of causing their pain, especially if you have little physical
contact with them. There may also be considerable unresolved
grief experienced by all involved family members long after the
divorce. Such grief may be complicated by the desire or expectation to "be happy" about the new family constellation. In reality,
one or more members of a family may still be grieving the loss of
the real or fantasied old relationship at the time of the remarriage.
For the children, and sometimes the adults, maintenance of this
grief, or a longing for the old relationship, may provide a continuity
that fosters a sense of security. For a stepfather who is desperately
trying to fit into a new family and to hasten a new integration, the
continuing connection to the past may be more than disconcerting.
Bud, a stepfather of eleven months, said, "I never know what to
expect from Irene or her kids. One minute she hates her ex and
wants to have him arrested for failure to make child-support payments, the next day she's quoting him like he was the expert on
our family . . . and the kids. . . . The oldest one is a real daddy's
girl. So she always tells him what's going on here, and she comes
back from weekends with him all sassy and pouting, finding fault
with me—uh, us. I want her to have a good relationship with her
dad, but I don't want to be treated like the cause of their divorce.
I never even met Irene until they were split. Even back then she

was angry at his withholding the checks and at his negative influence."

Russ, a stepfather of five years, was more sad than angry. He reported that his stepchildren had never accepted him and that his wife was ambivalent as well: "Sheila wants me and the kids to be close, but she also wants them to herself. With Travis, our mutual child, it's different. It's the three of us. But with the two older ones, she won't let them and me really interact much. She needs to get in the middle. That, and their feelings about their dad and his new family, make me a real outsider in my own home. I really like those kids too. I hope they know that."

Problems may also arise if the stepfather comes along after the original family has adjusted to life as a single-parent family. How will he be integrated into the single-parent system? Giving up their single-parent family may be difficult in and of itself. Furthermore that loss may reactivate grief about the divorce as well.

Each member of the new family is influenced by the "unfinished business" of the earlier marriage. Because children also need continuity with their past to foster a sense of security, this continuity must be provided at the same time that all members are evolving a new family form. The problem is that these forces may work against each other.

Competition for the Attention

When a man becomes a stepfather, he may be unprepared for the rivalry with his new stepchildren for their mother's time. Affection given to one may feel like affection withheld from the other. The ways time and money are shared may also become contested. It makes sense that such a competition would thrive in the early days of a stepfamily. Everyone is confronted with new roles, new living arrangements, new people with whom to relate. These changes naturally produce anxiety, which in turn produces a greater need for connection. It is typical for people to cling to loved ones until other relationships become normalized.

When a man brings a stepmother into his own family, he will

face a fierce competition for his time and emotional nurturance. Regular attempts will be made to split the new couple, and he will have to be the listener to complaints from children and new spouse. In addition, if the new wife also has children or if they attempt to have children together, he is faced with the "yours, mine, and ours" situation that makes for cute television sitcoms but is rife with divided loyalties and hurts in real life.

Fathers with Two Families

Many fathers today do have two families, with children of quite different ages. While there are truly a myriad of problems, in some ways it offers the opportunity to be a different kind of father. As one man said during a nationally televised interview, "It's different with the little boys than it was with Eric and Jenny. I was there at the births, I'm involved, I don't leave at seven A.M. and return after they're in bed. It's like God gave me a chance to really be a full father, not just a provider."

The chance to do it right this time may be more than a second opportunity. A man who succeeds at being a better father with his second family may feel some retroactive guilt about the way he was with the first. His older children may also feel envious as a result of how different their father is with their stepsiblings.

Hank related, "Even though I'm happy about my relationship with Emily, I know I owe the other kids something of me. Don't get me wrong. I did my best to provide for them. In those days that's what a dad was supposed to do. . . . But I was never around. It never occurred to me to go to their school plays or have special days with the little ones. I just worked and brought home the money. The rest was from their mother. . . . Well, now they are really close to her, and I miss them and feel like they don't know me at all."

Fathering Children with Two Families

Not long after the divorce of their parents many children find themselves in not one but two stepfamilies. They have a stepfamily with Mom and her husband and another with Dad and his wife. Adjustment to two unique cultures is problematic, and children will adjust to them slowly. The ages of children when the new family forms may also be significant. Very young children and children who are about to or who have already left the home generally have the easiest acclimation. By contrast children who are developmentally struggling with issues of separation and individuation (eighteen to thirty months; early adolescence) may have the most difficult time. Some clinical data suggest that adolescent daughters may have an especially hard adjustment. Elementary-school-age children are particularly prone to holding out hope of a reconciliation of their natural parents.

For the stepfather patience and a clear understanding that he will never replace the child's biological parent are essential. The easiest way for a stepfather to impede progress toward even limited acceptance is to obstruct contact between his stepchild and natural father.

Eleven-year-old Bart faced this very situation. His mother and stepfather demanded that he renounce his love for his biological father or face physical punishment from the stepfather and emotional exile from the remarried family. When he was referred for therapy by his minister, he was deeply troubled by nightmares of being deserted and ruminations that his biological father would be killed trying to kidnap him. Ultimately with the therapist's help he was able to move in with his biological father.

Although it may seem paradoxical, nothing helps a stepfather's relationship with his stepchildren more than openness and encouragement to maintain love for the biological father. In such an environment children can experience love as a growing rather than limited resource. The more that is given, the more there will be to go around. When the biological father does not respond to his children and increasingly absents himself from their lives, the stepfather is best suited to be a positive male role model who does not bring up or discuss negatives about the children's biological father.

Such patience in the face of one's own anxiety about acceptance and in the desire to get things done expeditiously may be trying, but it is often rewarding.

Eric, a fifty-five-year-old stepfather, tearfully and proudly described how his stepdaughter of five years told him for the first time that she loved him as she was leaving for college. He had been the only involved father she had known, but until that time she never called him by any name other than Eric. He said, "Those three little words coming from her in such a genuine way made me feel like a million bucks. I knew then that all the homework nights and high school visits were important to her as well as to me and my duty as a father."

Discipline and Authority

Often new stepfathers, trying desperately to be a proper paternal force and moral guidepost in the reconstituted family, are shocked to discover that their stepchildren reject their authority outright. Blended families have to begin anew in determining touchy questions such as how much and what kind of authority is given to a stepfather. Child discipline by stepparents must be painstakingly worked out.

Glenn describes his frustration:

My stepdaughter is nine and a half now, and our baby is two months. We've been married for fourteen months. It is very hard for me because my stepdaughter, Carolyn, is a good kid except when I try and discipline her. Then all hell breaks loose. She just says, "You're not my father. I don't have to listen to you." . . . I've supported her for two years because her natural dad is way behind in payments. He doesn't visit much either. I do the school things and the lessons . . . all of the "daddy" things she needs, but whenever her natural dad shows up, off she goes and forgets everything. She acts like he's the most wonderful guy on earth. He takes her out to movies and theme parks that we can't afford . . . because he doesn't send the child support. I don't want to favor the baby, but it's real hard. Her mom also is so angry at her ex that any discussions always end up with her blowing up. I feel like there's no reward for being the good guy here.

Often, in matters of discipline, the mother of the children is unwilling to have her new husband discipline her children. She may fear that he is intruding into her special relationship. She may feel threatened sharing that aspect of her children. Many wives express their ambivalence by requesting that their new husband help with discipline and then undercut his efforts by negating his authority with her children. Michelle described this well: "I know I want Mike to be a real father to the children, but then when he punishes them, I feel offended or think it's too harsh. Last week when my daughter came home after curfew for the third time, he told her that she couldn't use the car next week. So what did I do? When she came crying to me, I told her she could use my car. I know it was wrong. . . . He just shrugged and walked away when he found out."

Charles, a thirty-eight-year-old newly married stepfather, wrote,

My [step]daughter is age nine, and I have known her since she was three. When my wife and I were dating, I never tried to assume the father's role because I didn't feel it was right to do so. Lately I've been wishing that I had. Most of the time she is a really pleasant girl with a vivid imagination, but sometimes she is just off the wall. Screaming, yelling, kicking, name-calling, "you-don't-love-me," and all kinds of stuff come flying out at her mother. It really drives me nuts, especially the "you-don't-love-me's." When I hear this, I get all twisted inside and feel like paddlin' ass (which I know isn't right and don't do). The real problem here is that my wife insists on "handling it," tells me to "stay out of it." . . . It leaves me feeling useless or left out. Jennifer's natural father has not been available since infancy, and she just hasn't had any parental discipline when she throws tantrums. Her grandparents also give in to them. So I think I should do something, but end up caught in the middle and rejected. I feel like I'm going to explode sometimes. I don't, but I'm also no saint. I'm also worried because we have different rules for my involvement with our four-month-old son.

Charles is caught on the horns of a double dilemma. He and his wife have not agreed on discipline for the daughter. His wife sees it as her exclusive responsibility and will not allow him to be as involved as he might like. They have not yet developed uniform family rules for all children, and he is stuck with the double standard.

He either has to become involved with his wife in a redefinition of the rules of discipline, become more comfortable with backing up his wife's position even when he disagrees, or he needs to withdraw. This is complicated by the presence of their natural child. Part of Charles's concern is that he will relinquish his say in how his natural son is disciplined.

Until Charles and his wife can work through the discipline-and-sharing question, the best that he can do for his stepdaughter is to be available for her in a positive, caring, loving way, maintaining a firm and fair boundary that the child can test and count on. He may never be more than a father figure to the stepchild, which is different from being a father to his own child.

Financial Boundaries and Stress

It is not unusual for interpersonal conflicts to find expression in the financial arena. Particularly for men, finances often reflect deeper psychological needs and stresses. Allocation of financial resources is an important concern for stepfathers. Guilt and feelings of inadequacy often accompany the acknowledgment that there is less money to go around than desired. This is particularly a concern for men who have to support two families. Giving to the stepchildren may cause guilt about one's natural children going without; giving to the natural children brings up conflicts about the ex-wife and about the lack of resources for the new family.

Children may often express their sense of being "second-class" family members. Fathers may be especially prone to guilt over their children's pain at having less than others.

The reality is that most middle-class families require more than one income to survive well in the modern world. In most families the male earns the lion's share of the family income. Almost any man who has to provide for two families has an especial financial burden.

Some clinicians strongly recommend that the stepfather not attempt to deal with the financial issues alone. Instead they recommend that he involve the children and his wife in the development of the family budget. It doesn't take a nine-year-old long to understand the implications of the monthly bills balanced against income. If there is unhappiness about where the money goes, it may be of value to share in the unhappiness rather than to be the butt of it. When you involve them in the financial doings of the family, the stepchildren will also get the idea that you as stepdad are available for discussing other things that are important to them: fears, homework, friends, future plans, and so on.

Sexual Boundaries

How much affection is allowed or displayed may also be problematic. Two forms of sexual concerns can be unique to stepfamilies: sexual attraction between children from different marriages within the home, and sexual attraction between stepparents and stepchildren.

Many wives have expressed concern that their new husband will find their adolescent or older daughters more attractive than themselves. Sharon expressed her mixed feelings: "I get so conflicted, I want Martin and Charisse to be close, but then when he expresses affection toward her, I feel like she will take him away from me. She's young, thin, pretty, her body is a twenty-year-old's, not forty-five like mine. I know it's all in my mind, my insecurities, but I often get in between them. The other night they were playing cards and laughing, just enjoying the good times (which are not all that common lately), and I picked a fight with her about her boy-friend. It was worse because I knew what I was doing . . . like I was showing him how juvenile she was."

Sharon's fears may be exaggerated by her personal insecurity, but they are not groundless for other families. Classic stories such as Euripides' *Hippolytus,* O'Neill's *Desire Under the Elms,* Nabokov's *Lolita* keep these fears in the forefront of our consciousness.

Many stepfathers have responded with confusion and fear to sexual feelings for teenage stepdaughters. These stepfathers came into their stepdaughter's life suddenly, have less of an incorporated incest taboo, and have difficulty bonding with them. When they feel unaccepted as father figures, they may respond with inappropriate male-female reactions. These feelings are deeply troubling to most stepfathers. Although many stories promote the notion that stepfathers are more likely to cross the sexual boundary behaviorally, no clear research evidence supports it. John came into therapy when he became aware of "libidinous impulses toward my stepdaughter. It really upsets me. It isn't like I'm not attracted to her mother, my wife. It's just when she walks around the house in flimsy clothes, I find myself becoming aroused and then feeling guilty. . . . I'd never do anything, but I don't know why I find a sixteen-year-old so sexy. . . . She doesn't even react to me like a daughter or a friend. Mostly she talks about me rather than to me . . . like if she likes me, it'll be the end with her natural father."

Stepfathers may also be concerned when stepsiblings become sexually attracted to each other. When sexual relationships develop within a family, the results are likely to be traumatic to everyone living in the space. Mort reported, "Ruth and I had a long talk about the relationship developing between my son and her daughter. The young one started telling us of their kissing. We felt that we'd talk to them, but then we might need to send my daughter to live with my ex. What was so perplexing was that on the one hand their romance was like a stamp of approval on our marriage, while on the other it felt like incest.

RECOMMENDATIONS FOR STEPDADS

The primary relationship to work out is not the one with the children—it is the one with your wife. The two of you need to decide to create and keep a set of new family standards that are fair and consistent, no matter what external influences dictate. No couple will be perfectly consistent with such rules, but the act of pulling together and staying with jointly made agreements will cement the marital relationship and provide the children with a predictable pattern with which they can experiment, test the limits, and learn how to be in the new family. Most of all you need to nurture the new marital bond. Unless you spend the time and effort to make that relationship primary, the repercussions could be quite unfavorable.

Eli wrote the following on a national electronic bulletin board:

> I am an eight-year stepdad. My stepsons are ten and eleven, and I have a five-year-old son from this marriage. It's been a rough road, but we're making it work. For the first three years the boys' father had us in court almost constantly over custody, child support, and visitation. I'm amazed our marriage survived. I have some advice if anyone wants to take it. If you're excited about being a husband and instant dad, run, don't walk, to a counselor before the problems come up. The other thing is that although I'll never be a real father to the two older ones, my job is to help them prepare for fulfilling productive lives as adults. I'm the teacher, I don't need the credit. If they succeed, I succeed, whether they know what my contribution is or not. The thing is that the only way I can be that to them is to stay in their lives, and the best way to do that is to make it work with their mother, my wife.

That appears to be very sound advice. Following are nine specific guidelines:

1. If at all possible, support the relationship with the biological father. Do not try to replace him. You need to give assurance that you will not try to replace the biological father. It is important that your new wife and your ex-wife understand and support this resolve. Accept your lack of control or influence over the way that your stepchildren view their natural father. They will relate to him and to you differently. Do not compete with the natural father, especially if you think he is a "lowlife" or "jerk." There is nothing to win by proving your suspicions. If he is not a good father to the children, spend your energy offering them what you can and supporting your wife. She has had to deal with him far more painfully than you.

If support payments are infrequent or absent, there is no need to identify their natural father as a "deadbeat." He doesn't need to be mentioned at all. All that needs to be done is to realistically let the children know about family resources and expenses.

As a stepfather you must respect the relationship between children and their biological father. Sometimes that means *you* should be seen and not heard. If there is a problem, always go to the mother first and discuss the issue and potential solutions before approaching the child.

2. Accept the ambiguity of your role. Recognize that there are no road maps or manuals for being a stepfather. Most men find the experience frightening. It is important to recognize your doubt and fear and to approach the situation as a place to learn, rather than a place to perform. You will have to be very patient and wait for the emergence of comfortable working relationships with your new family members. What is most important is that you try to be yourself. Deal with your own ego needs and impatience privately or with your new wife.

3. Let the trust build slowly. Trust is earned over time. Like a great sauce it must simmer so that the nuances of flavor can blend together. Stepchildren will learn to trust you to the extent that you are predictable over time and situations. The more you are available for the children on a regular basis, the more they will accept you.

4. Do not expect instant love for or from the children. It is a myth that new families instantly fall in love. Your love for their mother will not fully carry over to the children. Furthermore they have no reason to love you instantly. In fact you will be seen as the person who embodies their loss of their original family.

Many children of divorce already feel rejected, frequently by their father. It is important to give them an opposite experience. By letting them know that they belong to and are an important part of your family, they have the opportunity to connect at their own pace. You cannot "make the kids come around," but you can provide the fertile soil in which they can grow.

5. If you take the role of disciplinarian, do it with the agreement of their mother. Do not expect to come in and be an authority in the family. When you feel ready to discipline the children, work out an agreement with their mother. Then, and only then, approach the children together and let them know specifically what role you will be playing. Stay within the boundaries discussed. Even with this preparation the children will likely test you repeatedly by refusing to respond to your authority or by end runs of appeal to Mom.

6. Try to set clear financial goals and limits. Let the children know what your fiscal limits are. Try not to engage in arguments about money with them. Instead make a serious budget and involve them to the extent that they can understand. If there are financial conflicts, try to separate the financial and emotional (i.e., guilt-based) decisions.

7. Face your feelings of guilt, fear, or shame. Many stepdads have terrible feelings of guilt about what they do not give to their natural children or stepchildren. This is an area that may have more to do with you and your own history than with the stepfamily situation. If you feel stingy, experiment with greater generosity. If you believe that you use money to replace time or presence with children, try to put in more time and see if the feelings change. A therapist may be particularly valuable in helping you resolve these inner conflicts.

8. Keep the marital relationship clean. There are all sorts of disagreements common to any long-term relationship. There are specific problems that come up in stepfamilies. Often family dynamics are such that the children act out the underlying conflicts between the husband and wife. If your stepchildren are being atypically unresponsive, they may be reacting unconsciously to a lack of connection between you and your spouse. Whenever difficulties arise in the family, consider finding the solution within yourself or between you and your partner first. It may not be the most obvious place for a solution, but it may be the most fruitful.

9. Get help. If there are problems in adjustment to the different rules or expectations, get to a family therapist, preferably one who can assess and work with the whole family system, the couple as a unit, or any of the individuals. Sometimes the difficulties are best addressed through individual therapy with the child or one of the adults, sometimes by focusing primarily on the new couple, and sometimes with the family as a whole. You may even benefit from a few sessions with the therapist and the "other" families all together.

Resources for Fathers

WHAT A FATHER NEEDS

In the first twelve chapters the many ways for men to be better fathers have been examined and encouraged. What has not been elucidated is what will sustain us while we engage in these endeavors.

I cannot become the kind of father recommended in the first twelve chapters without a certain amount of support, guidance, and nurturance to complement my expanding knowledge of fathering. Where will it come from? Some will have to come from within. The rest will depend on other people.

PERSONAL INSIGHT

Much of what a father needs to sustain him in his efforts to be a better father will be generated personally by exploration and examination of his own past, his feelings, beliefs, and behaviors. No parenting resource will ever be as powerful as our own mental health and stability. As we fathers gain insight into our unconscious needs and motivations, we are better equipped to make effective and consistent conscious decisions. Understanding where our "buttons" are, we will be able to father our children more by choice than by reaction. As more conscious fathers, we will be far more loving. We will be able to set firm, fair limits and to enjoy our children rather than try to force them into some preconceived mold that lies in our subconscious mind.

Normally insight is gained through hard experience, acknowledgment of personal limits, and careful reflection. There are few substitutes for hard and courageous work.

Psychotherapy

Perhaps the best, and potentially most intense, method of self-knowledge is individual psychotherapy. In this setting a man may have the luxury of paying full attention to himself. He need not perform. He need not solve any problems. He and the therapist engage in a mutual process of discovery, both of them fully focused on the client.

In therapy a man can explore his past, divulge his secrets, and examine his dreams without fear of ridicule, and with the likelihood of understanding and guidance. When I am vulnerable in a therapeutic setting, I need not fear reprisal or danger. Instead the therapist and I will explore my fears. I will be able to determine which are appropriate in a given situation and which are reflections of my childhood, feelings that block action inappropriately.

To help one best understand the process of fathering, I normally recommend that the therapist be an older male. That is not fully necessary. It is just more likely that he will have experienced similar concerns personally. If he has successfully resolved his feelings, he may be the most appropriate therapist.

For some men a female therapist may be the choice. If you are less threatened by women, or if you want to work without the potential of "assumed similarity" by the therapist, a mature female therapist may be your choice.

Whether you choose a male or female, you will ultimately have to make peace with the world of men, your brothers.

Group Therapy

Individual psychotherapy may not be appropriate for you. Another option, one that is financially less burdensome, is group therapy. I particularly recommend men's therapy groups. Normally these are co-led by two males and contain six to twelve members. In a therapy group men share their concerns, discuss options, assist each other's growth, and take risks in a safe public forum.

Experienced leadership is the safeguard and guarantee that the group will foster examination of intrinsically male concerns.

Many men find the group more helpful than the individual work. For them the vicarious learning and camaraderie are particularly beneficial.

Therapy is hardly the only source of support. In addition to, or in place of, therapy are several other growth-oriented pursuits.

Keeping a Journal

Many of us have written in journals from time to time. Often they are reserved for extraordinary events, such as trips or retreats. Some men write when they are troubled. Others use journals to jot down sayings or ideas that seem special at the time. The primary advantage of a journal is that it allows us to reflect on our lives, to explore those experiences that seem significant. Journals also contain a written record, one that may be reviewed. Unlike my memory, the entries in my journal will not change with time.

The time given to journal writing may be the only reflective alone-time in a man's day. That might make it particularly worthwhile.

Martial Arts or Self-help Programs

Among the paths to self-knowledge are a host of self-help programs. Some of the most interesting of these involve the martial arts. Judo, aikido, and the like coordinate a mental and physical discipline. Many men have gained confidence and a sense of being centered through these disciplines. As they challenge themselves mentally and physically, they face their fears, gaining some insight into the past and present.

Of course the martial arts are not the sole self-help philosophy that may be useful. Many educational and growth-oriented programs, available in almost every community and designed for individuals, couples, or people with special needs, allow for new understanding and connections with others.

Team Sports

Team sports can provide special challenges and camaraderie for many men. Competition alone will not likely help a man develop insight. Indeed it may work to minimize self-knowledge. However, sweating with peers, being part of a joint enterprise, and discovering personal limits allow a man to reflect on his personal drives, needs, and feelings.

NURTURANCE FROM OTHERS

As a man I am accustomed to solving problems myself. Like most men I have been trained to live my life in emotional isolation from other men. Whatever support or nurturance we men receive usually comes from our wives or the female members of our family. These are both important sources of support; however, it is unlikely that support for fathering can come completely from people who are not fathers themselves. Our misfortune is that we do not have male models, teachers, and supporters. Those are the sources I must cultivate. I will need to share with older men and with my peers.

A Lack of Friendship

In men's groups the first and most powerful need that emerges is a special form of loneliness: our relative isolation from other men.

Even men who have lots of acquaintances and active social lives decry the loss of their "buddy" from high school or college. Once we are out of school or the military, we often stop making close male friends. According to Larry Letich, most men past the age of thirty truly don't have friends. He claims that we have colleagues, work buddies, golf partners, and maybe one or two "couple" friendships where the bond is really between the wives: "If they say they do have a best friend, often it turns out to be an old friend whom they see or speak to once every few years.

"Sadly, for most men in our culture, male friendship is a part of their distant past. One man spoke for many at a recent men's conference in Montclair, N.J., when he lamented, 'I haven't made a new friend in 25 years.' "[1]

Our culture does not encourage intimacy and friendships among males. Among the pressures that are brought to bear are lack of time, questions about commitment, and suspicions about sexual orientation.

These pressures escalate when a man commits to marriage and when he becomes a father. The married man who leaves his family to "go out with the boys" is normally portrayed as being influenced by losers who engage in immature, antisocial, or anti-family behaviors.

Our society is quite uncomfortable with close male friend-ships. As the men's movement has picked up steam and men are rediscovering the importance of male friendship, a new phrase has come into being. We are told that what we are doing is "male bonding," which suggests some artificial chemistry. The inference is that of a sterile, possibly volatile, connection.

Additional pressures come from the workplace. Diminishing resources, massive fiscal deficits, economic recession, and baby-boom population numbers create a highly competitive, each-man-for-himself, advance-on-the-bones-of-others environment. Committed to providing for his family, a father finds himself in competition with other men who could be natural friends.

In addition, as America moves from a manufacturing to a ser-vice economy, the work setting becomes increasingly antiseptic.

Passion, sweat, and creativity through interaction are incompatible in the modern office cubicle. The high-pressure, time-consuming work stations at which most middle-class men are expected to succeed do not allow for time and energy for camaraderie.

Remember, our society's ideal man is not supposed to have any emotional needs. "Marlboro men" don't need "nobody." Since few men can actually live up to that questionable ideal, it's considered acceptable, even laudable, for us to channel all our emotional needs in one direction: toward wife and children. A man who has any other important emotional bonds (bonds that are not based on duty, such as an ailing parent) is in danger of being called neglectful, irresponsible, or weak, because forging emotional bonds with others takes time, time that could have been spent "getting ahead."

According to Letich, the only friendships allowed are those that serve a "business" purpose or those that can be fit effortlessly into leisure time. For many men "maintaining the lawn is more important than maintaining friendships." There are few rituals and little respect given to a man's friendships.

When was the last time you heard a grown man talk proudly about his best friend? Despite all the obstacles, it is possible to develop a real male friendship after the age of thirty; the kind we remember from childhood, high school, college, or military days. Many of us rediscover those same old friends after years of minimal contact.

To grow as a father, I really do need the emotional light and food offered by a buddy.

My Friends

I have known my two closest friends for over twenty years. We have visited and communicated with one another frequently during those years. In the past year I have had at least phone contact with each approximately weekly. Each of them is different. They are not friends to each other. Each offers me understanding, caring, and support. They know virtually everything about my life, at least everything that I have thought to share. I don't know of any area of my life that I would need to keep secret from either of these men. They do not compete with me, unless it is a clearly competitive game. They cooperate and, I believe, want what is best for me. It surely is mutual.

One of my friends has been a father for a lot longer than I have. He is a source of sage advice, encouragement, and a model of good fathering. The other has children who are a bit younger. He shares my angst, my doubts, and my learning.

I know that I can openly express my ignorance, my fears, or my sadness with my friends. I expect understanding and support in return. I have not often been disappointed.

If my child is ill and I tell my friend that I am scared, he will communicate that he understands the fear. He will ask questions about my child. He may offer advice. Most of all, he will offer me hope that my child will recover and strength to be a nurturing father.

I cannot imagine how much harder it would be to be a father without these other men to nurture and guide me.

Love, Romance, and Intimacy

A father needs a partner. Parenting is no easy task, even for two adults. A parent who is alone has particular burdens, not the least of which is the lack of a companion to share his experience. It is much easier to give to our children when we feel replenished by love, intimacy, and caring.

It is much easier for me, for example, to father and enjoy my children when my wife is supportive and encouraging (as opposed to demanding and irritable). When I feel that we are a team, I am freer to take risks and make errors. Someone else will be available to help if I need it.

It is important that my partner knows me. When she knows the inner me, she will be able to reach me in ways that I will understand. When my wife truly senses who I am, she can show me love and affection that will penetrate my protective shell.

This past year my wife encouraged me to accompany our

daughter on a school field trip with her class to Yosemite National Park and on a summer trip to Europe. She used three unimpeachable arguments: (1) don't worry about the money; (2) you can enjoy it and you need a break; (3) it's good for our daughter.

It is clear to me that although the first and third were necessary to persuade me to go, the second was the most important. Had Susan not been focused on what would be good for me, she would not have been as able to produce the other reasons that allowed me to convince myself to go.

She was right on all counts. The trips were wonderful for my daughter and for me.

My world as a man, and as a father, is often hard. I become duty oriented. I lose sight of my own needs. My lover can help me fill the tank before I embark on my daily quest, and at the times when I most despair of the journey's conclusion.

I also get nurtured by giving to my partner and to our relationship. Robert Bly believes that the most damaged part of the psyche in modern man is the "lover," meaning not just the ability to make love but the ability to love life, to feel, to be either tender or passionate. Passion and the capacity for intimacy are essential for friendship. Intimacy is the only antidote to mortality.

Models or Mentors

I was speaking with a client recently. He is a successful businessman in a national firm. He is also a homosexual. As we spoke about models, he confessed that he had no appropriate male models that inspired him. Of the men who shared his sexual orientation, he couldn't identify a single one who had endured the rigors in his professional world and come out on top. Where was he to find a gay man whom he could emulate as a hero, someone he could identify with, who was a success? For Tony straight men were not models, because they "had it easier" in the corporate world, and gay men were caricatures—sexually promiscuous, "queens" or effeminate, primarily known for their behavior in bars or social gatherings.

For Tony sexual preference became an obstacle, but I'm not certain that most men have realistic models. Ask a man who his mentor for fathering is and you'll likely get the answer Charlie provided: "I'd like to say my own father, but that wouldn't be true. Our lives and our approach to fathering are so different. He was from the era when fathers were supposed to be distant. The truth is that I'm pretty much learning it on my own. On-the-job training, you know."

It's unfortunate that most of us feel isolated in our experience of fathering. It sure would be helpful to have a positive example to help us through the rough spots, someone who would minimize the need to learn everything for the first time. Few fathers have such mentors. Most are destined to learn the craft on the job, from inadequate or out-of-date models, or from their female partners.

If you can find a man whose fathering you admire, you may want to cultivate that relationship. If you approach him with respect and a desire to learn, he will probably be most open to sharing his knowledge with you. Many older men know the pitfalls and the pathways to good fathering. We need to find them, honor them for their experience, and learn what they have to offer.

When these older mentors are not available, we may have to rely on our contemporaries: men who can share the experience but lack the overview that is only possible for someone who has been through it all. Our buddy may not know where the path leads, but at least we'll be reassured by walking on it together.

CHECKING THE TIRES, BRAKES, AND OIL

To grow as fathers we need to be in a position to do so. Here are some basic ways that we may contribute to our own growth:

1. Keep yourself as healthy as you can. Often we do what we need to do instead of keeping ourselves strong enough to be a continuing resource. For me the statement that is

repeated on all airline flights is important: "If you are traveling with a child, and the oxygen masks appear, put yours on first. Then help your child." You won't be of much help to the children if you are (oxygen) depleted.

2. Keep a sense of humor. Don't take what the children do or say as a personal reflection or insult. Do enough self-reflection to let small hurts roll off your back. You need to be strong for the big ones.

3. Ask for help. I know that as men we are congenitally unable to ask for directions at a service station in a strange land, but at times we need the assistance of others. We do not have to always do it on our own.

4. Keep focused on your contribution to your children and to your world. Dedication is a powerful motivator. Finding meaning in life helps keep us alive. Set reasonable goals and enjoy it when you attain them.

5. Set your own priorities. Keep them. Beware of taking others' priorities as more important than your own. Gather all the information, then choose your own direction.

6. Seek the spiritual source beyond yourself. Whether it is a supreme being, an ethical way of life, a connection to all creatures, a love of your fellow man, or what Robert Bly calls the deep masculine. When you are in touch with things greater than yourself, you may find a special path to yourself and to your children.

QUESTIONS AND ANSWERS

Over the last ten years I have been giving talks, lectures, and workshops on fatherhood to a wide range of audiences. In that time a number of excellent questions have repeatedly been posed.

In this chapter I present and respond to the most frequently asked questions from men about being fathers and from women who wish to understand better their husbands' and boyfriends' process of relating and parenting.

QUESTIONS ABOUT A FATHER'S HISTORY

- *If my father was an alcoholic (mental patient, criminal, etc.), should I dare to have children?*

    You may well wish to be aware of any genetic deficits that are present in your and your wife's family. In addition you may want to get some insight into particular patterns of childrearing you experienced as a child. All of these could influence your parenting and affect your children. Alcoholism does tend to run in families, for example. There are some genetic components (like an allergy), and some social ones. Forewarned is protected. You might have to be aware and to adjust. Whether or not you decide to have a child is always an emotional decision, as well as, sometimes, a practical one. If you truly want children and fear passing a genetic defect along to another generation, consider genetic counseling to get as much data as possible. Seriously consider adoption.

- *My father just retired and "sat down" when he was fifty. I'm forty-eight now . . . ?*

Your father's behavior is not your destiny. It may be important to understand what was going on for him when he "sat down" and gave up. You may well want to probe your own depression or feelings of giving up with a therapist in order to avoid that. Some things are passed down from one generation to the next (that's why our parents and our children always seem like caricatures of our worst traits), but insight can add flexibility to behavior.

- *My child has the potential to be a great virtuoso (baseball player, computer genius, etc.). How do I encourage that?*

Be sure that it's what your child wants. If it is something you wanted to do in your life but fell short, be cautious. Your child will be miserable trying to live out your dreams instead of his or her own. Make the lessons and opportunities available to the child, but let him or her take the lead. Encourage practice, but don't make it a battle. If your child truly has a gift, and you make the resources available, chances are he or she will use the opportunity.

PSYCHOLOGICAL QUESTIONS

- *Whenever my wife and children are late coming home, or I'm away overnight, I worry that something terrible will happen to them. Does that make me neurotic?*

If the fears of harm coming to your children are fleeting and they promote more connection between you and them when you are together, it is not neurotic; the condition is called parenting. If you really obsess about these concerns and begin to become very restrictive about your children's behavior, you may want to seek help from a therapist. Over time that level of anxiety may be harmful to you or your children.

- *I know this sounds crazy, but sometimes I actually fear my own son's aggressiveness. Isn't that strange to be afraid of my own child?*

On a rational level it makes little sense, but emotionally there are viable reasons. For one thing your son is your replacement in this world. When he is a full-grown man, he will be a father, and you will predecease him. His aggressiveness reminds you that his job in part is to push you out of the way when you are no longer a functioning member of society. In addition by the time he is three years old, he has laid a claim on your wife's affections. In that sense he is your rival. As a little boy he can win that battle to some extent.

Little boys' aggression also can be painful physically. They seem to have uncounted numbers of elbows and knees. They will regularly lay Lego and action-figure traps for Daddy's bare feet in the dark. Finally, their lack of socialization unconsciously brings up fears of annihilation by adult aggression. The little boy's ability to hurt and break animate and inanimate objects is a reminder of the beast within and the thin veneer of agreements we call adult society. He scares us because he reminds us of our own repressed hostility.

The antidote to this fear is to respect it, to love your son openly, and to help him channel the energy into socially acceptable motivations.

- *I don't know what gets into me, but sometimes I just lash out at the children, calling them names, even spanking them out of my frustration. What can I do to stop?*

Raising children is inevitably frustrating. They do not respond well to verbal correction (e.g., "If I've told you once, I've told you a thousand times . . ."). They always seem like caricatures of our own worst traits. In addition the goal of our job as parents is achieved by becoming obsolete, hardly an exciting prospect.

It is no wonder that parents become frustrated. The important thing is to recognize your frustration, not respond to it unconsciously. The best way to avoid visiting your frustration on your children is to take care of yourself. When you are on an even keel, you will have a lot more slack and patience. Optimally this is achieved by working on a mutually nurturing relationship with your spouse and examining your own motives and inner life. Psychotherapists are very well equipped to assist in both endeavors.

NONTRADITIONAL FAMILIES

• *I am an older father. Will my children suffer?*

For one thing you are not alone. Warren Beatty, Jack Nicholson, David Frost, and a spate of other celebrities have ushered the older first-time father into prominence. There are some special advantages and disadvantages for most older fathers.

Older fathers are usually better established in their careers. They are usually past the obsessive need to get ahead and prove themselves elsewhere. They may also have a better sense of their priorities. Many older fathers report being much more patient than they could have been as younger men. They are usually more financially stable. Older fathers are less likely to feel threatened by their children or by their relationships with their wives.

On the negative side we older fathers are surely less energetic or strong and are less able to keep up with our children. Older fathers may also be more prone to age-related illnesses.

We are not as closely tied to them generationally. It may be harder to share our "Dark Ages" experiences with our children. We may also be quite a bit older than our wives, a situation that also has pluses and minuses.

Most of all, it is important to father our children in a loving way. Given good health and a reasonable financial situation, age is unlikely to be a crucial factor in how we father our children.

- *My son is only seventeen and he's a father. What advice would you give him?*

    It is hard to imagine a more difficult relationship than the one experienced between teenage parents and their children. Often adolescent fathers are completely left out of the family unit, restricted by parents or in-laws. They probably have little or no say regarding adoption, abortion, custody, and even sometimes marriage.

    Many teenage fathers are quite concerned about their babies and want to be involved in paternal decisions. But like teenage mothers, they are probably unprepared to assume the role of parent and provider. Most have unrealistic expectations and lack knowledge of human growth and development. Because of the quality of prenatal care and nutrition, children of adolescent parents will usually have more infant health problems, developmental lags, and high infant mortality. They also have a greater likelihood of being abused.

    Adolescent fathers have many special problems. It is unlikely that they can both stay in school and fulfill their paternal responsibilities. If they drop out, they may be relegating their future to low-paying, entry-level jobs. Emotionally they report feeling isolated, because their friends cannot share their experience. They do not find peers or adults who understand their sense of responsibility and involvement with their baby or partner. Many feel rejected and are intimidated by their girlfriend's family.

    This is a time for both families to pull together to support all three children. Family therapy involving the girl's family as well as your son's that focuses on finding solutions as opposed to recriminations can be most helpful. As a therapist I would actually give you, the parent of a teenage father, more advice than I would your son. It is a time for you to show him plenty of love and support, even if you disapprove of his sexual behavior.

- **Both my boys were born while we were in the service. Is there anything dangerous about kids growing up in the navy?**

Millions of American children have been born to military families. In some ways the military is a conservative culture that reflects general American values. In another sense there are commonly some additional concerns for military dads.

In addition to the realistic fears of losing a parent in combat, military families face unusual situations. The typical military family will move frequently and will be unable to set down permanent, extended-family roots in their communities. Relationships of family members are often governed by the rank structure of the husband. Fathers in the military have to pledge first allegiance to the service and "keep their children in line." Troublemaking children often cost fathers promotions: a situation that reverberates throughout the family.

It is common for military families to be dual-income families, particularly for men in the lower ranks, which places additional demands on fathers to become active parents. It is also somewhat common for military fathers to have significant periods away from their families. In the navy, for example, some servicemen, such as submariners, are home for six months and gone for six months at a time, forcing major adjustments for their families.

The lack of stability of military families, high stress levels, and generally younger parents from lower socioeconomic levels of society make child abuse more common in military families.

These are all potential negatives. However, families who live on military bases often report more family time, less drug abuse, and better grades in school compared with children in equivalent civilian communities. Family Life Centers, which were instituted in the early 1970s on many bases, provide resources for military families. Race relations have also been less volatile, particularly in the air force.

The crucial challenge for any military family is to maximize their family time and take the necessary steps to circumvent additional difficulties.

- **My wife and I just adopted a child. Is that different from having our own?**

There are a number of differences between adoptive and biological parenthood. You may have to endure some additional struggles in bonding. For one thing the child comes suddenly. You do not have those precious nine months for preparation. For another, full bonding may be delayed through a lengthy waiting period, until you are sure that the birth mother will not reclaim the baby. The child will not share your genetic makeup or certain biological proclivities that can bring family members closer. Generally over time you should feel the same kind of love for the child as biological parents do. The one additional caveat is the child's potential future need to connect with his or her natural parents.

- **We are a blended family with kids from three marriages and different last names. What should we watch out for?**

The biggest issues have to do with loyalty conflicts, guilt feelings, merging different family cultures and identities, and adjusting to different allocations of time, money, and affection. You may also have to face guilt about family members who are not in your home, in-laws, grandparents, and problems that continue after the divorces. Do not expect miracles. Working out these issues takes a lot of time. Concerns to anticipate include discipline, authority, affection, and family boundaries.

Keep the couple relationship as the center of everything. Work hard to keep it open and functional. Seek community resources. Don't delay seeking help with persistent problems.

QUESTIONS ABOUT STRATEGIES

- **How do I tell my teenage daughter about what guys are after without making myself look like a jerk?**

Your daughter is unlikely to see you as a jerk if you have a long-term relationship with her. If your first serious interactions with her are judgments about her dating, she will not be very interested in listening. By contrast, if you have a strong bond, your ideas and information may be welcome. Just be sure you don't need her actually to acknowledge that she is paying attention or that she will heed your warning.

If you are truly concerned about her sexual experiences, it is never too early to try to instill values that you consider important. It is less important what the boys may want then what she thinks about herself, the teen clique to which she belongs, and her developing moral values.

It is not necessary to relate specifics about your own personal dating experiences. It is much more consequential to listen to what is important for her. If you understand her needs, you may be able to help her find several ways to succeed. When she feels respected by her father, she may well demand the same respect from males her age.

Basically the most important communication with your adolescents occurs when they are much younger. When youngsters are accustomed to a pattern of reciprocity and respect from adults they will usually listen.

- *How am I supposed to be close to my kids when they only want their mommy and she encourages that?*

You need to stand up for your time and space. It is always easier to let her do it, but the longer you allow that, the harder it will be for you to take over. Children are always attracted to the familiar, so if she always reads a good-night story, you're a substitute. If you want the connection, insist on your nights and times with the kids (even when your three-year-old is screaming invectives).

A good strategy is to talk to your wife calmly, out of the home, about your wish for her to make what Marty Greenberg calls space available. Don't blame her for being too controlling. Instead, try to educate her about your needs, then stick to your guns. It won't happen overnight. She had this child inside her. Her connection to her baby is partially physical. She doesn't understand the kind of emotional connection you have with a child.

- *How can I get my husband to be more involved with the kids? Even when I watch and supervise his interactions, he's all thumbs.*

   Get out of his way. Jointly decide your mutual and individual responsibilities. Then when it's his time with the children, make yourself unavailable. I usually recommend that mothers physically remove themselves from the house. That way fathers will develop their own relationship and style with the children.

   Incidentally you used a word that might be an important clue. You said *supervise*. If you end up as the supervisor, you will believe that you have the "right" way to approach the problem. His suggestions will be as a worker, asking for permission. That will simply not promote his personal involvement. It will always be mediated through you. If you want a full parenting partner, you will have to share the control as well as the responsibility.

QUESTIONS ABOUT MALE-FEMALE DIFFERENCES AND RELATIONSHIPS

- *What am I supposed to do when my wife asks me how I'm feeling and I don't know?*

   The first step is to recognize that you don't know. Second, don't assume you have to know on her timetable or according to her style of question. Then try to discover what feelings you do have. Men are not unfeeling. More likely they don't put words to those feelings. There are only about ten primary emotions (e.g., fear, anger, sadness, happiness, terror, rage, love, anxiety), and each has a primary locus in your body. The feelings' location will be consistent within each individual and different than in other people. Notice where you feel sadness for example, where you feel joy, and so forth.

   Later when your feelings are requested, take a few moments to check out your body and explore where there are physical "feelings." If you know the spot, you'll also know what the emotional feelings are.

Be careful: If the feelings do not have a body location, you are probably saying "I feel" and producing a judgment. Often people will say "I feel" as a preface to their negative impressions.

- **Is it true that women really talk about their feelings? Sometimes I think that my wife's "feelings" are just an excuse to blame me.**

    It is something of a myth that women are always more feeling oriented. Sometimes women do use feeling words to be critical and blame. True feelings or emotions always have a locus in the body. If you feel sad, for example, there is a physical location where you feel it most. If your partner is judging rather than feeling, meet her with your feelings and request hers. Remember, there is only a short list of feelings. Let me give you a brief example:

    SHE: I feel that you never talk about your feelings to me. [*a judgment*]

    HE: Well, right now I'm feeling sad at being put down. [*expression of feelings*] What are you feeling right now? [*open question, asking for reciprocity*]

    SHE: Lonely. I want to be closer to you, but I'm afraid of being rebuffed. [*her feelings*]

- **How can I get my boyfriend to open up? I know he has a good heart, but he just never says anything.**

    First, allow him the space to do so. Many men process feelings much more slowly than you might like. Don't fill up silences with more questions, helpful suggestions, or demands. Give him time. If his time line is excessively long, ask him to give you a time when you might discuss the matter.

    Second, find out where he is open. Is he more talkative around friends, family, children? Replicate the safety of those situations. If he talks best while he is doing something, plan to talk when the two of you are engaged in some mutual activity. If it's around kids and play, try to talk in playful settings.

    Third, help him label his feelings. When he says something,

comment on what you hear. Don't skip steps or share your reaction directly.

Finally, most males begin talking about emotional topics at a specific level rather than a general one. If you want him to talk about his feelings, let him do it in his way.

Two questions that often come together:

- **Why do women always want to talk things into the ground? Can't they leave well enough alone?**
- **Why doesn't my husband ever want to say anything?**

In almost every couple there is one partner who thinks the other is noncommunicative and another who thinks the partner won't shut up. Many women talk to connect as much as to communicate information. When your wife is endlessly thinking out loud, opening and reopening "settled" discussions, it may be because she feels insecure and wants more contact with you. Try to maintain the contact, but let her know how annoying the "babbling" is for you. Just be prepared to continue talking. When your partner seems particularly quiet, it may be that he has nothing to report. He doesn't connect by talking; he finds closeness physically. If what you want is closeness, you might want to adjust your method; talking, especially face-to-face talking, may not be the way. If you really want to talk, you may need to slow down to his pace and style of verbalization.

- **Why do the words "we need to talk" fill me with such dread?**

Because we are conditioned to believe that whatever follows those words will indicate some unhappiness with us. There will be "a problem." Most of us automatically react to problems with a need to fix them, without delay. You may also unconsciously fear that a rejection is imminent. These "talks" may remind you of talks with your parents when they were about to be critical or punitive.

- *Ever since the baby came along, my wife seems uninterested in sex.*

A number of factors may be causing her lack of interest: (1) she may be so fatigued that even pleasure would be a chore; (2) she may have so much skin contact with your baby that she craves a chance to be *out* of touch; (3) she may be depressed or angry with you because of the current state of her life; (4) she may be feeling a lack of intimacy with you. Remember, for a man the pathway to intimacy is sexual contact; for a woman, sex is the culmination of intimacy. Try to discover what she is feeling in general. Open conversations about those topics. Try to unburden her as much as possible. It may also be helpful for you to talk to her about wanting to be more connected with her physically because you feel left out, attracted to her, and so on.

QUESTIONS ABOUT DILEMMAS

- *How can I be the strong one all the time and then be "sensitive" with no warning?*

You can't! This is the premier issue that couples must confront. Men must give up the power role in order to be sensitive, and women must learn to assume the power role in order to give men the break. Let your wife know that you are confused by what she is asking.

She cannot expect you to get up in the middle of the night to investigate the sounds downstairs and then expect that you will come back to express your feelings about that without some transition from one role to the other.

Transition between roles is important in other instances as well. When you come home from slaying the dragons (or rush-hour traffic), you may not be ready just to settle into home life. Tarzan needs to watch TV, read the paper, take a bath, go for a run or whatever before he can be a loving husband to Jane and father to Boy.

She needs to understand that you can only do one thing at a

time, and you need to be her guide, because she will not instinctively know whether you are in Alan Alda or Sylvester Stallone mode.

You can't blame her for what she wants. Wouldn't you like to have a husband who supported you financially, protected you, and sensitively nurtured you? If she wants all that, she may need to give it to you in return.

- *How can I get my family to see that I don't do anything but work and I don't get any respect for it?*

For one thing you need to do some accurate data collection. Take a few weeks and chart the hours of the day and how you spend them. Ask your family members to do the same. Then chart the things that are necessary as well as those that are free and fun. The comparisons may provide some eye-opening revelations.

In addition you may want to reexamine your own priorities and discover why you always seem to be at work. Perhaps you are unconsciously avoiding some other form of relating. You may need help from your family to break out of the rut. They will probably prefer it if you were available for fun activities more often.

- *How do I get over being too cautious with my children so I don't stifle them, but don't endanger them either?*

This is the perennial question for all parents. How much freedom, how much security? It's always a delicate juggling act. When do you let your daughter go out on a date with a boy in a car? When do you let your preschooler climb to the top of the jungle gym without a warning cry (which could precipitate a fall)? When do you give your son or daughter the keys to the family car? Do you let your son play football? Do you encourage your daughter's gymnastics? Are there friends you want them to avoid? When do you put your foot down about family rules?

There are no easy answers to such difficult questions. Basically you and your partner must explore and uphold your personal family values. Most parents consult with the parents of their children's friends to get a sense of community standards. Many parents tell their children what they believe and leave some of the final decisions up to the children. There is also a time for you to just set limits as a parent. If the limits are not too strict or too rigid, it may be the best you can do.

You may also have to separate your own predilections and unconscious fears from the situations your children get into. Your childhood messages may find their way into your mouth before you carefully consider them. Awareness of your own needs will surely assist your judgment of your children.

- ***What do I tell my kids when their mom is unfaithful?***

A lot depends on what is happening in the relationship. A general rule of thumb is not to discuss your, or your partner's, specific sexual activity with your children. Do teach them about sex, but eschew mommy and daddy examples. Another consideration is that your telling the kids may be in place of your talking to appropriate adults about this (e.g., your wife, counselors, clergy). That's using your children improperly to satisfy your own needs.

If they want to know about infidelity, they will find out. What's more important is the way you handle the information yourself and what you choose to do about it.

As a therapist the rule of thumb I use is that infidelity is about the primary relationship. A second rule of thumb is that therapy to help resolve the damaging effects of an affair is at least four to six times as long as therapy that occurs before anyone has had one.

If either you or your wife is unfaithful, I would encourage you to run, not walk, to a competent couple's therapist.

- ***How can I get my spouse to live on a budget?***

Rules are always difficult, as is talking about difficult topics. In our culture money is the big taboo for discussion. As a therapist I can attest to the fact that my clients will share intimate details of their sexual life far before they will discuss money.

Whenever you discuss finances, two issues are simultaneously at risk: money and emotions. Finances are almost intertwined with emotions from the past. Does spending symbolically send another message? Is it anger at you for being unavailable? Is it a statement of freedom? Are you being cautious in spending because of your own childhood injunctions?

If you really want to explore the budgetary issues, first examine the consequences of the current situation. What is the impact of her staying off the budget?

One couple with whom I worked used their finances to avoid each other. She would seriously overextend her spending. He would get angry and withdraw. She would view his withdrawal as a sign that he didn't care and expressed her anger by spending more money. The greater the spending, the greater the distance. It was only after considerable time in therapy that they were able to understand that they were afraid of being too close. They stumbled onto an expensive and painful, yet effective way of protecting themselves.

My experience is that if both people agree on a budget and then one breaks the agreement repeatedly, there is more than money at issue. A third party may be necessary to help you work it out.

- ***What can you tell me about being a father and being gay?***
For one thing you are not alone. There are estimated to be close to a million gay fathers in America. A lot depends on your lifestyle. Are you still married to the child's mother? Are you living with her? How are you expressing your homosexual preference behaviorally? Have you come out of the closet? Are you living a double life? Are you in a monogamous gay relationship? Do your children know that you are gay? Many homosexual men have a double dilemma: identifying as gay in the straight world and identifying as a parent in the gay world.

There is no research evidence that suggests that gay men are better or worse fathers to their children. If they have close, loving relationships at home with their partner and children, it may not be much different from positive straight father-child relationships.

There are, however, special difficulties that gay fathers face. There will of course be the problems customary to gay life. In addition, no matter how enlightened or open the home environment is, your children will probably be picked on at school because of your alternative lifestyle and because of the homophobia that is particularly rampant during the preteen and early-adolescent years.

- *I am a househusband. My wife is the wage earner. Is that likely to harm the children?*

Only if you or your wife is uncomfortable with the arrangement. Nobody is born knowing how to parent. You are probably the person in your family who is best suited to do the work. The biggest challenge for men who are the primary caretakers for their children is isolation. You need support from other men or women who do similar work. I do recommend that you read Kyle Pruett's *The Nurturing Father.*

If you are doing it voluntarily, commit yourself to this alternate lifestyle, and get support from extended family and friends, it could work out wonderfully.

- *Both my husband and I work outside the home, but he won't lift a finger at home. How can I get him to see that he has to do the housework just like I do?*

I'd want to know a lot before I began to answer that. Does he agree with your assessment about what each of you does at home? Is your work outside the home of equal duration and intensity? What does he do when you are doing the housework? What time does he give the children? Do you feel responsible for the home work? Who sets the standard for success? Do you act as supervisor?

I usually recommend that each person in the couple take a two-week period and chart the work time (home and away) and play time. Then compare the lists. Sometimes the results are astonishing. Some couples find that the discrepancy is massive. Others find that they are both overworked. Only when you have the data can you attempt to even it out.

- *I am very anxious about my wife's current pregnancy, but I don't want to upset her.*

It is very common for men to have a host of pregnancy anxieties. You do need to talk about your concerns, and your wife is the best person. Her openness and availability may surprise you. She may be reassured that you feel as she does. If she is not available, talk to other expectant and recent fathers. Consider my book *When Men Are Pregnant;* it suggests a host of strategies.

- *I miss my kids, but every time I see my ex-wife, I get so mad, I can barely stand it. Any ideas?*

Yes, several. Keep your priorities straight. If the most important is being with your children, prepare yourself for the scene, but get the time with your kids. Second, work on yourself. You will not be able to change your ex-wife, but you can make internal peace with that marriage. If she still gets to you that strongly after a year, there are still some hooks for you in that relationship. Perhaps you need her to like you or approve of you. You need to let go of your need for her to be a certain way. Individual therapy may be very helpful for you to accomplish that.

Keep in mind that the longer the two of you fight, the worse it is for the kids. You don't ever need to be friends again. You do need to co-parent. Try to interact on the parental level versus the personal one. She probably wants what's best for the kids also. When you stop taking the personal provocation, the kids will benefit.

- *Where do you find time to father and to work and do the chores?*

That seems like the most common dilemma in our times. I wish I had good answers and could personally follow them. I think the most important factor is prioritizing. If the children are high on that list, you may want to try to restrict your work to the workday, when the kids are in school or activities. When you can't, maybe you could try to be available to your children for a few hours in the evening and on weekends. Sometimes that is not the best time for them, but we can try to compromise.

I have learned one thing through my own battles with that

dilemma: not to try to do both at the same time. The quality of the work suffers, and you don't enjoy the time with the children.

The other thing I have learned is to work it out with your partner. If you support each other, there will be more energy and quality time with the children, both together and alone.

V

DEAR CHILDREN

A LETTER TO MY CHILDREN

Dear Natasha and Gabriel:

It's difficult to try to say everything I feel about being your father in a short letter. I know it's important to somehow communicate some of it to you. You made me a father, and the love I feel is so unique and so deep, it defies any description or prior understanding I have ever had.

This fatherly love I feel has several unusual qualities. It is very protective. It surely is paradoxical. It wants to keep you the same and wants you to grow. It knows you will leave. It seeks your approval and also needs to set standards for you to live by.

I worry so much about your health, safety, and happiness. I worry about the world we are leaving you. I fear that I get so caught up in providing financially that I fail to supply your daily emotional daddy needs. I worry in a micro way about your doings, habits, trials, and tribulations. I wonder a lot at what I'm doing

writing a book about fathering and spending hours away from my
own children. Yet you inspire the book, and most of everything else
that I do.

My life certainly isn't the same as it was twelve years ago.
Things seemed so much easier then. I wanted children, but I really
didn't know what that meant. (I guess I don't have that excuse
for you, Gabriel, I did know.) I never anticipated all the fears or
frustrations. I certainly never envisioned the joys you would bring
me. Like most men, I didn't foresee the plethora of interruptions
your lives would bring. I had no idea that going to the market
could turn into a major ordeal. I also didn't imagine that it could
take hours to do things that previously took minutes. More than
anything, I didn't expect to feel so vulnerable, nor so fulfilled.

You don't know very much about my life before you were
born. I want to tell you, but I want it to be when you ask. I really
want to give you all the good I got from my own father, and of
course all the things I missed out on as a child. I want you to be
able to move in this world with fewer fears than I have. I want you
to be able to enjoy more adventures. I'd like to know that Mommy
and I will prepare you better than I felt prepared.

Often I feel that I owe you an apology for not being better, or
more natural, at this fathering enterprise. I lose my temper too
easily and my patience too often. Keep in mind that I love you the
way a daddy loves. I will never love anyone else the way I love you
both. I will probably never feel as guilty as I do when I don't do
enough to express that love.

As I write this, there are screams coming down the hall. You
are fighting about something. Did one of you cross the imaginary
geographic center line on the couch? Did you both think the tall
glass held the most milk, or the other's plate the larger piece of
dessert? Or are you just letting me know that it's time to leave the
computer to pay attention to what's important? When I come into
the family room, will you tell me to go back to the computer, or ask
me to act as judge? Perhaps it is just none of my business. Perhaps
it's only a sign that Mommy is momentarily on the phone or re-
viewing homework. I will have to check, you know. I'll need to be

assured that you are both okay. I may need to do my job and set some fatherly limit ("Okay that's it, if you two keep fighting, nobody will get the larger piece"). I think that was my father talking through my mind and mouth. Perhaps I should raise my voice and order you two to lower yours. One of the best things about being a daddy is the right to be silly.

There are so many things about you as people that enliven me. I love your joy and excitement as you master new skills. I love when you take my hand as we cross a street. I love when you ask me for help, and when you ask me if you might help me. It's great when you want to go for a ride with me on some family errand. I love helping you with school projects, mastering the computer, VCR, or remote controls, using encyclopedias, and so on. I especially love it when you show each other love. I wish I told you more often how much I enjoy those things.

I know I've done a lot of things right. I certainly deserve some credit for providing you with such a good mom. I deserve some credit for how she and I keep our relationship strong and overcome rocky times. I know I am good at listening to you, and I feel good about setting reasonable limits. (I may have to reassess that evaluation once you reach adolescence.) I know that I've worked hard to keep up with you, to understand you, and to try to talk things out. More than anything else I have always loved you.

When you were born, Natasha, a joy filled my heart that rekindles each time I see you or think of you. It is a joy unbounded by my own knowledge or previous experience. It finds crevices in my soul and fills them with an inexplicable and beautiful feeling. You have amazed me from birth, and that never stops.

Gabriel, your birth gave me a son. As a man you will follow me. You are meant to take my place in this world. I pray that you will far surpass me, in your heart and in your deeds. I admire your energy and bravado. I hope you channel it well. I pray that your beautiful spirit is never broken. I eagerly look forward to playing catch and shooting hoops together. That will be special.

If I have failed you in some inadvertent way, by my obsession with work and providing financially, or by my personal limitations,

I am truly sorry. I pledge myself to be a better father in the future. I will not stop trying to improve that wonderful pursuit. The greatest joy in my life is a reflection of your faces lit up with happiness.

This book is rightfully for you. The inspiration comes from you. The raison d'être is that I want to be the father to you that I wish my father had been for me.

I love you both.

Daddy

NOTES

CHAPTER ONE

1. The term *father hunger* is credited to psychiatrist and psychoanalyst James Herzog. His article "On Father Hunger: The Father's Role in the Modulation of Aggressive Drive and Fantasy" can be found in Cath, S. H.; Gurwitt, A. R.; and Ross, J. M., *Father and Child* (Boston: Little, Brown, 1982).

2. Andrew Lloyd Webber, "The First Man You Remember" from *Aspects of Love* (New York: Polygram, 1989).

3. In a letter to Sara Gilbert, author of *What's a Father For?* (New York: Warner Books, 1975), p. 223.

4. Gilbert, S., *What's a Father For?* (New York: Warner Books, 1975), p. 32.

5. Parke, R., *Fathers* (Cambridge, Mass.: Harvard University Press, 1981), p. 105.

6. An excellent description of fathers who provide the primary care for their children can be found in Pruett, K. D., *The Nurturing Father* (New York: Warner Books, 1987).

7. It is important to distinguish here between expectation and reality. The fact is that a diminishing number of women today have the number of choices delineated here. However, most women still expect to have the options. Men do not. For many women the reality that they do not have the choice to balance work, child care, and homemaking is a rude shock.

8. Greenberg, M., *The Birth of a Father* (New York: Continuum, 1985), p. 19.

9. Shapiro, J., *Men: A Translation for Women* (New York: Dutton, 1992), p. 15.

10. It is to be hoped that the result of federal (Title IX) guidelines mandating equality for women's sports programs, as well as the culture's ability to see women as athletes, will allow girls and young women the same opportunity in this generation. It is now possible, for example, for a young woman to play basketball, where for her mother the only way to participate would have been as a cheerleader.

CHAPTER TWO

1. The climate for what is commonly called male bashing emerged with the second phase of the women's movement. During the early 1970s many women and media commentators began to define femininity by contrasting it with masculinity. In a reversal of historical trends, the latter was denigrated and blamed for the suffering of the former. A spate of popular-psychology books and the national TV talk shows have capitalized on these feelings and promulgated them as factual.

2. Hayward, F., "Male Bashing," in Thompson, K., *To Be a Man* (Los Angeles: Tarcher, 1988), p. 73.

CHAPTER THREE

1. Kipnis, A. R., *Knights Without Armor* (Los Angeles: Tarcher, 1991), p. 262.

2. Keen, S., *Fire in the Belly: On Being a Man* (New York: Bantam, 1991), p. 28.

3. Corneau, G., *Absent Fathers, Lost Sons* (Acton, Mass.: Shambala, 1991).

4. An October 18, 1992, news item carried by Associated Press claimed that 70 percent of married households are dual-income households.

5. Farrell, W., *Why Men Are the Way They Are* (New York: McGraw-Hill, 1986).

6. Studies on gender are particularly susceptible to political rather than scientific conclusions. Much of what is "common knowledge" reflects inaccurate conclusions from partial statistics that are then popularized in the media. Examples of these "politically correct" errors include the discrepancy of women's and men's work weeks (based on interview studies of small samples of women and no men), and the often-repeated notion that educated women in their thirties have a better chance of being hijacked than married, a conclusion beautifully debunked by feminist writer Susan Faludi.

7. Best sellers such as *Women Who Love Too Much, Smart Women/Foolish Choices, Men Who Hate Women and the Women Who Love Them,* and

Secrets About Men Every Woman Should Know are but a few examples of contemporary thinking that portrays women almost universally as victims and men as scum.

8. One such study in our laboratory asked thirty husbands and wives of different socioeconomic strata their reasons for marrying. For men the top two reasons were (1) love and (2) the timing was right. By contrast for women love was third (and timing fifth) behind (1) social status and (2) his earning power. Clinical studies of couples in therapy also supports these data.

9. Location is a key determinant of housing affordability. According to the August 1992 survey of the National Association of Home Builders, between 6.7 and 23.6 percent of median-income families can afford to purchase a home in the San Francisco Bay area. In Jackson, Michigan; Brazoria, Texas; and Lincoln, Nebraska, 90 percent of median-income families can afford to buy one.

10. Ironically it was antiwar demonstrations by veterans that hastened the end of the war. When a hero leaves his medals at a demonstration, it has a greater impact on policymakers than when a person who is intellectually opposed states his opinion.

11. Tannen, D., *You Just Don't Understand: Women and Men in Conversation* (New York: Morrow, 1990).

12. Blumstein, P., and Schwartz, P. W., *American Couples* (New York: Morrow, 1983).

CHAPTER FOUR

1. Richard's choice of a male therapist was specifically to "find a positive, successful father figure." This may have made some of his early therapeutic work easier. He may also have felt more understood by a male. A competent, experienced female therapist could also have provided him with the safe yet confrontational environment he desired.

2. Herzog, J., "On Father Hunger: The Father's Role in the Modulation of Aggressive Drive and Fantasy," in Cath, S. H.; Gurwitt, A. R.; and Ross, J. M., *Father and Child* (Boston: Little, Brown, 1982), pp. 163–174.

3. Shapiro, S. A., *Manhood, A New Definition* (New York: G. P. Putnam's Sons, 1984), p. 97.

4. Corneau, G., *Absent Fathers, Lost Sons* (Acton, Mass.: Shambala, 1991).

5. Merton, A., "Father Hunger." Originally appeared in *New Age Journal.* Reprinted in Scull, C., *Fathers, Sons and Daughters* (Los Angeles: Tarcher, 1992), p. 18.

6. Secunda, V., *Women and Their Fathers: The Sexual and Romantic Impact of the First Man in Your Life* (New York: Delacorte Press, 1992), book jacket.

CHAPTER FIVE

1. Ross, J. M., "Mentorship in Middle Childhood." In Cath, S. H.; Gurwitt, A. R.; and Ross, J. M., *Father and Child* (Boston: Little, Brown, 1982), p. 250.

2. Tessman, L. H., "Fathers and Daughters: Early Tones, Later Echoes," in Cath, S. H.; Gurwitt, A.; and Gunsberg, L., *Fathers and Their Families* (Hillsdale, N.J.: The Analytic Press, 1989).

3. The figure of seventy-four cents is according to the *San Francisco Chronicle* of June 20, 1992. Estimates of actual figures of unequal pay for equal work vary widely. The cited data are often based on insufficient research or political rather than scientific goals. It does seem clear that among blue-collar workers and older workers there is a significant gender-based difference in remuneration. Among young, college-educated, white-collar professionals the gap may not exist.

4. Part of the discrepancy involves the nature of data obtained. Early studies of relative amounts of work were based entirely on interviews with women, who tended to overestimate their own contribution compared with that of their spouses. Later studies also relied heavily on interview data. It is clear from these that both husbands and wives believed that women put in more combined hours (although not the quantity suggested in the earlier studies). Time-chart studies, which minimize the effect of subjective belief by objectively measuring exactly how each member of a couple spends time, show that the discrepancy between women's and men's work week, on the average, is negligible. It is important to note that many couples who see equivalent amounts of work time for each partner still attest that the woman works more. This is an example of political rather than statistical interpretation of research in the gender area.

5. Shapiro, S. A., *Manhood, A New Definition* (New York: G. P. Putnam's Sons, 1984), p. 97.

6. Use of the masculine pronoun is not intended to exclude or to slight our daughters. I use the male pronoun purely for the sake of simplicity.

7. Corneau, G., *Absent Fathers, Lost Sons* (Acton, Mass.: Shambala, 1991).

8. Tom Brokaw's *Focus on the Family*.

CHAPTER SEVEN

1. Osherson, S., *Finding Our Fathers* (New York: Free Press, 1986).

2. Gilligan, C., *In a Different Voice* (Cambridge, Mass.: Harvard University Press, 1982).

3. Robert Bly and Bill Moyers, *A Gathering of Men* (New York: Mystic Fire Video, 1989).

4. Pittman, F., "Bringing Up Father," *Family Therapy Networker,* May/June 1988, p. 22.

CHAPTER EIGHT

1. Maitland, S., "Two for the Price of One," in Scull, C., *Fathers, Sons and Daughters* (Los Angeles: Tarcher, 1992), p. 28.

2. Osherson, S., *Finding Our Fathers* (New York: Free Press, 1986).

3. Robert Bly and Bill Moyers, *A Gathering of Men* (New York: Mystic Fire Video, 1989).

4. Rubin, L. B., *Intimate Strangers* (New York: Harper & Row, 1983).

5. Jonson, B., *Timber: or Discoveries Made upon Men and Matter* (1640).

6. Groth, A. N., *Men Who Rape: The Psychology of the Offender* (New York: Plenum, 1979).

7. Osherson, S., *Finding Our Fathers* (New York: Free Press, 1986), p. 22.

8. A mature female therapist may be equally effective for many men. The predominant reason that I recommend an older male therapist is the higher likelihood that he will have a deeper, more immediate understanding of the issues and provide a male mode of feeling in return. Generally men who are doing this exploration are well served by someone who has had to face his own personal dilemma of finding his own inner father.

CHAPTER NINE

1. Opening lines from the film *Field of Dreams*.

CHAPTER TEN

1. Shaving of course is only an example of masculine ritual. It's a curious one for the author. Neither his wife nor his children have ever seen him without his full beard.

2. Reported in Shapiro, J. L., *When Men Are Pregnant* (San Luis Obispo, Calif.: Impact, 1987).

3. May, K. A., and Perrin, S. P., "Prelude, Pregnancy and Birth," in Hanson, S. M. H., and Bozett, F. W., *Dimensions of Fatherhood* (Beverly Hills, Calif.: Sage, 1985).

4. These "couvade symptoms" are often the object of humor. They are far more common than earlier thought. Almost 50 percent of expectant fathers, emotionally wanting to be closer to the pregnancy, unconsciously find a physical way to do so. Among the most common symptoms are weight gain and lower-back pain. Some men have "morning sickness," and a few actually experience labor pains.

5. Lamb, M., *The Role of the Father in Child Development*, 2nd ed. (New York: Wiley, 1981).

6. Parke, R. D., *Fathers* (Cambridge, Mass.: Harvard University Press, 1981).

7. Bozett, F. W., "Male Development and Fathering Throughout the Life Cycle," *American Behavioral Scientist*, 29, no. 1 (1985): 41–54.

8. Hanson, S. M. H., and Bozett, F. W., *Dimensions of Fatherhood* (Beverly Hills, Calif.: Sage, 1985).

9. Greenberg, M., *Birth of a Father* (New York: Continuum, 1985).

10. Roberts, C. L., and Zuengler, K. L., "The Postparental Transition and Beyond," in Hanson, S. M., and Bozett, F. W., eds., *Dimensions of Fatherhood* (Beverly Hills, Calif.: Sage, 1985), p. 196.

11. Keen, S., *Fire in the Belly* (New York: Bantam, 1991).

12. Cath, S. H., "Vicissitudes of Grandfatherhood," in Cath, S. H.; Gurwitt, A. R.; and Ross, J. M., eds., *Father and Child: Developmental and Clinical Perspectives* (Boston: Little, Brown, 1982), pp. 329–338.

CHAPTER ELEVEN

1. Pruett, K. D., *The Nurturing Father* (New York: Warner, 1987), pp. 260–261.

2. James Levine, former head of the Fatherhood Project at Bank Street College in New York City, is a frequent lecturer, consultant, and writer on the influence of men's careers on their family life.

3. Greif, G., *Single Fathers* (New York: Free Press, 1985).

4. MacFarland, T., "Disposable Daddies," *Mothering*, 61, Fall 1991, p. 117.

5. Marie's decision would not have been upheld by the New York State law. Despite her expressed desire, Thom would have been legally responsible for child support.

6. I contacted five attorneys who specialize in family law (one a professor at a local law school and four who are practicing divorce attorneys) to ask about these examples. Each was personally aware of at least "a few" such cases. One attorney reported that she had litigated "ten or more." One of the attorneys reported that her husband was in such a predicament with his first marriage.

7. Krantzler, M., *Creative Divorce* (New York: M. Evans, 1974).

8. Estimates vary from 70 to 90 percent.

9. Although a father's frustration is understandable, this solution cannot be condoned. A father who takes the law into his own hands is further jeopardizing the children he loves. The trauma could cause severe psychological damage. In a worst case the children could be deprived of both their mother (by the kidnapping) and their father (by imprisonment). Ultimately, fairer treament of fathers in the courts would mitigate this problem.

10. There is no question that in any divorce, the woman may be financially ruined, while the man experiences a slight "blip" in his financial life. Any number of examples can be cited of men hiding money, instigating affairs, and trying to ruin their ex-wife's life emotionally and financially. This chapter is focused on single fathers, and the examples drawn are to highlight the problems for that group of individuals. There is no suggestion that either gender

has a monopoly on vindictiveness, insensitivity, or pain either during or following a divorce.

11. Although it is not fully relevant here, clinical data suggest that the loss of a child may be the most devastating loss in a family. Parents are supposed to predecease their children. Even if it occurs suddenly, a parent's death is more acceptable psychologically.

12. Some children of divorce also claim to be permanently affected.

CHAPTER TWELVE

1. For a more complete description of stepfamily structure see Bohannan, P., "Stepparenthood: A New and Old Experience," in Cohen, R. S.; Cohler, B. J.; and Weissman, S. H., eds., *Parenthood: A Psychodynamic Perspective* (New York: Guilford, 1984).

2. Two books that stand out in this field are Emily and John Visher's *Stepfamilies: A Guide to Working with Stepparents and Stepchildren* (New York: Bruner/Mazel, 1979); and Judith Wallerstein and Sandra Blakeslee's *Second Chances* (New York: Ticknor & Fields, 1989).

CHAPTER THIRTEEN

1. Letich, L., "Do You Know Who Your Friends Are?" *Utne Reader*, May–June 1992, pp. 85–87.

BIBLIOGRAPHY

SOME SIGNIFICANT BOOKS/PERIODICALS
ON FATHERHOOD

Bozett, F. W., and S.M.H. Hanson. *Fatherhood and Families in Cultural Context*. New York: Springer, 1991.

Cath, S. H., A. R. Gurwitt, and L. Gunsberg. *Fathers and Their Families*. Boston: Little, Brown, 1989.

Cath, S. H., A. R. Gurwitt, and J. M. Ross. *Father and Child: Developmental and Clinical Perspectives*. Boston: Little, Brown, 1982.

Corneau, G. *Absent Fathers, Lost Sons*. Acton, Mass.: Shambala, 1991.

"Fathers and the Family," *Family Therapy Networker* (May/June 1988 Special Feature).

Gilbert, S. D. *What's a Father For?* New York: Warner, 1975.

Greenberg, M. *The Birth of a Father*. New York: Continuum, 1985.

Hanson, S.M.H., and F. Bozett. *Dimensions of Fatherhood*. Beverly Hills: Sage, 1985.

Keen, S. *Fire in the Belly*. New York: Bantam, 1991.

Kimmel, M. S., and M. A. Messner. *Men's Lives* (2nd ed.). New York: Macmillan, 1992.

Kipnis, A. R. *Knights Without Armor*. Los Angeles: Jeremy Tarcher, 1991.

Klinman, D. G. *Fatherhood U.S.A.* New York: Garland, 1984.

Lamb, M. E. *The Role of the Father in Child Development*. New York: Wiley, 1976.

Levant, R., and J. Kelly. *Between Father and Child: How to Become the Kind of Father You Want to Be*. New York: Viking Penguin, 1991.

Osherson, S. *Finding Our Fathers*. New York: Free Press, 1986.

Parke, R. D. *Fathers*. Cambridge, Mass.: Harvard University Press, 1981.

Pruett, K. D. *The Nurturing Father*. New York: Warner, 1987.

Schwartz, A., ed. *To Be a Father*. New York: Crown, 1967.

Scull, C., ed. *Fathers, Sons and Daughters: Exploring Fatherhood, Renewing the Bond*. Los Angeles: Jeremy Tarcher, 1992.

Secunda, V. *Women and Their Fathers*. New York: Delacorte Press, 1992.

Shapiro, J. L. *When Men Are Pregnant: Needs and Concerns of Expectant Fathers*. New York: Delta, 1993.

Thompson, K. *To Be a Man*. Los Angeles: Jeremy Tarcher, 1991.

A FEW RECENT FILMS

I Never Sang for My Father
Dad
Field of Dreams
Hook

INDEX